CREATI... ...ARNING

Boston   Burr Ridge, IL   Dubuque, IA   Madison, WI   New York   San Francisco   St. Louis
Bangkok   Bogotá   Caracas   Kuala Lumpur   Lisbon   London   Madrid   Mexico City
Milan   Montreal   Ne...   ...pore   Sydney   Taipei   Toronto

The McGraw-Hill Companies

Higher Education

Published by McGraw-Hill, an imprint of The McGraw-Hill Companies, Inc., 1221 Avenue of the Americas, New York, NY 10020. Copyright © 2008. All rights reserved. No part of this publication may be reproduced or distributed in any form or by any means, or stored in a database or retrieval system, without the prior written consent of The McGraw-Hill Companies, Inc., including, but not limited to, in any network or other electronic storage or transmission, or broadcast for distance learning.

 This book is printed on recycled, acid-free paper containing a minimum of 50% total recycled fiber with 10% postconsumer de-inked fiber.

1 2 3 4 5 6 7 8 9 0 QPD/QPD 0 9 8 7

ISBN: 978-0-07-295497-5
MHID: 0-07-295497-3

Vice President and Editor in Chief: *Emily Barrosse*
Publisher: *William R. Glass*
Executive Editor: *Christopher Johnson*
Director of Development: *Kathleen Engelberg*
Executive Marketing Manager: *Nick Agnew*
Developmental Editor: *Lynda Huenefeld*
Developmental Editor for Technology: *Julia D. Akpan*
Project Manager: *Carey Eisner*
Manuscript Editor: *Kay Mikel*
Art Editor: *Emma Ghiselli*
Photo Research Coordinator: *Nora Agbayani*
Senior Designer: *Preston Thomas*, III
Text Designer: *Adriane Bosworth*
Cover Designer: *Jenny El-Shamy*
Senior Production Supervisor: *Richard DeVitto*
Composition: *10/12 Minion by Techbooks*
Printing: *45# Scholarly Matte Recycled, Quebecor World*
Cover: © *Gene Einfrank*

Library of Congress Cataloging-in-Publication Data

Brehm, Mary Ann.
Creative dance for learning: the kinesthetic link/Mary Ann Brehm, Lynne McNett; photography by Gene Einfrank.
p. cm.
Includes bibliographical references and index.

ISBN-13: 978-0-07-295497-5
ISBN-10: 0-07-295497-3

1. Dance–Study and teaching–Textbooks. I. McNett, Lynne. II. Title/
GV1589.B74 2007
792.8071–dc22   2006048817

The Internet addresses listed in the text were accurate at the time of publication. The inclusion of a Web site does not indicate an endorsement by the authors or McGraw-Hill, and McGraw-Hill does not guarantee the accuracy of the information presented at these sites.

BRIEF CONTENTS

Contents

PREFACE

Through the making of art, creative dance nurtures and affirms each dancer's spirit.

We have witnessed joy for three decades now as our students have explored movement problems using the kinesthetic sense as a guide. The miracle of movement comes not only in baby's first step or in athletic glory but also in simple awareness of common actions. This "movement sense" is vital to life: it enables people to feel, interpret, coordinate, and craft physical experience. *Creative Dance for Learning: The Kinesthetic Link* is the outgrowth of our many years of experience as dance educators and our continuing passionate commitment to arts education.

When movement is informed by the kinesthetic sense, it is a powerful medium of expression and learning. The rich modality of movement can be drawn on to integrate many goals of education. In the United States, dance has now been recognized as one of four artistic disciplines that students are expected to study. Even so, dance is commonly absent from the educational environment. We feel that this is due, in part, to a shortage of resources for understanding dance principles and practical ways to teach dance in schools. *Creative Dance for Learning* seeks to fill a gap and meet existing needs for preparing teachers to include movement and dance as a regular part of learning. In this book we approach dance both as an art form standing on its own and as an art activity that enhances learning across the curriculum. It is both a textbook for education courses and a resource for current dance educators; for classroom teachers at all levels; for drama, music, and visual arts specialists; for physical educators; and for counselors and therapists. In all these situations, dance speaks to the need for movement activity and creative endeavor in people's lives.

Creative dance differs from most kinds of dance in that it is improvised, or made up at the moment of dancing. It is conceptually based rather than technical. It is accessible to all abilities and offers great opportunities for developing individual and group problem-solving skills. These traits make creative dance perfect for school settings as well as for use in studios or by specialists in many other situations.

Creative Dance for Learning provides theoretical and practical guidance on teaching creative dance, particularly in educational settings. As a comprehensive teaching guide, it addresses the "what," "why," and "how" of creative dance. Our approach is heavily influenced by Barbara Mettler, Margaret H'Doubler, and Rodolf Laban, all legendary figures in the field of creative dance. Their theories are combined with our own insights to:

- Validate dance as art education, adaptable to all ages and abilities
- Highlight the kinesthetic sense as a guide for creating dance forms
- Explain dance theory in common language
- Provide methods of linking movement across the curriculum
- Address cultural material through creative dance
- Outline teaching progressions that develop student skill and understanding
- Guide readers into building and presenting lessons of their own
- Provide models for assessing student learning
- Relate creative dance instruction to achievement standards in dance and other disciplines
- Offer more than twenty-five well-tested lesson plans and forty lesson adaptations that extend the lesson material

Pedagogical features that link theory to practical application throughout the book include the following:

- Creative Toolboxes offer specific activities to try with students or while reading the text.
- Concept Spotlights summarize theoretical information.
- Lesson Worksheets and Brainstorming Lists focus the lesson planning process.
- Charts summarize material for easy reference.
- Teaching Resources include music, literary, and multicultural resources.
- Many photographs and illustrations further illuminate the text.

Much of our work has taken place in elementary schools, but we also teach this same material at universities, studios, and in other community settings. Plentiful examples from classroom experience illustrate how movement can be used to help students learn concepts, solve problems, and thereby understand core academic subjects. The sizable section of lesson plans spans many subject areas. These lessons are realistic for school day schedules and can be adapted to a wide range of age groups and settings. The practical information, in combination with detailed explanation of the process of linking dance to curricular topics, empowers teachers to make this work their own.

Creative Dance for Learning builds from the strongest creative dance traditions and synthesizes them with current educational theory. It offers fresh theoretical insights and cutting-edge practices that take dance off the pedestal that separates it from common human experience, making the art of body movement accessible for all. It is our hope that *Creative Dance for Learning* will help make dance widely available by giving teachers the tools to make movement expression a more natural, comfortable, and joyful part of their students' lives.

Acknowledgments

In the spirit of group dance, this book is a sum of many contributing parts. The support we've received has been a huge help for the content and to our enjoyment of the process. First, a thank-you to those who helped us get this project off the ground by letting us meet in your homes for early planning sessions: Nancy and Walter Lob, and Peg and Jim Runnels. David Brewster, Judy Mishew, and Pat Cattini steered us in the right direction with their early editorial advice. Technological support came in many forms, and often at critical times, thanks to Anastasia Joy Nelson and Walt Brehm.

Special attention is deserved by these professionals for lending their expertise to different sections of the book: Joann Keali'inohomoku, PhD; C. Sue Pfaffl and Carol Kestler (multicultural connections); Rima Faber, PhD (dance education standards); Barry Oreck, PhD (assessment); Aleene B. Nielson, PhD (multiple intelligences); and M. Cate Deicher, CMA (Labanalysis). A big thank-you to all.

We deeply appreciate the contributed ideas and scrutinous reading eyes of many fellow educators. Classroom teachers include Toni Wade, Carol Drummond, and Pete Duranceau. The wealth of knowledge and creativity of Grace Levin, A. A. Leath, Nancy Lob, Rachel Fitzgerald, Margo Taylor, Melissa Rolnick, John Snavely, D. Mus, John Wilson, PhD, and George Brehm broadened the scope of this book.

Without the help of dedicated dancers, this book would not have been possible. Our collegial dance organization, the International Association for Creative Dance, has nurtured this seed of creativity for many years, providing us with a community within which to dance new ideas, and, of course, the "laboratories" for our lessons were classrooms of students.

Our deepest gratitude to the following art programs and schools for their support and participation: Arts Genesis, Inc., Opening Minds through the Arts Project of Tucson Unified School District, Tucson/Pima Arts Council, Project DISCOVER of the University of Arizona, Lesley University Creative Arts in Learning Program, Washington State Arts Commission, Western Washington University, Allied Arts Education Project, Bellingham School District, Burlington-Edison School District, Mt. Vernon School District, Anacortes School District, and Shaftsbury Elementary School Arts and Basics Program.

Our photographer, Gene Einfrank, demonstrated amazing patience and skill behind the camera in catching dancers in these diverse groups: Happy Trails Pre-School and Kindergarten, Peter Howell Elementary School, Third Street Kids, Miles Exploratory Learning Center, St. James Methodist Church Sociable Seniors, Zuzi Dance Company, Dunham Elementary School, Tucson Magnet High School, and the Tucson Creative Dance Center studio group and community dancers. Marcia Berger, Susan Schoon, Margo Taylor, and Sheryl Oden were instrumental in gathering these dancers. Special thanks to Peggy Lane for the use of the beautiful Tucson Creative Dance Center for studio photography.

Thanks also to Helen Roberts, at the National Resource Center for Dance, University of Surrey, England, and Robert Dodd of Mettler Studios for permission to print photographs of Rudolf Laban and Barbara Mettler, respectively.

We thank developmental editor Lynda Huenefeld for her spirited enthusiasm and confidence in our project as well as Vicki Malinee, who saw the merit of our ideas and opened the door for us to create this text. We extend many thanks to Carey Eisner, production editor, for getting the final details just right; Kay Mikel, copyeditor, for her impressive red penciling; and Tara Davis, marketing coordinator, for her timely responsiveness to our suggestions.

We thank classroom teachers and dance professionals who reviewed manuscript for this text:

Karen Bradley, CMA, *University of Maryland*
Mary Alice Brennan, PhD, CMA, *University of Wisconsin–Madison*
Hollie Newman, PhD, *Florida State University*
Rima Faber, PhD, *National Dance Education Organization*
C. Griffin Goehring, *Green Mountain Creative Dance Center*
Joann Keali'inohomoku, PhD, *Cross Cultural Dance Resources*
Emilee Kellermann, *Kellison Elementary School*
Carole Marlowe, *Tucson Unified School District*
Elsa Posey, *National Registry of Dance Educators*
Naima Prevots, PhD, *American University*
Angela Rice, MM, *Rockwood Summit High School*
Jill Szczublewski, *Sandhills Intermediate School*
Douglas Victor, *Lesley University*

Finally, our heartfelt gratitude to our families, friends, and fellow dancers. Your patience and faith have seen us through.

Mary Ann Brehm
Lynne McNett

About the Authors

Mary Ann Brehm has a PhD in Dance from the University of Wisconsin–Madison and has taught dance at the University of Wisconsin–Whitewater, the University of Wisconsin–Madison, and the University of Vermont. Currently she travels throughout the United States to teach the course "Creative Movement: Kinesthetic Learning across the Curriculum" for Lesley University's Integrated Teaching through the Arts Master's Program. She is a former member of the Barbara Mettler Dance Company and is on the Board of Directors of the International Association for Creative Dance.

Dr. Brehm has been a dance teaching artist for nearly 30 years, using dance in relationship to school curricula in several nationally recognized, award-winning arts education programs, including the Tucson Unified School District's Opening Minds through the Arts Project, Arts Genesis, Inc. (Tucson), the Shaftsbury (Vermont) Elementary School Arts and Basics Program, and the University of Arizona's Project DISCOVER. All of these programs integrate the arts into the ongoing classroom curriculum in communities with high rates of poverty.

Dr. Brehm is the author of several publications that explore the use of dance for a variety of educational purposes, such as building community, supporting curricular learning, fostering the development of multiple intelligences, and promoting individual growth. She was one of three artists nominated for the Buffalo Exchange Arts Award in 2005.

Lynne McNett has a BA in Dance from Western Washington University and 30 years teaching experience. She studied Children's Creative Dance with Virginia Tanner in Salt Lake City and Creative Dance Improvisation with Barbara Mettler in Tucson. For two decades she has been teaching dance in educational settings from pre-school to college, developing dance curricula to align with state standards and presenting her work at dance and art conferences nationwide. She has taught as adjunct faculty at Western Washington University.

Currently Ms. McNett works as a professional development consultant for the Allied Arts Education project in Bellingham, Washington, training and mentoring dance art educators and classroom teachers in methods of dance instruction in schools. She is on the Board of Directors for the International Association for Creative Dance.

CHAPTER 1

BREAKING GROUND

Learning Objectives

1. Gain insight into teaching a first creative dance lesson in a school setting.

2. Connect the authors' early experiences of teaching dance to their reasons for offering dance in school.

3. Recognize the authors' main influences on creative dance theory and pedagogy.

✎ *Portrait of a Lesson*

In they traipse. A straggled line of second graders jostles its way through the door. An occasional shoestring flops, and a few shoulders droop under the weight of a heavy coat. As the line circles round, I assess our first task—getting ready to dance. This will be a whole new experience for many, yet creative human nature is on my side. We have here the usual, but ever unique blend of kids. I notice the special-needs kids right away as well as those who apparently speak a language other than my own. The self-appointed seven-year-old Student Teacher is making sure her neighbors fully understand the directions I haven't yet given. It's easy to spot the popular crowd, even at this age. Mr. Cool is already rolling his eyes; he doesn't do as well as some to restrain his cringe when I affirm that we are here to dance. The kids I notice last are the ones who have quietly done what I've asked: Form a circle. Some of these will be my helpers. Thank heaven for them.

I really want to get moving, and they are already wiggly. But this is our first time together, and we have a few things to talk about. A quick but dead serious run-through of rules emphasizing safety is imperative. Then a little humor lightens things up as I try to dispel some of the fears I sense. No, we are not dancing ballet or ballroom. And everyone is an artist.

People love to watch movement. Watching the human body in action is something all kids can relate to from their own physical experience, so I demonstrate the concepts of today's lesson through movement. I show them the "space bubble" (the space surrounding oneself) and how it can be filled with movement, changed in size, and moved from place to place. Vocabulary includes names of movements and parts of the body that can be moved. It also includes words about space: size, shape, directions, and levels. My three-minute solo emphasizes the basic message of the day: group safety. Now it's my job to see that each student leaves in thirty minutes knowing that he or she can be safe in my class and that the group can move safely. We're on our way.

We spread out and claim our spots. Already I can see that some have a hard time staying on track. I'll stay on my toes to hold their attention. Others are plopped on the floor like futons you could barely move with a forklift.

Our movement actually begins (hurrah!) as the children "paint" the inside of their own space bubble and fill their space up with movements of named body parts or the whole body all at once. Following my verbal directions, they make up their own movements, finding their own way to explore their range of movement. Sometimes I encourage them to close their eyes and feel the sensations of movement, noticing that stretching, curling, shaking, and swinging produce very different feelings in the body. The Futons begin to sweat, and Miss Wiggles has just about exhausted herself into slow speed. With the blessed help of an aide, the autistic boy seems to be hanging in there and having fun. The English language learners (ELLs) are flushed and smiling, ready for more. So far, all of our movements have been done in one place. We have discovered many ways to "move" without going anywhere. It's a novel idea to some and a very safe way to dance. Now comes the challenge: moving around without "popping bubbles." Can we do it? Sure we can!

Near the corner of the room there's a shy pair of overalls that looks unconvinced. He barely got moving inside the safe haven of his own space, and now he's supposed to face the traffic? So we start by walking slowly—maybe just a few kids at a time. We take our time to discover many other ways we can move through space, such as skipping, hopping, or crawling. Mr. Cool finds a way to show off his athletic prowess and relinquishes embarrassment to the challenge of big leaps. He also gets one bench time for clobbering someone with poor judgment. Still, we all survive the traffic (even Overalls). By the end of the lesson we can all move at the same time without bumping. Yes! It's the beginning of group work and maybe fewer casualties on the playground will result.

By defining a space bubble, individuals create a safe place for movement exploration.

A quiet moment completes our lesson. We draw our focus inward and let our bodies rest. Curled up in a little ball, Student Teacher can forget her responsibilities and relax. With her head on her knees, Miss Wiggles cannot see anyone to distract her, and Overalls knows he's invisible now. The boy with special needs trusts his aide enough to help him soften into himself. And the Futons are finally doing what they're good at, giving in to gravity. The ELLs are lying with eyes wide, wondering "What next?" When it's time to go, they look surprised yet pleased with themselves. As they line up, they chatter among themselves, giving words to their nonverbal experience. I sigh my relief that we've had a successful lesson. We can all be proud of that.

Already I know most of the aforementioned characters by name and personally bid them farewell as they leave. I also become aware that there are names I don't know. These are the kids who were less demanding because of their attention, responsibility, and receptivity. I never had to coax them or make a big deal out of their small successes. They simply did what was asked of them, silently blending into the rhythm of the lesson. When a student displays obvious needs, like those I noticed first, it is easy to see the benefits of creative movement. We can wake them up, calm them down, raise awareness, build self-esteem, and even teach English. But what about the rest of the children? What do they get out of this experience?

The answer is worthy of this book. What creative dance can do for each and every student, regardless of age, gender, race, or ability is profound, yet as basic as bones. Without knowing the personal experience of other teachers, this is what we see going on with our students: the physical body is exercised and developed toward its best abilities; movement feelings are recognized and expressed; the cognitive mind is brought to task as movements are chosen and sequenced; creative problems are solved, and language is given to abstract concepts; each person's spirit is nurtured and affirmed as he or she creates art, communes with peers, and learns new perspectives.

This is why we like to dance and why we want to share this huge reservoir of learning with teachers and students everywhere. Movement is easily accessible and, as you will see, brimming with educational value. Students need this kind of activity, and teachers do well to grasp this great opportunity to enrich their teaching with movement.

❧ Formative Experiences in Teaching Dance

The learning power of creative dance was revealed to me (Lynne) in studio classes with four-year-olds. Creative dance helped my students to develop physical, emotional, intellectual, creative, and social skills. For example, Rosio's disabled left leg (a physical limitation she was

One of the first skills required for traveling safely in a dance class is to look for and move through "empty space."

born with) became stronger to the point she could bear weight, even jump on it. Jenny's fear of moving backward (reflecting her lack of confidence) was eventually overcome. Todd's difficulty with verbal communication diminished as he learned a new way to express himself and become accepted by his peers. Annie, a natural born star, learned how to accept diversity in others and temper her flamboyance in exchange for meaningful movement.

These young minds ordered, remembered, and reconstructed complex patterns. They worked cooperatively in groups yet maintained a strong sense of themselves. But above all I saw that these young children expressed themselves artfully and more easily than we do as adults. The expression of inner beauty and the need to create something new appears to be intrinsic to human nature.

Because of the learning I observed in those one-hour lessons, taking dance to school made perfect sense: out of the studio and into the classroom I leapt. Impassioned by the values of creative dance for children and the desire to be a good teacher, I was able to bend to less than ideal circumstances for teaching dance, which had not been an issue in the studio where students attended my classes by choice and without distractions. The school classroom was an entirely different environment and audience. Not only did many students and teachers need convincing that this was an activity worth trying, but we had to create space among desks, bookshelves, piles of paper, and science experiments. Sometimes my artistic goals were considered secondary to the physical activity. I found that more validity was given to the creative dance time if I could connect it with the academic curriculum. I emulated teachers' management and presentation skills and picked their brains for curricular material that we could explore in dance. Together, those teachers and I learned how powerfully dance could be integrated into learning.

I (Mary Ann) began my teaching career in a second-grade classroom in a small rural school. Because of my background in dance, I was eager to include it as part of my curriculum. I was in the lucky situation of being somewhat loosely overseen, having freedom to explore—and even fail—with experimental curriculum. Several teachers in the school were interested in stimulating creativity and in learning by doing. Children were given rich sensory experiences—such as observing at the local pond—and those experiences became the focus for writing, reading, math, and visual arts activities. I started bringing dance activities into this format. I often taught a visual arts lesson that related to a science, social studies, or language arts topic we were studying. Now, I began to block off time to dance about these topics first and then do a visual arts lesson. These lessons often stimulated story writing, and I noticed that making movements about the topic brought out increased attention to detail. The students' interest in the curricular material was expanded because they had experienced it in their bodies. The dance work was also enriched because it wasn't an isolated activity; rather, it was related to what students were studying and thinking about the rest of the day.

In small ways I worked to bring movement into the school day. After the flag salute and show-and-tell, we would spend a few minutes standing by our desks stretching, twisting, and loosening up freely. At that time I didn't realize that students could focus internally while moving. Nor did I understand the importance of moving with full concentration on movement feeling. I learned that later. Each day I was expected to introduce a phonics element. The children enjoyed forming their body shapes into those letters as we discussed their sounds. They also liked making themselves long or short depending on whether I said kite with a long *i* or kit with a short *i*. I remember sitting down with the list of second-grade behavioral objectives (a new thing that year) and coming up with movement activities to address most of them. These activities helped students remember what the class was studying and made abstract ideas concrete.

I became convinced that we could dance about anything, but I was short on conceptual knowledge of how to organize and develop this material. For instance, I once had taken a course on Children's Dance in which the instructor said, "Of course you can see how this activity could be developed in an infinite number of ways." I racked my brains and couldn't think of even one way to extend that activity. Although it had been fun, I had no framework to understand how that particular dance related to anything else. It wasn't until I studied with Barbara Mettler that I began to understand the structure of dance, which gave me a tool for relating it to the curriculum. Soon I changed my emphasis from classroom teacher to working as a specialist in dance, helping classroom teachers integrate dance into their curricula.

We (Lynne and Mary Ann) began collaborating after meeting in a course taught by Mettler and realizing the commonalities in our approaches to teaching. From Mettler, we gained a sense of clarity and simplicity in approaching dance. We acquired an appreciation for the need to feel movement in order to create with it. We learned how freedom of movement and awareness of the movement feeling enable us to create meaningful dance forms. We attained a sense of how natural movement can become the substance of rhythmically satisfying dances. And we discovered the joys of group dance improvisation. These personal dance experiences have changed the way we teach.

Major Influences: Barbara Mettler, Rudolf Laban, and Margaret H'Doubler

The approach to teaching creative dance presented in this book is highly influenced by our study with Barbara Mettler as well as by the work of Rudolf Laban and Margaret H'Doubler. These pioneering dance theorists/educators saw dance as an art that enhances human potential. All three used an analytical framework to organize movement material. Because their work was geared to meeting a basic human need, their theories and methods easily apply to dance study that is meant for all people. Furthermore, their use of a broad analytical framework clarifies the relationship of movement to other topics, making dance's link across a school's curriculum readily apparent. These influences will be referred to throughout this text. For more information, brief biographical sketches of all three are provided in Appendix A, and their writings are listed in the bibliography.

The teachings of these individuals have had a great impact on us and figure strongly in our theory and practice. Their influences and our many years of applying this work in educational settings have carried us well beyond our first efforts at teaching dance. In this book we have woven together an approach to creative dance that works in schools as well as being highly adaptable to many other situations.

CHAPTER SUMMARY

- In a typical creative dance lesson at school, you may have to engage individuals with an assortment of abilities and personalities. Introductory lesson goals need to be simple and reasonable to ensure student success.
- Creative dance can be powerfully harnessed in the classroom to introduce, parallel, or enrich study across the curriculum.
- The approach to teaching creative dance presented in this book is influenced by the work of Barbara Mettler, Rudolf Laban, and Margaret H'Doubler, all of whom saw dance as a basic human need and used an analytical framework to organize movement material.

REVIEW QUESTIONS

1. What are reasonable goals to expect from an introductory creative dance lesson in school?
2. What led the authors to offer dance at school?
3. Why is the work of Mettler, Laban, and H'Doubler applicable to educational settings?

CHAPTER 2

PRINCIPLES OF DANCE AS CREATIVE ART ACTIVITY

Learning Objectives

1. Explain how creative dance improvisation grows out of natural kinesthetic experience.

2. Describe how the kinesthetic sense functions and how it is used by creative dancers.

3. Relate sensory experience to kinesthetic choices in movement expression.

4. Define rhythm as an organizing principle in life and dance.

5. Discuss the integral relationship of art to all of life.

6. Explain how dance making is creative problem solving.

7. Discuss the natural relationship of sound to movement and how creative dance develops musicality independent of recorded accompaniment.

8. Relate creative dance principles to standards of dance education.

9. Describe the adaptability that makes creative dance accessible to everyone.

❧ Creative Dance Improvisation

A simple way to describe creative dance is to say that the dancers create their own movements rather than having them choreographed by someone else. Generally creative dancers **improvise,** which means that the dance is created spontaneously while dancing. This is done by paying attention to movement sensations and feelings in the body and letting them be the guide for finding movements that are satisfying and meaningful. The process that regulates and guides voluntary movement is called the **kinesthetic sense,** or kinesthesis. Based on careful attention to what is going on right at the moment, kinesthesis is a process that involves both movement awareness and decision making. Improvised movement becomes the material of dance, an expressive art, when kinesthetic attention is brought to creating **movement forms** or patterns that are aesthetically fulfilling.

A kinesthetic approach to dance improvisation uses the nature of human movement expression as the basis for organizing movement forms organically. Creative dance brings the dancer closer to nature because it is based on inherent biological, developmental, and psychological characteristics of humans. In creative dance, human nature is affirmed as being a part of all nature. By keying into the *nature* of human expression, one learns to express his or her natural "humanness" in the same way a cat's movement expresses "cat-ness" or a tree's movement expresses "tree-ness."

Focusing on the nature of *movement* expression affirms the link between human movement and all movement. Creative dance works with the elements common to all motion, be it the movement of people, clouds, earthquakes, bulldozers, or birds. These links are very important for understanding dance as an integral part of life. This point of view helps in finding structures used in teaching creative dance and provides a basis for making connections between dance and other areas of school curriculum. (Linking dance across the curriculum is discussed in detail in Part III.)

There are many ways of looking at movement, and it can be studied to many ends. In addition to its aesthetic value as expressive art, dance material has functional value for physical development and therapeutic value for healing. Through the utilitarian realm of movement, students learn to be comfortable with movement, learn about their bodies, and increase their health and fitness. They learn skills that enable them to function efficiently and perhaps even to perform as athletes and artists. When movement is studied as an artistic form, however, a mindful attitude gives meaning to movement and bridges the physical with the expressive self. Movement skills are used as a resource for expression.

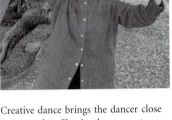

Creative dance brings the dancer close to nature by affirming human nature as part of all nature.

❧ The Kinesthetic Loop

Art making in any medium demands the use of the senses, and different art forms emphasize different senses. Dance relies primarily on the kinesthetic sense. Here is the story of how this resource of internal information operates as a loop of communication uniting body and mind (Fee, 1971–1972).

Movement Awareness: Sensing and Feeling

Receiving objective information and interpreting it subjectively make up the awareness phase of the kinesthetic loop. When movement occurs, **sensory nerves** in the muscles, tendons, joints, and inner ear send signals to the brain about what is going on in the body. This tells a person where the parts of the body are in relationship to each other, how fast one is going, and how tight or loose the muscles are. The brain receives this information as objective sensation, or **proprioception.**

These movement sensations are processed by the mind in relation to all other experience. Some sensations may feel familiar, others unfamiliar. They may feel pleasant or unpleasant; they may trigger memories or evoke emotions. The mind also orders and arranges incoming information into patterns. Interpreting, ordering, comparing, and responding emotionally to movement sensations in relation to personal experience constitute the subjective aspect of the kinesthetic sense. Thus the mind receives objective movement sensations and interprets them within the context of subjective associations. These associations give the experience of moving its richness and meaning.

In this understanding of movement perception, there is a difference between "sensing" a movement and "feeling" a movement. **Sensing** refers to the objective aspect of noticing movement sensations, and **feeling** refers to the subjective associations triggered by that movement. These two are intertwined and happen almost simultaneously. Highly skilled kinesthetic awareness involves being able to both sense and feel movement. For brevity's sake, except when the distinction is required, we often use the word *feeling* to denote both sensations of movement and the subjective feeling states triggered by movement.

CONCEPT SPOTLIGHT 2.1

Aspects of Movement Awareness

Objective	Subjective
Sensing	Feeling
Receiving information	Interpreting information

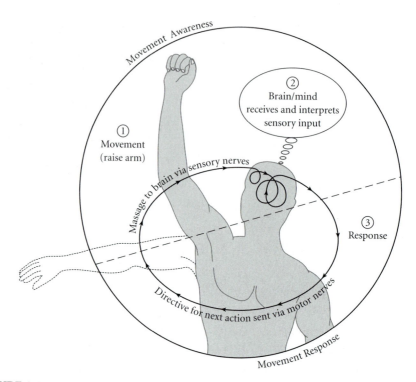

FIGURE 2.1   *The Kinesthetic Loop.*

Responding with Movement Expression

After the incoming message from the muscles has been received and processed by the mind, the next phase of the kinesthetic loop is for the brain to respond. Based on the input just received, it sends a message through the **motor nerves** to the muscles telling them how to continue or not continue moving. The muscle contracts or releases in response to that directive, producing movement expression. This new movement stimulates more kinesthetic sensations for the brain to receive. Thus kinesthetic experience is a loop of communication running back and forth between the moving parts of the body and the brain. The two phases of the kinesthetic experience are (1) awareness of the objective and subjective experience of moving and (2) expression based on that awareness (see Figure 2.1).

The kinesthetic loop is completed in milliseconds and is constantly processing feedback from the muscles and sending messages to them. Much of the time this

---

2.1 CREATIVE TOOLBOX—TRY THIS!

Awakening Kinesthetic Awareness

To awaken kinesthetic awareness in a dance class, ask students to close their eyes and move their hands slowly, paying attention to what they are feeling. Point out that they know what their hands are doing because nerves send a message to the brain from the muscles. Then contrast moving slowly and moving fast. Each student has his or her own feeling of just how slow is "slow" and how fast is "fast." Here students use the mind's ability to make subjective interpretations of the incoming information. To stimulate awareness of the emotional response to movement, ask students how slowness feels versus how fastness feels. You may get responses such as calm, lazy, or bored for slow and hurried, agitated, or excited for fast.

neuromuscular process goes on unconsciously. Everyone has familiar movement habits that send similar messages to the brain day in and day out. People get used to these messages and recognize them as the sensations associated with being themselves. The familiarity of these sensations often dulls the mind's attentiveness to them, and they slip below conscious awareness (Hanna, 1988).

It is possible, however, to heighten awareness so that much of this process is available to consciousness. By paying careful attention to kinesthetic information, movement sensations and feelings reveal subtle details often missed in everyday life. Such experience awakens the feedback (or awareness) part of the kinesthetic loop. The study of creative dance cultivates this kinesthetic awareness. Creative dance also develops the output part of the kinesthetic loop, in which a message is sent on to the muscles directing them in movement expression. Here the kinesthetic sense is used not only to feel what is happening in the body but to control the response.

The kinesthetic sense guides dancers in making movement choices.

✎ Sensory Experience and Kinesthetic Choice

Art is born from awareness. It requires attention to both the fine details and the overall patterns of one's experience. H'Doubler (1940/1998) wrote that "self-identification with experience . . . is the very core of creative effort" (p. xxi). By "self-identification with experience" she meant being aware of your emotional relationship to information coming to you via the senses. That is, when you see the pattern of bare tree branches against the sky, you notice the feeling that experience evokes in you. It may provoke you to move in response to what you see, such as stretching your arms upward. Your self-identification with the visual experience of seeing a tree produced the creation of a movement form. This is the seed of dance experience.

Any kind of sensory awareness can prompt dance expression. If you tune into the subjective associations that arise with sensory experience, you can recognize feeling tones in the body because your body reacts to all sensory input. For example, if you hear a loud crash or an owl call, smell a foul odor or a sweet flower, see a child in danger or an old friend coming toward you, muscles respond to the subjective associations the mind creates while processing this sensory information (Damasio, 1999). This stimulates the kinesthetic receptors and starts the kinesthetic loop. Because the impact of sensory awareness is felt throughout the body, cultivating that awareness can bring a feeling of merging with the external world as it is being perceived through the senses. This kinesthetic response to outside sensory information can then be used as the source for movement expression.

2.2 CREATIVE TOOLBOX—TRY THIS!

Engaging Kinesthetic Choice

As an introduction to the function of the kinesthetic loop in creating organic movement forms, have students make a single movement at a time, basing each successive movement on the sensations and feelings generated by the previous movement. After each movement, have students pause. Ask them to make the next most natural movement, based on what feels right. It is at the point of making a new movement that the dancer listens to what the body says to do next. It is quite obvious whether students are using their kinesthetic sense to make movement decisions or are deciding intellectually about what movement to make. The kinesthetically felt movements evolve naturally from each other. The thought-inspired movements are often stilted and hesitant.

Not all forms of dance cultivate identification with experience in the way that creative dance does. Much of the time learning to dance involves replicating movements rather than basing movement expression on the feeling perceived in the body. Missing is a conscious attention to kinesthetic experience. In creative dance, movement forms are sought that allow full experience of the movement, with all its subjective associations, through the kinesthetic sense. Dances based on kinesthetic perception have a feeling of wholeness and are rich expressions of the dancer's originality, authenticity, and integrity.

Rhythm as an Organizing Principle

In everyday language, the term *rhythm* is commonly used to talk about the beat patterns in music. This is certainly an important manifestation of rhythm. It is the aspect of rhythm that occurs in time. Rhythm, however, goes beyond timed beat patterns to encompass all patterns of life as they naturally organize themselves. **Rhythm** arises from polarity: it is created by reciprocating patterns of activity and rest, expansion and contraction, flow and ebb. All body movement is characterized by such rhythms because the contraction and release of muscles is rhythmic. Exertion is naturally followed by recuperation. Cueing into the rhythm of a phenomenon can help the dancer find its structure, its meaning, and its liveliness.

Rhythm is the interplay of opposites: Understanding the rhythmic nature of movement means understanding movement on a continuum between opposites. The material in this book is often organized in polarities such as forceful/forceless, tight/loose, large/small, or fast/slow. This emphasis on polarities reflects a reliance on rhythm as the organizing principle for approaching dance and the teaching process, and it opens a full range of expressive qualities for students.

Identifying Rhythm through the Elements of Dance

For dance, elements of movement provide a structure that helps students develop their natural artistic vision of rhythmic patterns. The guiding framework of the approach to creative dance presented here analyzes movement in terms of four elements: the **body,** which is the instrument with which dance is created, and the three abstract elements of movement material: force, time, and space. Movement occurs with an exertion of force through time and space (Mettler, 1960/2006). The **force element** refers to how energy is expended in movement, the **time element** refers to when movement happens, and the **space element** refers to where movement happens. These elements are described in detail in Part II. All of the elements of movement occur in every movement, and each element contributes to the creation of rhythmic patterns. These patterns are experienced as a "binding together of related parts into a whole" (H'Doubler, 1932, p. 1). This feeling of wholeness is what gives rhythm its satisfying quality and makes it a basic organizing principle for finding form in art. Creative dance rides on that rhythm; it is the art of body movement and the art of rhythm.

Giving Form to Feeling

In creative dance, the form of the dance evolves by following the feeling of the movement and the body's natural rhythmic patterns. Essentially, dance making as an art process involves tuning in to the rhythmic nature of reality and playing with it to discover a satisfying form. Whether the content being expressed is pleasant or unpleasant, the form is satisfying because through it one recognizes a natural beauty in what has been created. The rhythmic ebb and flow of movement can be used to organize material by individual dancers and it can be the basis for group dancing. Expressing individual uniqueness and finding fulfillment as part of a group are two complementary pillars of creative dance.

Because humans have innate abilities and needs to function as a group, spontaneous **group forms** sometimes emerge as people dance together. As dancers together explore the rhythmic relationship between the elements of dance, they learn to sense compelling forms for group expression. Using these forms—unison, complement, and contrast—solidifies movement themes and provides a means for them to develop.

Unison means that all dancers do exactly the same thing. Their bodies do the same movements; they move with the same timing; they make the same spatial patterns; and they use the same degree of force in their movements. Finding unison in group dance improvisation is natural yet extraordinary as individual dancers become unified through their awareness of all four elements of dance. In group dance improvisation, unison is achieved by dancers adapting to each other and finding a consensus of unified movement.

Movements that **complement** are similar and support each other to enrich or complete a theme. Within the force element they may be of similar energy level or emotional tone. In time, complementary movements may fit into the same metered pattern but be part of different subdivisions of beats. In space, they may extend or complete a design.

Contrast, on the other hand, juxtaposes different movement qualities to highlight their opposite properties. For example, combinations of forceful and forceless, slow and fast, or high and low movements may create contrasting forms but still retain a dynamic, rhythmic relationship with each other.

Rather than relying on these serendipitous forms to emerge by chance, creative dance identifies the skills needed to develop improvisational group dancing by cultivating the nonverbal capacities humans have to sense the rhythm of group movements. These are the same abilities for recognizing group movements that in nature enable fish to school, birds to flock, and bees to swarm. Using such skills, dancers can easily and consistently recognize group movement themes and build on them, enabling individuals to have the very satisfying experience of being part of something larger than themselves, of creating something they could not create alone.

In this unison swing, all individuals in the group move with the same feeling and form.

✎ Art in Life

Mettler, Laban, and H'Doubler viewed dance as an art activity wholly linked with life. Creative acts of exploration and adaptation are necessary for our survival as humanity. In fact, they operate continually in daily life, even at a cellular level. H'Doubler (1998) observed that a single living cell needs to adapt and change to respond to its situation and environment. She stated that "life's creative principle of adjustment . . . is an inherent biological principle before it is an art principle" (p. xxix). This is one indication that art is a basic human need. Because creative adaptation is needed for survival, H'Doubler viewed creativity as a fundamental quality present to some degree in everyone. This view of creativity supports an approach to art making in which students have freedom to explore within carefully defined limitations. Such limits encourage creativity by demanding that students adapt to a given situation.

A group form can contain both complementary and contrasting elements. The two open individual shapes, which are complementary, are positioned in contrasting high and low levels. The single closed curved shape of the third dancer contrasts with the open straight shapes of the others.

Although art experiences grow out of inherent human need, an art experience can be truly extraordinary—like entering another world. The material of the "art world" is the same as in the everyday world; it is just experienced differently. The art world feels like you are creating it and like it is being created for you and from you at the same time. If it is a collaborative effort, the effect is further startling because a new world is co-created. The art experience requires being fully present in a place where, paradoxically, you are both acting with control and being led by the flow of a situation. Art is about both discovery and creation.

❧ *Aesthetic and Utilitarian Consideration*

One's relationship to art can be both aesthetic and practical. One can delight in the shape of a well-crafted bowl as well as in its properties of being a container. A Tiffany lamp gives off light and provides something beautiful for that light to illuminate. A beautifully prepared meal is satisfying both to the stomach and to the senses of taste, sight, and smell. Fine architecture provides both shelter and beauty. The utensils, body coverings, and rituals of traditional cultures wherein art is not divorced from life serve both utilitarian and artistic functions.

In dance, everyday movements can be appreciated both for function and enjoyment. Mettler (1980b) gives a wonderful example of how the experience of walking can be the seed of an art experience. "When I walk home from the store, my satisfaction may be both in the form of my walk, (its forward stride, regular step, knee spring, arm swing) and in the fact that I am bringing home a loaf of bread. If the esthetic aspect of the experience completely dominates the utilitarian, then I am dancing. It is the beginning of art" (p. 2).

From this point of view, an art experience shifts consciousness to look with wonder at things encountered in the world (whether household objects, people, flowers, emotions, sound, or one's own movements). It becomes an attitude of opportunity to explore the nature of the thing and mold it in beautiful, satisfying ways. Children dwell in this kind of world often, but art is more than just child's play. It is a conscious cultivation of that natural ability to approach the world with fascination and to discover its essence by spiritedly arranging and rearranging its elements.

This is the spirit in which creative dance promotes learning. Integrating dance with education does not diminish the endeavor's artistry in service of the practical; dance is used in both its utilitarian and aesthetic functions. When students explore the basic nature of a curricular topic, they apply the artistic principles of developing and organizing sensory experience through aesthetic play. Kinesthetic links to learning involve tuning in to the rhythm of an experience through the kinesthetic sense and using the nature of the instrument (the body) and the material (movement) to guide dance making. In this respect, art stays fully rooted in life.

❧ *Dance Making as Problem Solving*

The problem-solving methodology used in creative dance helps students discover new ways to move by stimulating the students' movement imagination. For the most part, students are not asked to copy a teacher's movements but are encouraged to discover their own kinesthetic solutions and express them through clear movement choices. This may also involve decision making between alternatives they have discovered. Students' choices from their explorations feed into the dance forms they create. Such problem solving happens on many levels throughout the lesson—while initially sensing movements, exploring concepts, working alone or with others, and, finally, putting together a culminating form.

Creative dance studies are generated from an objective framework of the elements of dance: the body, force, time, and space. These analytical categories provide fertile territory for creative problem solving. Offering limitations within the elemental material of dance focuses attention on the exploration of distinct kinds of movement possibilities without dictating the outcome.

A creative dance teacher builds lessons from an analytical framework, but students use the very personal modality of the kinesthetic sense to discover solutions to creative problems. Here exists an interplay of an objective problem and a subjective solution. This meeting of objectivity and subjectivity contributes to dance being both universal and, at the same time, intensely intimate. Students are reinforced in their capacity to be unique individuals while at the same time sharing a common focus with the group of which they are a part.

2.3 CREATIVE TOOLBOX—TRY THIS!

Problem Solving in Practice

Concept: Large Shapes and Movements

Lessons are developed by building meaningful progressions of creative problems based on the framework of analyzing movement by its elements. Let's look at an example. As a beginning exploration, students might be asked to make a large shape, and from that large shape to make a large movement. This is a very specific directive, yet it allows for many possible solutions. With reference to the analytic framework of the elements of dance, students are exploring the objective element of space. More pointedly, students' focus is limited to the aspect of shape and size. Even more specifically, their choices are limited to large shapes and movements. As a solution to the problem, one student may be splayed out on the floor, fanning arms and legs. Another may stand tall, then let the whole torso drop into a swing. In different ways, both are successfully solving the problem. Next, students could be asked to develop the movement in a way that takes them from place to place. The sequence of the two movement problems is a meaningful progression because the concepts have a natural, and now personalized, relationship within the element of space. From several such studies, material can be chosen to be developed into a culminating dance that ties together the focus, or objective, of the lesson.

By making up movements as they dance, students use their perceptions and imaginations to explore new ideas, opening doors in the mind to improvisational and experimental thinking. Intellectually, actively, and emotionally, dancers evaluate experience and recycle it in relation to ever changing situations. By creating and choosing solutions to movement problems, students gain experience in facing predicaments with many variables. This builds courage and a suppleness of mind that will aid them in other situations requiring flexibility, judgment, and decision making.

❧ *What about Music?*

Music and dance are intrinsically linked. In early societies there was no separation between dancers and musicians. As these art forms developed, however, they became specialized and their roles grew separate. The link between music and dance originates from the fact that any sound—vocal, body percussive, or instrumental—requires movement. Conversely, every movement creates sound, even if it is at a very low decibel. Music and dance arise from this common origin.

Playing an instrument while dancing unites the roles of dancer and musician.

Many people come to creative dance through experiences of listening to music and dancing freely to its inspiration. Music gives them the container they need to release their attention from utilitarian movement and to match their rhythm to the rhythm of the music. Without any instruction, people can enjoy movement expression simply by letting the music lead them. When chosen carefully, the vast array of wonderful recorded musical creations can act as an aid to expression by providing a mood or beat. Although it is the norm in modern culture, this practice of dancing in response to music (rather than music responding to movement) reverses the natural relationship of sound growing out of movement. In its purest form, creative dance stands on its own without the use of recorded music.

To develop freedom of expression, awareness of movement feeling, and control over the relationship between sound and silence, students benefit from opportunities to

The drummers are following the movement impulses of the dancing boy to create the musical accompaniment.

work without the support of external music. Creative dance lessons cultivate the relationship between music and dance by allowing dancers to discover their own internal rhythms and express them in both movement and sound. This is not a rejection of the importance of music for dance but a recognition of the unity of sound and movement. Emile Jaques-Dalcroze, a Swiss music educator of the early twentieth century, felt that understanding rhythm in a musical sense depended on awareness developed by movement. He created a system of teaching musical rhythm through movement experience. Called eurhythmics, this system is still a widely followed approach to music and dance education (Findlay, 1971; Jaques-Dalcroze, 1930). Making sound and creating music while dancing or while watching others dance develops the dancer's musicality and exponentially enriches the dance experience. This includes freeing the voice to reflect movement feeling; establishing and maintaining steady beat patterns; matching complicated irregular patterns of movement with sound; playing instruments while moving or in response to others' movement; and clapping, stomping and singing while dancing.

The power of music can work both for and against dance expression. Music can easily dominate or even unduly conflict with what a dancer is feeling or the nature of a study. This creates tension between the music and dance, making it very frustrating for individuals to follow and create their own authentic rhythmic patterns. One student insightfully observed that he had trouble attending to his own kinesthetic sensations because he was distracted by the mood of the music. We recommend using recorded music judiciously and with sensitivity to the relationship between sound and movement. Simply turning on music, which may or may not bear a relationship to the study being presented, dulls the senses and clouds students' appreciation for the natural relationship between sound and movement, music and dance. When dancing without recorded music, dancers are able to find movement feeling without the influence of external sound. Dancers need to be able to work in complete silence at times, and they need to be able to make their own music as they dance.

None of the lessons presented in this book requires the use of recorded music. Under most circumstances, a hand drum is adequate when musical support is desired. If a drum is too percussive for a study, other handheld rhythm instruments can be used to convey appropriate qualities. See Chapter 11 for details on matching rhythm instruments with movement qualities. You will also find some suggestions for recorded music in the Lesson Notes that follow lessons in Part V. Appendix F includes a music resource list that will lead you to further sources of music for creative dance. In general, any style of music can be used as accompaniment for creative dance, so follow your natural inclinations to find inspiring music for the dance studies you teach.

Relating Creative Dance Principles to Standards of Dance Education

As is true in other disciplines, educational standards have been developed for dance on the local, state, and national levels in the United States (see Box 2.1.) The standards developed by the National Dance Education Organization (NDEO) for teaching and learning dance in the arts were devised from a broad movement perspective and are applicable to a variety of dance styles and approaches. Rather than prescribe instructional methodology or curriculum, the standards are meant to be guideposts for developing and planning dance programming and curriculum in any dance genre. They help to assess individual student progress and reveal whether a program is providing balanced emphasis in different content areas of dance education. These standards

---

Box 2.1

Dance Standards: A Historical Perspective

In December of 1991 the U.S. Department of Education and the National Endowment for the Arts granted one million dollars to the Consortium of National Arts Education Associations to develop "world class" national standards in the arts of dance, music, theatre, and the visual arts. In 1994 the consortium published content and achievement standards outlining "what every young American should know and be able to do in dance" in the benchmark grades of 4, 8, and 12 (National Dance Association, 1994). This was the first time national standards were defined for dance education in the United States. They were accepted by Richard Riley, Secretary of the U.S. Department of Education, on March 11, 1994, as "voluntary" standards, meaning states could choose whether or not they wished to adopt them. By the year 2000, forty-nine of the fifty states had adopted the standards, but states unilaterally used the national standards to inform creation or revision of local, state, and district standards.

The National Dance Education Organization (NDEO) was formed subsequently to address the needs of dance education in the arts. Under its direction, *Standards for Dance in Early Childhood* were developed in 2002, and in 2003 NDEO organized a task force with representatives from professional studios of dance, K–12 teachers and administrators, arts agencies, and U.S. and state departments of education to revise the 1994 standards and develop *Standards for Learning and Teaching Dance in the Arts* (ages 5–18; K–12). Both sets of standards were finalized in 2005 and are available on the NDEO Web site, www.nedo.org.

Source: Contributed by Rima Faber, PhD, chair of the task force that developed *Standards for Learning and Teaching Dance in the Arts: Ages 5–12 (K–12)* for the National Dance Education Organization (2005).

serve as a model for states and school districts, which establish their own standards of dance education.

Currently, dance standards have been developed for early childhood education and for kindergarten through grade 12. Both sets of standards provide a continuum of learning organized to coordinate with the National Assessment of Educational Progress (NAEP) in the three overarching categories—performing, creating, and responding—plus a fourth category, interconnecting. Within these areas, achievement standards delineate the specific understanding and skill levels that are expected for early childhood, ages 2 to 5; and grade bands K–4, 5–8, and 9–12. As presented in *Creative Dance for Learning*, creative dance shares a compatible understanding of movement and dance with the current organization of dance standards of the United States, so the two work well together. How creative dance fits into the categories of these standards is described next.

Performing

Performing refers to the skills and knowledge involved in the execution of movement. Performance can include preset exercises or choreographed steps as well as improvisational explorations. Performance is evaluated by looking for the dancer's skill in using all of the elements of dance: the body, force (called "dynamics" in the standards), time, and space. Creative dance approaches performance and skill building primarily through exploration using the elements as building blocks for organizing a dance curriculum.

Creating

Creating involves movement invention and the organization of original movements into patterns that communicate meaning. The meaning of a movement is kinesthetically sensed and communicated by expressing what the body feels. Therefore, a movement may or may not represent anything beyond its own kinesthetic experience or form. Movement forms may be improvised or set into repeatable choreography, which is a problem-solving process. Once again the dance elements of force (dynamics), time, and space guide the framework for generating movement. Creative dance works with the same understanding of how to pose and find solutions to movement problems. These are seen in the exploration section of lessons wherein the movements are improvised, or in culminating forms, wherein the movements may be improvised or set into choreographed compositions.

Responding

Perceiving, analyzing, and synthesizing are important for any art experience. Responding to dance is integral to the acts of performing and creating, and also to the role of an audience. Responses can be made in a variety of modalities: movement, oral, written language, or another art form. In creative dance, responding is built into the exploratory process in both individual and group improvisation. Individual students learn to perceive and respond to verbal cues of the teacher and to kinesthetic feeling. In partners and groups, dancers can respond to each other in studies of moving and being moved, following a leader in unison, echoing movement, and in group creative improvisation. Responding skills are further developed by critical analysis at dance showings as well as in discussions, journal writing assignments, and follow-up activities that should be integral aspects of creative dance study. These provide opportunity to develop the perceptual and synthesizing skills necessary to respond to dance with insight.

Interconnecting

Creative dance is a discrete subject that interconnects to other arts, other academic disciplines, other historic eras, and life outside the classroom. It can also be a means to study diverse cultures. Characteristics of a culture's dance reflect the values and beliefs inherent in a society. These can be explored creatively, thus promoting understanding of different peoples. Creative dance promotes physical development, teaches social skills, encourages a healthful lifestyle, and provides avenues for personal fulfillment through artistic endeavors. The study of creative dance relates to other art forms through shared artistic forms and elements. Curricular links to science and math, language/literacy, and social studies are made through the insights and communication inherent in movement experiences such that academic standards in those subjects can be addressed as well. All of these interconnections between dance and other areas are recognized and affirmed by the NDEO standards.

Because the NDEO standards are written in such a way as to encompass all forms of dance, they encourage a broad interpretation. They need not standardize terminology, mandate teaching methodology, or dictate aesthetic values. That would stifle creative exploration in teaching and art making, the concern of many when facing the prospect of standards in education. Using the standards as they are intended, as a tool, opens one's teaching to a wide perspective and can ensure that a creative dance curriculum offers a full range of dance opportunities for students.

❧ Everyone Can Dance

In a free, creative approach to movement expression, everyone can dance, and each dancer brings his or her unique abilities to the dance work. Creative dance has a natural appeal to kinesthetic learners, and highly energetic children love the opportunity to be athletically challenged. At the same time, shy students feel the safety of tuning in to their own movements. Because creative dance encourages students to move in ways that feel natural and comfortable to them rather than imposing a specific style of movement, people who might balk at dancing can find an easy avenue into movement expression.

The kinesthetic sense works in combination with the other senses during dance, yet the dancer need not use all the senses in order to dance. Creative dance can be done in silence or with closed eyes. Dance improvisation uses the kinesthetic sense to develop the inner sense of sight through embodiment of spatial form and the inner sense of sound through moving to a beat. This is done whether or not there is actual stimulus from the eyes or ears. The blind and deaf can dance and gain immensely from the experience. Although physical disabilities can be limiting, they need not interfere with the ability to dance creatively. Everyone is encouraged to move in his or her own way.

It is not unusual for the word *dance* to conjure up scary connotations that lead people to say "I can't . . ." or "I don't dance." In this book we work to dispel a mislearned attitude that gives dance an exclusive choir: the idea that only certain people can dance. Building trust for the less inclined is an

Physical limitations need not interfere with the ability to dance creatively.

important step in teaching dance and in bringing dance into the lives of those who thought it was unavailable to them. Especially when cultural mores have inhibited movement expression, many beginners need a trusting environment to be able to dance. If the word *dance* puts off your audience, use the word *movement*. But what you will see from your students in the lessons of this book will be dance.

Creative dance is often associated with young children; less prevalent is the realization that creative dance improvisation is one of the most sophisticated and demanding of all dance forms. It requires spontaneous choices, high-level thinking skills through continual problem solving, and authentic attention to the kinesthetic sense. Creative dance is adaptable to all ages, physical abilities, and levels of experience. Its study is seated in concepts (the elements of dance) that apply to all dance forms, and the skills it teaches will make any dancer more expressive.

Chapter Summary

- Creative dance improvisation means creating movement forms while dancing. Using movement as material, it is based on kinesthetic awareness and the nature of human movement expression.
- The kinesthetic sense is a loop of awareness and response. The awareness phase involves both objective sensing and subjective associations. Movement expression is based on this awareness.
- Any sensory experience produces a kinesthetic response. Cultivating awareness and identifying with one's experience informs expressive choices in dance and any art making.
- Rhythm is the organizing principle used to create dance forms and to guide the teaching process.
- Creativity is a natural and necessary human behavior, making art integral to life.
- Art can serve both aesthetic and utilitarian needs.
- Creative problem solving takes place in all parts of a creative dance lesson. Dance making involves finding and choosing movement solutions to studies posed as problems whose solutions are not yet known.
- Music and dance arise from a common origin. Creative dance cultivates the dancer's internal sense of musicality. This can be done with or without sound.
- Creative dance relates to the National Dance Education Organization's dance standards through a compatible understanding of principles of dance as an expressive art.
- Creative dance is accessible to all because it is based on dancers moving in their own way.

REVIEW QUESTIONS

1. What is meant by a kinesthetic approach to creative dance improvisation?
2. How is movement expression related to kinesthetic awareness?
3. How does sensory perception affect artistic choices in dance?
4. Explain how rhythm relates to life, dance material, and group forms in dance improvisation.
5. Write a statement that affirms creative art as a human need and ability.
6. In what ways does creative dance involve problem solving?
7. How can musicality be developed in creative dance without the use of recorded music?
8. Describe the kind of creative dance activity that connects to each broad area of the NDEO dance education standards: performing, creating, responding, and interconnecting.

CHAPTER 3

CREATIVE DANCE

A COLLAGE OF LEARNING

Learning Objectives

1. Understand how creative dance enhances the natural development of the body and movement skills.

2. Discover how creative dance engages the senses.

3. Learn how creative dance interconnects all of the arts.

4. Understand how creative dance stimulates thinking skills.

5. Learn how creative dance helps to establish basic communication skills.

6. Discover how creative dance can build literacy.

7. Learn how creative dance can shape behavior and increase responsibility.

8. Understand how creative dance can help teach individual and group skills needed for community building.

9. Learn how creative dance enriches the quality of all areas of life.

Why dance? In Chapter 2 we emphasized how dance fulfills basic human needs for creating and expressing through movement. In this chapter you will learn how creative dance promotes individual and group growth from so many perspectives that it is truly a collage of learning. Its practice can make a difference in the world.

Creative Dance Develops Healthy Bodies

In a noncompetitive atmosphere, creative dance teaches confidence and proficiency in using the body as a tool for functional tasks, athletic competition, communication, and the expressive art of dance. Moving in healthy ways builds self-respect and boosts an individual's physical and emotional well-being. Offering the opportunity for successful movement experiences is especially vital during physically awkward stages of development.

With sedentary activities such as watching television or playing video games on the rise, it cannot be taken for granted that today's youth receive adequate movement opportunities. In general, young people are not as active as in times past, and childhood obesity is on the rise (Newman, 2004). Physical activities are less a part of children's normally active early years, pointing toward future potential health hazards for society. Although schools may have some sort of physical education program, physical activity is not a standard part of every school day. For example only 32 percent of U.S. high school students took physical education classes in 2001 (Newman, 2004). In some schools even recess time is being cut back. Creative dance can infuse movement into students' lives and set the stage for lifelong physical activity.

Creative dance is a great stress releaser. Relieving stress through exercise and relaxation facilitates efficient brain functioning and promotes mental and physical wellness (Hannaford, 1995). Learning to modulate both tension and relaxation helps individuals control their bodies. Contracting the muscles aids stability in movement and provides a

A dancer awakens the kinesthetic and tactile senses in preparation for dancing.

base of strength for forceful movements. Letting go of tension aids flexibility and enables ease and lightness in gentle movements.

One of the many goals in dance is body awareness. Students gain awareness of the possibilities of their physical bodies as they are guided through explorations of movement. Body awareness helps students recognize healthy alignment, which aids balance and prevents injury. As students move among others, body awareness helps them to avoid accidents by being proactive with physical self-control. Gaining awareness and trust in the body helps individuals make natural and effective kinesthetic choices. This is the beginning of efficient coordination and grace.

Creative Dance Awakens the Senses

Dance provides opportunities to balance many kinds of sensory awareness. Those who work at cultivating the kinesthetic sense are paying attention to who they are, where they are going, and what they are doing. Although the kinesthetic sense is the main player in dance, the sense of sight is called upon for perceiving visual designs in movement; hearing is sensitized as movement and sound are integrated; and the tactile sense is engaged when dancers contact parts of the body, other dancers, supporting surfaces, or objects. Kinesthetic dance experience is profound in its integration with life and is conducive to learning on many levels. The multisensory nature of dance contributes significantly to the critical role that movement and sensory perception play in physical and neurological development (Hannaford, 1995). Combining other kinds of sensory awareness with the primary kinesthetic sense helps students to integrate experience and knowledge within the arts and offers diverse ways of solving problems. Movement increases students' chances of success through activation of many sensory learning modes.

Creative Dance Interconnects the Arts

Art sparks imagination and encourages students to explore and celebrate being human in an increasingly technological era. Concepts learned through creative dance build a solid foundation for understanding all of the arts: music, drama, and the visual arts. Mettler (1980b) saw dance as primary and central to all the arts because all other art forms stem from movement. Throwing a pot, placing fingers on a keyboard, and the air flowing over vocal chords all result from movement. Without movement, a paintbrush would have no stroke, a guitar could not be strummed, and actors would have no physical support for their voices.

Each art form has an inherent relationship to dance through the elements of movement. Dance shares the element of time with music, and creative dance studies that emphasize time patterns and sound integrate with music. Spatial studies in dance are also design studies, sharing the space element with the visual arts. Dance integrates with drama through the force element, which calls forth emotions and the dramatic nature of interacting forces. These intrinsic connections between dance and the other art forms enable creative dance to act as the common thread when integrating the arts with each other and when infusing the arts in cross-curricular studies.

Creative Dance Exercises Thinking Skills

Harvard clinical psychiatrist John Ratey (2001) stated that movement not only relates to the motor functions of the brain but also "is crucial to every other brain function, including memory, emotion, language, and learning" (p. 148). These brain functions evolve from and depend upon movement. Why is this so? The same neural circuits that regulate physical tasks are used with thinking processes because they involve recalling, evaluating, and sequencing actions. The brain "walks through" these actions as it remembers, plans, and makes decisions. Eric Jensen (2000) noted that movement activity is needed at fairly frequent intervals for the brain to assimilate new information.

Movement helps stimulate brain activity by coordinating different areas of the brain. Because the two sides of the brain control different sides of the body, contralateral movements (that cross the midline of the body or counterbalance the sides) activate neural connections between the sides of the brain. Activities such as reading and logical investigation require cross-brain integration. Brain Gym movements developed by Paul and Gail Dennison (1994) harness this connection between movement and thinking. Bonnie Bainbridge Cohen (1993) has also demonstrated how developmental movement sequences promote intellectual growth. While it may not be necessary to "dance" to allow these important nerve connections to mature, dance offers movement opportunities that stimulate and ground them. The natural movements of creative dance wake up the brain of the dancer.

As described in Chapter 10, the broad ability of creative dance to exercise thinking skills can potentially tap all of Howard Gardner's multiple intelligences. Gardner (2004) looks upon intelligence in terms of problem-solving and product-producing abilities in a variety of modes. One of the most profound intellectual values of creative dance lies in its rich opportunities for creative problem solving. Because of the exploratory nature of creative dance, the answers to problems are often unknown, and students must call upon resourceful kinesthetic thinking. Problems often have several correct solutions and there are several ways to arrive at each answer. People practice higher level thinking skills when they create dances for artistic expression and also when they combine dance with academic themes and concepts.

Creative Dance Is Basic Communication

Early in life the qualities of common movements communicate expressive meaning. How a baby reaches his or her arms out—eagerly, desperately, languidly—communicates meaning without words. Even after children learn to talk, they continue to use movement to enforce their words or as a way to say something without any words. A shrug, a hug, a wave, or a start of surprise—each expresses a message that can be clearly understood. Facial expressions, body gestures, and postures add personality and meaning to spoken language. Body movement can also reveal contradictions to what is being said. Movement may communicate where words fail, and creative dance keeps this channel of communication alive.

When words are removed from communication, movement expression becomes especially significant. A simple action such as walking can speak eloquently. Sally's walk has a spirited lightness to it, Anna's walk is intent and strong, and Celia's is stiff and awkward. The walk carries with it attitudes and subconscious habits. The unique style a person lends to any movement demonstrates a personal characterization. If the quality lent to movement is a conscious choice, the dancer is crafting the communication of movement feeling. Genuinely expressed feeling can evoke kinesthetic empathy from those who are watching. When sharing dance with an audience, the dancer communicates movement feeling, beyond words.

Creative dance also enables individuals to practice the skill of effective movement communication through group work. In nonverbal leading and following studies, dancers use movement to communicate directives to their receptive and attentive followers, who respond accordingly. The leader's movements must be clear for the intended result to occur. These kinds of dance studies teach the importance of sensitive observation on the part of leader and follower. They are interactive, fun, challenging, and powerful in building communication skills.

This third grader is expressing the meaning of the word *exuberant.* The movement expression indicates and anchors her comprehension of the word's meaning.

Creative Dance Builds Literacy

Literacy tops the list of educational goals in the United States. Reading, writing, and communicating skills further education throughout a person's life. Dance contributes to literacy in many ways, from stimulating the brain to linking with the elements of language and composition. Examples of these links are found throughout this book.

Movement is important in the development of the physical and neurological skills needed for reading, writing, and language. An essential neurological connection is made between movement and sight. Activation of peripheral vision, which occurs during large movements, facilitates tracking and focus of both eyes. The more the body and head move (as they do while dancing), the more the muscles of both eyes work together. Efficient eye teaming enables students to focus, track, and concentrate while reading (Hannaford, 1995). Making letters through positions and pathways in movement supports the physical act of writing. Hannaford also points out that "ease with language requires the words and proper sentence structure from the left [brain] and the image, emotion and dialect from the right. This integration allows ease of reading and writing as well as comprehension and creative access" (p. 81). Kinesthetic exercises, cross-lateral movements, and large motor skills such as crawling, walking, running, skipping, and leaping use both sides of the body and the brain.

Creative dance studies engage linguistic intelligence. Some of the many creative dance activities that address literacy skills include expressing the meaning of vocabulary words and words that exemplify phonetic rules, working with the quality of phonetic sounds and the beat of a word's syllables, and interpreting the meaning of story characters, plot, setting, and mood. Dance also provides memorable experiences that can stimulate creative and descriptive writing. The acts of composing a story, essay, or poem in written language and composing a dance with movement both involve creating a form that communicates meaning. There are many parallels between written and dance composition. See the section on Linguistic Intelligence in Chapter 10 for more discussion on promoting literacy through dance. Chapter 8 and the lessons of Part V also provide many detailed examples of using creative dance to build literacy.

Creative Dance Shapes Behavior and Responsibility

When teaching dance, words like *stability, flexibility, tension,* and *relaxation* are used in a physical context. These attributes can be applied in a social context too. Awareness of one's body and knowledge of how to control it provide experiences that build confidence, coordination, and control of the whole self. Knowing that one can control and adapt movement leads one to be able to control social and emotional actions as well. Through creative dance, students learn to trust themselves and others, gaining courage to be individuals and greet the unknown. They learn to take control of their actions and their lives. Confidence mounts and creativity unfolds. From a strengthened personal awareness, individuals build self-esteem and confidence as a strong foundation for interaction with others. They are more able then to offer their full potential to society.

Laban and those who extended his work on effort into the field of psychology (Bartenieff, 1981; Laban and Lawrence, 1974; Lamb, 1965) discovered how different movement qualities express different personal strengths. A well-balanced personality is reflected in the ability to manifest many different movement quality combinations. Undeveloped strengths show up with a limited range of movement qualities and in the inability to respond to a given situation with the appropriate behavior. Therefore, providing students with a wide variety of movement experiences is useful for balancing behavioral attitudes and promoting healthy integrated personalities. The aggressive person benefits from practicing gentle uses of force, contained uses of space, and slow-paced movements. A timid person is encouraged to open up by use of general space, large movements, and exploration of the stronger aspects of the force element. Recognizing the needs of a group can guide teachers' choices for material to work within movement. Gentle movements may serve to calm down or focus a class. Strong movements can provide a group with a release of restrained energy or help them express dramatic feelings.

Creative dance builds life skills and is an excellent avenue for character building. Effort and perseverance go into mastering new skills. A good deal of practice is necessary for the physical control and athletic skill demonstrated in a finished dance. Students polish a movement study to the point where they are pleased with it and are willing to demonstrate the dance decisions they've made. Even when the teacher or their peers are the only audience, performance demands excellence. Making a dance, no matter how short it is, indicates that dancers have chosen what seems to them to be the best way to communicate an idea in the form of movement. Showing dances develops confidence and demonstrates commitment. Dancers make decisions. Dancers stick to it. Dancers perform.

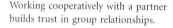

Working cooperatively with a partner builds trust in group relationships.

All creative dance lessons can affect behavior by developing both self- and group awareness. Individual security and self-respect found in movement activities bring strength to a group and contribute to interactive relationships. These experiences in creative movement influence attitudes and behavior, helping students to recognize the appropriateness of different types of behavior in life situations.

◈ *Creative Dance Builds Community from Diversity*

Throughout history people have come together to dance and to make art as an expression of their culture—a preservation, perhaps, of their heritage. The power one feels through making group art is personally satisfying and at the same time encourages a community feeling among the participants. Strong communities are made up of strong individuals. Their health depends on the ability of an individual to contribute strength to the larger group or to receive strength from others.

Creative dance lessons teach individual and group skills that are needed for community building. Beginning with individual development, creative dance encourages each student to find and express his or her uniqueness. When students feel safe and individual needs are fulfilled, they are more able to accommodate group needs. Group studies in each dance element contribute to gathering a feeling of community. Dancers learn to form group bodies. They learn to accommodate their use of force in relation to each other's needs. They synchronize as a group on a beat pattern and move in spatial forms—such as a group circle or line—that create a feeling of unity. Leading and following exercises and unison movements build sensitivity to perceiving group needs and making contributions.

Pride and a sense of belonging strengthen successful group work. Life skills such as cooperation and caring are developed as students create collaborative artworks with the needs of the group foremost in mind. By dancing together and contributing their own strengths to a larger entity, dancers form bonds that can last a lifetime. This provides a basis for building relationships with others in any area of life. Creative dance experience promotes the ability to work with others harmoniously at school, in the community, and in society at large.

Intergenerational dancing creates a sense of community.

P art II provides a prose glossary and an analytical structure of terms and concepts used in creative dance teaching. The terms being described are printed in bold type and are summarized on the Elements of Dance chart starting on page 60.

Our major influences (Mettler, H'Doubler, and Laban) all analyze movement around categories similar to those presented here, yet each has his or her own organization and point of view. In general we have chosen to define our framework with terms that are simple, are broadly applicable, and in our experience have helped students understand movement in a way that has consistently stimulated creative expression.

CHAPTER 4

THE INSTRUMENT OF DANCE

The Body

Learning Objectives

1. Distinguish between the body as the instrument and movement as the material of dance.

2. Identify aspects of the body's structure that provide useful focuses for instrumental training.

3. Describe basic in-place (axial) body movements.

4. Define basic locomotor movements in terms of how the body shifts weight from one part to another.

5. Understand how the physiological functions of kinesthetic sensory awareness, muscular tension and relaxation, breathing, heartbeat, and dynamic alignment contribute to instrumental skill in dance.

6. Recognize the difference between group body and individual body movement.

❧ *The Relationship of the Instrument to the Material of Dance*

Each art has an instrument with which to create its particular form. Violins, carving tools, and word processors are all instruments of expression in different mediums. In dance, the instrument is the body in the same way that a brush is the instrument of painting. And just as the elemental materials a painter works with include line, color, and shapes, the material of dance includes force, time, and space—attributes that characterize movement. A dancer uses the body as an expressive instrument to create movement forms by manipulating and molding qualities of force, time, and space. Developing instrumental skill for dance enables the body to give clear form to a feeling.

Just as musical instruments need to be tuned, tools need to be sharpened, and computers need to be programmed, body coordinations need to be practiced and honed. Ideally, basic movement skills are discovered and learned as the body follows a natural course of physical growth and development. Creative dance training augments this natural development. Beyond athletic control and a pure enjoyment of movement, dance coordination primarily means using the body as an instrument of expression. Through skillful use of the instrument, dancers learn to express themselves safely and effectively in the art of body movement. Even though lack of instrumental technique need not prevent a person from having beautiful dance experiences, such skills help the body to break through physical limitations that might hamper creative expression.

Because the body cannot be separated from the movements it makes, the distinction between instrument and material is a subtle one. This distinction, however, is crucial to dance as a creative art. When focusing on the instrument, dancers are paying attention to their own bodies—that is, to themselves. Focusing on movement as material to be molded takes the dancer beyond that personal focus. On an artistic level, the purpose of developing instrumental skills is in service of creating movement forms that express and communicate meaning. When this purpose is not understood, overemphasis may be

CONCEPT SPOTLIGHT 4.1

Relationship of Instrument and Material

Body as instrument	Movement as material
Focus on oneself	Focus on quality and form of movement
Personal/concrete	Abstract

CONCEPT SPOTLIGHT 4.2

Aspects of the Body Element

The main areas addressed within the body element are:

  Structure
  Basic movements
  Physiological functions

These provide focuses for exploration in instrumental studies.

placed on what the body can look like and do rather than what it can say. Ultimately, the heart of dance experience lies in putting attention not on instrumental work but on the feeling and form of the movement material.

✍ The Body's Structure

While focusing on body structure, dancers explore how parts of the body move independently and in combination with each other. Each part of the body plays its unique role in forming a coordinated whole body movement.

Within the **torso,** the central trunk of the body, lie several key areas that are crucial for coordination of the **whole body.** The **center of gravity,** or center of weight, generally located in the middle of the pelvis while standing, is the point around which the weight of the body balances. When exerting force (as in lifting, pushing, and pulling), control around the center of gravity is important to stabilize the body and maximize power. This requires awareness and strength in the abdominal muscles. Martial arts systems such as karate, aikido, and t'ai chi emphasize stability around the center of gravity. These ancient traditions recognize that this is the base of power in movement.

Many instrumental skills revolve around coordinating the body as the center of gravity shifts. When one changes body position (moves an arm or a leg, for example), the weight shifts and the body must adapt to a new position to stay balanced. If a person shifts the center of gravity far enough in space, her base of support will change and she will take a step or roll or fall.

In addition to the center of gravity, Rudolf Laban (1971) recognized a **center of levity,** or lightness in the upper torso. Residing near the sternum bone, this is the center of buoyancy, the point around which the body floats (Hay and Reid, 1978). Moving from the center of levity is an instrumental skill that supports the dancer's ability to express the feeling of lightness by moving with minimal force and delicate discrimination. Even rough and tough fifth graders are able to render beautiful, poignant expressions of gentleness when asked to "lift from the heart" or "feel a string pulling upwards on the sternum."

Ascending in the torso, the **spine** sports a design that adjusts subtly with every movement. Its structure of twenty-six separate vertebrae arranged vertically with cervical, thoracic, lumbar, and coccygeal curves permits a natural rippling of movement from

Lifting from the chest (the center of levity) aids the expression of lightness.

one vertebra to the next. In this way, the spine spreads movement through the center of the body toward or away from the extremities. The head, arms, and legs, which radiate out from the center of the body, connect with each other through this central column of the torso.

The extremities are attached to the torso in a way that enables them to move independently from each other and the torso as well as in concert with the whole body. The **shoulder girdle,** connecting the arms to the upper torso, rests like a yoke on top of the **ribs.** Lower extremities connect through the **pelvis** at the hip sockets. The hip and shoulder joints are designed to allow great freedom of movement, but it is not uncommon for people to be limited by tightness or instability in these areas. By practicing awareness and control while freely exploring movement, dancers can develop their bodies in healthy, natural ways without the risk of damaging these vulnerable joints.

Developing kinesthetic sensitivity in the hands and feet contributes to expression in a dance.

Practiced instrumental use of extremities in relation to each other and in coordination with the whole body adds noticeably to the expressiveness of a person's movements. The connection of the **head** to the spine is important for whole body coordination. When the head is held on the neck too tightly, movement in the whole body is restricted. When the head moves freely at the top of the spine, movements of the whole body are more efficient and graceful. Although in most aspects of life the **legs** and **feet** are used primarily in a utilitarian manner to transport us from place to place, in dance the legs take on an expressive role beyond the utilitarian. The extremities of **arms** and **hands** are commonly used in everyday life as people gesture to express feelings. Dance expands that gesture language into expression with the whole body. It is a wonderful experience to work with the head, feet, and legs to wake up their kinesthetic sensitivity with the intent of making them as expressive as arms and hands.

The **vocal cords** come into play in creative dance as the voice is used by the dancer while moving. In creative dance sound unites with movement; the quality of sound generated by the flow of breath over the vocal cords naturally matches the qualities being expressed in the rest of the body.

The structure of the musculoskeletal system as it combines with the functioning of the muscles determines the nature of basic human movement. Without the armature of the skeleton, human bodies would be an amorphous mass. **Bones** provide a framework for the body shape, and muscles provide the power that makes movement happen. Being connected to the skeleton, muscular action moves the bones through space. How muscles attach to the skeletal system and the way bones fit together at the **joints** determine how the bones move in relation to each other and, consequently, restrict the basic movements the body can do. See Appendix B for an anatomical model of the skeletal system.

❧ *Basic Body Movements*

The physical vocabulary for creative dance is derived from the natural functions of the musculoskeletal system. Natural human movements very clearly reflect the body's structure and how it developmentally learns to move. The following basic body movements are roots for all movements. Learning to do these actions gracefully and with efficiency is an instrumental skill that provides a base for expressive forms of movement.[1]

Stretching wakes up movement feeling at the beginning of a class.

The joints of the body are primarily built to extend, flex, and rotate. These functions correlate with the basic body movements of **stretching, bending,** and **twisting,** respectively.

Twisting is a rotational movement.

When twisting continues full circle, it becomes **turning. Opening** and **closing** emphasize abduction and adduction combined with extension and flexion as well as outward and inward rotation of the limbs. Each of these movements requires muscular tension and control. Other basic body movements require the muscles to relax. The body moves loosely in such movements as **flopping** and **dropping.** These movements have a heavy feeling because the weight of the body is released into gravity. **Falling** movements result when the body completely gives in to gravity. **Shaking** can be done either loosely or tightly. Loose shaking and **bouncing** actions help the body let go of tension. The basic movement of **swinging** combines both release and control: the release allows the movement to drop into the swing, and control powers and guides the movement. Because every single movement involves both contraction and release of muscle fibers, it follows that any movement needs to have some degree of swing. Bouncing is an excellent preparation for swinging because it requires releasing the knees, which is necessary to express the dropping quality of a swing.

Undulating movements highlight the characteristic successional movement of the spine, wherein one vertebra pushes on its neighbor in a wavy manner. Successional movement is very important because it is among the earliest to develop and thus serves as underlying support for more complicated movements. This kind of movement can be transferred to the legs and arms so that the softness of the waving movement gives the extremities a curvy feeling, even though the bones of the legs and arms are straight. When teaching successional coordination to young children, undulation may be too difficult a word. **Waving** is a useful term although it needs to be clearly shown not to imply waving hello or good-bye with the hands. **Rippling** is another word that denotes especially small undulations. Choosing the right word to introduce this movement will depend on the context, age, and language development of the students.

The actions of these basic body movements are typical of what the body structure can naturally do **in place.** That is, their primary action is around one or more axes of the body. For this reason they are called **axial movements.** Because they ask the body to move in ways that are characteristic of its structure, involve both relaxation and tension, and are free of the challenge of moving through space, these axial movements are a useful way to prepare the body as an instrument at the beginning of a dance class. They are a major component of The Moving Body lesson in Chapter 14.

The body as an instrument also moves from place to place. **Locomotor movement** involves moving the center of gravity through space and changing the support of weight from one part of the body to the other. Most of the time, weight shifting is done from foot to foot. **Walking** shifts weight from one foot to the other foot and maintains some contact with the ground at all times. One can also shift weight between other body parts without leaving the ground as in **rolling, crawling,** and **slithering.** Movements that make a weight shift while the body is in the air are referred to as having an "air moment." These include movements that go into the air and come down on the same foot (**hopping**), land on the opposite foot (**running** and **leaping**), or land on both feet (**jumping**).

Galloping and **skipping** are more complex locomotor movements. A single gallop or skip involves two movements, one of which takes a longer time than the other. A gallop is an uneven run in which one leg consistently moves the longer amount of time. This

---

4.1 CREATIVE TOOLBOX—TRY THIS!

Undulating

Undulating is a good basic movement for focusing on the kinesthetic sense. This can be done by making large wavy movements with the whole body and then directing students to make the waves smaller and smaller while closing their eyes. Even young children enjoy making ripples so small that they can barely be seen, yet are felt moving within their bodies.

4.2 CREATIVE TOOLBOX—TRY THIS!

A Sneaky Approach to Skipping

Sometimes children have a difficult time learning to skip. If so, they need to return to practicing more basic skills such as crawling, jumping, and galloping rather than being drilled intellectually on the mechanics of skipping. Well-meaning attempts to break down the skip into a step and hop are often unsuccessful because the muscular control to step and then hop develops later than the ability to skip. Here, overintellectualizing hampers the developmental process. Children can not skip (or do any other complex movement) until they have developed the coordination that supports that action. After students can gallop with ease, a good strategy for teaching skipping is to have students exaggerate a bouncy walk until it turns into a skip. This is an example of what Margaret H'Doubler's students called her "sneaky approach" to teaching movement skills (Brehm, 1988 p. 57).

---

means that weight is transferred from one foot to the other, while leaving the ground, with an uneven beat pattern. The simplest way to cue a gallop is to say that one foot leads. A skip is an uneven step and hop with more airtime than contact with the ground. This gives skipping a lifted feeling. In explaining the difference between a skip and a gallop, one third-grade student noted that in a skip the legs take turns. Although they require different coordinations, galloping and skipping can be done with the same irregular beat pattern.

Exaggerating a bouncy walk is an effective way to teach skipping.

As babies and young children progress through developmental motor stages, they spend a lot of time building the instrumental skills of shifting weight from one part of the body to another. They start with lying, lifting the head and upper torso, rolling, and crawling. These activities provide the foundation for walking, jumping, running, galloping, skipping, and leaping. This motor development sequence in humans parallels the movement coordinations of other animals as they evolve from simple to complex organisms (Cohen, 1993). All humans begin life moving in an undifferentiated way, opening and closing around the center of the body much like a jellyfish or starfish. This develops into moving the spine in snakelike slithering. Movement progresses to rolling, then to pushing and reaching with both sides of the body at once as a frog does or when swimming the breast stroke or bouncing on two feet at once. The next pattern to evolve is moving one side of the body at a time like a lizard does. In a standing position children usually exhibit this coordination when asked to gallop or to "move like Frankenstein." This pattern is followed by the developmental coordination of contralateral movement, an ability shared with amphibians such as salamanders and other mammals. In contralateral movement, the arms and legs of opposite sides of the body balance each other. This can be done while crawling and by swinging the arms while walking. When the right foot steps, the left arm swings forward. Contralateral movement is also used in running, leaping, skipping, and most other complex movements. It is the most advanced coordination of the body and requires integration of both hemispheres of the brain (see Figure 4.1).

In human development these movement coordinations are usually explored horizontally at floor level first and then vertically while standing (Cohen, 1993; Hannaford, 1995). When there are no developmental hindrances, and if given the opportunity to practice them, children will naturally do these movements, which then become part of their movement vocabulary. Returning to more basic coordinations such as crawling and rolling supports the ability to perform difficult, complex coordinations. Children seem

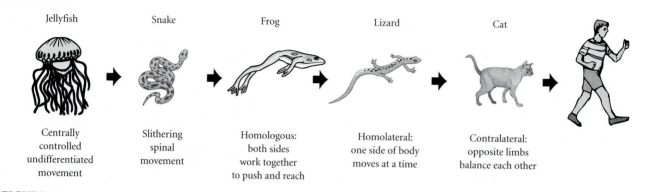

Jellyfish   Snake   Frog   Lizard   Cat

Centrally   Slithering   Homologous: Homolateral: Contralateral:
controlled   spinal   both sides   one side of body   opposite limbs
undifferentiated   movement   work together   moves at a time   balance each other
movement   to push and reach

FIGURE 4.1   *Human motor development follows the same sequence as the evolution of animal movement.*

to know this instinctively. Possibly that is why, even in the intermediate grades, students enjoy getting down on the floor and crawling around. The body wants to do these movements.

❧ *Physiological Functions*

Although all physiological functions are required for normal life and movement, the following functions are highlighted because of their special significance for helping dancers create expressive movement forms.

The **kinesthetic sense** (described in Part I) comes into play in the body element as the dancer is precisely aware of what the instrument is doing and how the movement feels. In dance the body does not just perform mechanically coordinated movements; it expresses feeling. Instrumental skill in dance requires developing the kinesthetic sense so that dancers can make physical and expressive choices based on movement feeling. Also, incorporating the use of other senses such as hearing and seeing into dance expression builds upon this kinesthetic base. Because the kinesthetic sense is so important in preparing the body for dance, each dance lesson ideally begins with a few activities geared toward awakening the kinesthetic sense.

A single muscle fiber has two physiological functions. It can contract, and it can release. These conditions are felt in the muscles as **tension** and **relaxation.** When contracted, a muscle feels tight; when released, it feels loose. Human movement occurs between the two poles of tension and relaxation. The key to efficient movement is to contract only the muscles necessary to achieve the movement desired. In extreme tension, the body is locked into no movement because opposing muscles hold it rigidly in a position. When there is extreme relaxation, the body rests with no overt movement because the muscles are not exerting any force. Between these poles, the flow of tension and relaxation underlies body actions and the expression of different qualities of movement.

Learning to coordinate the interplay of tension and relaxation in the muscles is an important functional skill for expressiveness in dance. Heavy-feeling movements can be achieved by relaxing the muscles. Of course, the body does not in fact gain mass as muscles loosen. But with the help of gravity the muscles let go, and the weight of the body sinks easily into loose, heavy movements such as rocking or flopping. A small amount of tension to stabilize the center of gravity and lift the center

Held tension creates a tight position.

of levity will tend to elevate the body out of its loose heaviness and allow gentle, light movements such as tapping or floating. A greater amount of tension is needed for forceful movements such as pushing and pulling, which rely on strong contraction of the muscles.

An individual muscle fiber can only be either tight or loose at any given moment. Because of the on/off nature of how muscle fibers work, they can only make one movement at a time. Yet a single movement requires a synchronous coordination of contraction and release of many different muscle fibers. Because muscles are grouped so that complementary muscles contract when opposing ones release, there is a flow of tension and relaxation to create a succession of movements. This has implications for how a dancer develops skill in letting one movement naturally flow out of the previous one. In creative dance, this is not done by logically thinking about what movement to do next. It happens by feeling the movement.

Complete relaxation results in a loose position.

Even though every movement experience is unique, some general principles apply to the succession of one movement after another. For example, after body parts have moved away from each other, as in opening, they will naturally want to come together again and close. An arm that has been lifted will at some point want to descend. Creative dance making is based on the natural functioning of the body wherein movements evolve organically one after another. This approach to body movement aligns with the basis of early modern dance as opposed to more conceptual approaches to dance making.

The movement of **breathing** coordinates the rhythm of tension and relaxation in all natural body movement (Mettler, 1980b). The primary muscle governing respiration is the diaphragm, a horizontal domelike muscle that separates the lungs and the abdominal organs. As such, it lies between the centers of gravity and levity. The diaphragm is aided by the intercostal muscles of the ribs and the abdominal muscles. The inhalation phase of breathing normally occurs as the diaphragm contracts and moves downward. This movement enlarges the space available for the lungs, creating a partial vacuum and attracting air into the lungs. In normal exhalation, the diaphragm relaxes and moves upward, compressing the lungs and causing air to be released out of the body through the nose and mouth. The abdominal muscles come into play during a forced exhalation, contracting and adding to that upward and outward movement of air by strongly pushing the diaphragm even higher into the chest (Calais-Germain, 1993).

Certainly, inhalation and exhalation are vitally important in respiration's primary role of providing oxygen to the body. In addition, coordination between the diaphragm and abdominal muscles in the mechanics of respiration plays an important role in how breathing supports instrumental skills and creative expression in dance. Breathing out and contracting the abdominal muscles strongly during a forced exhalation tends to stabilize the torso, making forceful movements more efficient and effective. Because exhalation involves both relaxation of the diaphragm and contraction of the abdominals, the outbreath impulse can match exerting as well as releasing impulses. Exhalation naturally occurs both at the moment of greatest exertion (such as in chopping movements) and at moments of release (such as in loose, floppy movements). This can be seen in the natural tendency to mark the impulse of strong movements with sound such as the "Hyah!" that accompanies a karate chop and to audibly exhale in a sigh when relaxing. Cultivating this natural synchronization of exhalation with the beginning of a movement can be especially useful when working with force and time rhythms.

Because breathing is both voluntary and involuntary, it can be controlled. In therapeutic, meditative, and yoga practices, both inhalation and exhalation phases of the breath are sometimes controlled and manipulated. The question arises of how much to control the breath while dancing. Mettler (1980b) recognized the coordination between exhalation and muscular action and stressed the importance of exhaling on movement impulses whether they involve taking hold or letting go. She taught that, for dance, breathing should be as natural as possible because holding or unduly patterning the breath stifles freedom of movement and creative expression. If exhalation is allowed to naturally coordinate with movement, breathing in will usually take care of itself because, in terms of rhythmic movement expression, inhalation is primarily a preparation for exhalation. If too much attention is paid to moving exactly with the in and out rhythm of the breath, the movement may become locked into a rigid pattern that lacks artistic liveliness. Likewise, thinking too hard about movement often results in holding the breath and hesitant, uncoordinated movement. Tense intellectual concentration and the disconnection from the breath that goes with it can be avoided by following the feeling of movement; that is, by using the kinesthetic sense as a guide. A kinesthetic approach to breathing and movement frees both the breath and the flow of movement, making it easier to integrate the breath while dancing.

Another body function important to expression is the **heartbeat,** an internal drumbeat that makes working with beat patterns in time alluring and natural. Directing students to listen to their heartbeat while resting quietly can heighten awareness of the beat pattern happening inside them. The resting heartbeat is an example of an ongoing beat pattern that exists in life.

The body's dynamic **alignment** is crucial to skillful performance of dance movements. Viewing alignment as dynamic recognizes that posture is not a static position to be held. It is a constantly changing relationship of body parts—the coordinated functioning of the neuromusculoskeletal systems. A well-aligned body allows the dancer to move with more freedom and grace. It allows the body to move to its optimal range and ability to balance. Since the early twentieth century, many complementary approaches have been developed for studying efficient movement function from the standpoint of kinesthetic experience. These are called somatic approaches because they study the body from the standpoint of experience and function. They include, among others, the Alexander Technique (1984), Feldenkrais (1972), Hanna Somatics (1988), Body–Mind Centering (Cohen, 1993; Hartley, 1995), Bartenieff Fundamentals (Bartenieff, 1981; Hackney, 2002), and Sensory Awareness (Brooks, 1986; Littlewood, 2004) from the tradition of Gindler, Jacoby, and Selver. Somatic approaches to alignment are helpful to creative dancers' instrumental skills because they work from a kinesthetic base and cultivate natural movements.

❧ Group Body

Thus far the body element has been addressed in terms of an individual dancer. However, in group dancing, attention to the **group body** also becomes important. Structurally, both individual and group bodies are made up of different parts. In an individual body those parts include the head, torso, arms, legs, and so forth. The group body consists of the individuals that are members of the group. The group body is characterized by the number of members, the skills and temperament of its members, and their arrangement in space. Each dancer's body is part of the group body, but group movement does not occur merely by adding individual movements together. Just as the separate body parts need to synchronize to produce coordinated body movements for an individual, the dancers in a group need to synchronize their bodies to produce coordinated group movements. In practical terms, this often means simplifying individual body movements so that the form of the group body becomes clear. Mettler (1960/2006) noted that group body movement "is a different *kind* of movement" from individual movement

A group body is formed by the integrated functioning of all its parts. Each individual body contributes to the whole.

(p. 388). How the group body functions within the different elements of dance is addressed in Chapters 5, 6, and 7.

CONCEPT SPOTLIGHT 4.3

Individual Body versus Group Body: Opening and Closing

Opening and closing involves parts of the body getting farther apart and closer together. For an individual body, this means the arms and legs move away from each other and then come together again. When a group body opens and closes the focus is on the members of the group separating and coming together. The relationship of individual body parts is relatively insignificant.

Attention to the structure, function, and basic movements of the body constitute the domain of the body element of dance. The terms described previously provide topics upon which to focus a dancer's attention in instrumental studies. In creative dance this primarily takes the form of thematic improvisations such as body part studies or exploring the feeling of different basic body movements. Specific movement patterns can also be given as exercises to guide the student in finding the kinesthetic feeling of a particular body coordination. (See Chapter 14, The Moving Body, and Chapter 15, Body Parts, for lessons that address the body element.)

Having focused on aspects of the body as the instrument of dance, we can now turn our attention toward the material of dance. Throughout Chapters 5, 6, and 7 on movement material, references are made to instrumental body element themes that support expression of each of the formal elements of movement.

CHAPTER SUMMARY

- The body is the instrument of dance; movement is its material.
- Instrumental studies for dance can be generated by considering the structural aspects of the body; that is, the parts of the body that move.
- Basic movements are a natural part of developmental sequences and normal movement experience. Basic axial movements stay in place. Locomotor movements shift weight in patterns that travel from place to place.
- Physiological functions that especially support creative dance include the kinesthetic sense, muscular tension and relaxation, breathing, the heartbeat, and dynamic alignment.
- The group body is made up of individual bodies, which creates a different kind of movement from that of an individual body.

REVIEW QUESTIONS

1. What is the relationship between creative dance studies that focus on the body as the instrument of dance and studies that focus on movement as the material of dance?
2. As key areas of the body's structure, how do the centers of gravity and levity facilitate the expressiveness and coordination of whole body movements?
3. Generate a sample sequence of basic axial movements, including movements that engage muscular tension as well as movements that promote muscular relaxation.
4. Make a chart that categorizes locomotor movements by the following criteria:
   - Manner of weight shifts between body parts
   - Whether there is an air moment
   - Even or uneven beat pattern

5. How do each of the following physiological functions contribute to skilled dance expression?
   · The kinesthetic sense
   · Muscular tension and relaxation
   · Breathing
   · Heartbeat
   · Dynamic alignment

6. What factors determine the nature of movement created by a group body? How does this compare to (or differ from) individual movement?

Note

1. The sequence of movements Mettler (1960/2006) recommended as instrumental preparation and awakening of movement feeling provided the starting point for our list of basic movements. To stimulate a range of kinesthetic sensation, they encompass many movement qualities. H'Doubler (1950) groups these actions somewhat differently. Although not listed as such, stretching, bending, twisting, opening, and closing are incorporated in her analysis of joint actions. Movements such as swinging, undulating (sequential in H'Doubler terminology), and shaking (vibratory) are addressed as qualities. This comparison illustrates how the same movement phenomena can be looked at through different lenses for different purposes.

CHAPTER 5

THE MATERIAL OF DANCE

The Force Element

Learning Objectives

1. Identify force, time, and space as the movement elements that are the material of dance.
2. Define impulse and discuss how awareness of impulse and creative pause contribute to finding organic dance form.
3. Discuss dynamic polarities that connect creative dance to natural patterns of balance.
4. Describe how shifts in force create accents.
5. Explain how the force element underlies dramatic expression.
6. Discuss how the interaction of activity and receptivity underlies group work in dance.
7. Identify specific instrumental skills that support expression in the force element.

Movement as the Material of Dance

When working with the material of dance, students put their attention on the forms or patterns of the movements they are making rather than on their bodies. Movement occurs from an impulse of **force** exerted in **time** through **space.** All movement, not just human movement, can be analyzed in terms of these three attributes. When approaching movement as the material of dance, the elements of force, time, and space provide a concrete framework within which to work. This gives both teachers and dancers an objective focus that is very liberating, especially to those who may feel intimidated by the idea of improvised dance or movement expression. Understanding movement in terms of these three elements helps teachers focus students' attention on one aspect of movement at a time and gives teachers access to materials that can stimulate a full range of expressive movement responses from students. This helps teachers to be clear about what they are teaching and why. Movement analysis is not an end in itself. In this context, it is purely in service of the dancer being able to feel the rhythmic ebb and flow of movement that generates a rich dance experience.

Organic Dance Form

The element of force brings focus to how, or in what manner, a movement occurs.[1] In humans and other animals, the force of a movement is produced by a movement **impulse,** a contraction of muscles that requires energy or effort. When force is exerted, movement occurs. When there is no force, there is no movement. Mettler (1960/2006) describes a movement impulse as a "single wave of activity beginning and ending in rest" (p. 108). In daily life most people are unaware that activity alternates with rest in every movement. Rest is apparent in some movements such as the pattern of breathing when the body is relaxed or

---

CONCEPT SPOTLIGHT 5.1

One Movement at a Time

Although organic form studies are more appropriate for advanced students, beginning students can benefit from making one movement at a time. The term *organic form* might not be introduced in early lessons, but asking students to make single movements one after another helps them to discover the way movements naturally emerge one from another. This is an excellent way for beginners to focus on the feeling and form of a movement and to open doors to kinesthetic creativity. For choreographers, organic form offers insight into natural transitions and progressions of movement.

---

asleep. There is a natural pause at the end of the exhale before the next inhale begins. The force pattern of exertion followed by recuperation is the origin of rhythm in movement.

Fritz Klatt (1923) calls this moment of repose between movements the **creative pause,** and it contains the seed of the next movement. When students are keyed into how one movement is born out of another, they can begin to get a sense of what Mettler calls **organic form.** Dance studies introducing organic form focus on making one movement at a time. They reveal how one movement impulse naturally flows out of the stillness at the end of the preceding movement. By exaggerating the pause between movements and sensing their bodies as they move and pause, students can discover how they want and need to move next. The dancing that results is organic because its form is determined through awareness of the nature of the movement itself rather than through intellectual or arbitrary considerations. Organic dance form is alive. Its growth and development emerge spontaneously from the dancer's ever changing kinesthetic feeling (Mettler, 1960).

✆ *Dynamic Polarities*

Organic dance forms grow out of the natural phases of activity and rest in the body. Characteristically, force expended in movement happens as fluctuations between poles of opposites. An example of this is the way muscles function: to make a movement, a muscle fiber must contract; it then has to release, or rest, before it can contract again. The body's movements mirror the basic activity/rest rhythm that characterizes all of life in such cycles as day/night, growing/withering, and living/dying. If dance is approached as a natural activity that follows natural patterns of the world, it must be framed in a system that acknowledges the balancing effects of polar opposites.

Opposites are very evident in the analysis of the force element. Movements use varying degrees of force. Those which use a lot of force are **forceful.** They are **strong,** assertive movements such as pushing, pulling, pounding, and squeezing. Movements using little force are relatively **forceless.** They have a **gentle** quality such as in tapping, brushing, threading, or floating.[2] Forceful movements require a lot of muscular exertion. Although forceful movements can be made in an upward direction, they are easier to make downward because the force exerted by the body can be combined with the downward force of gravity. Unlike the downwardness of heavy movements that release into gravity, forceful movements require active engagement of the muscles. Forceless movements require just enough muscular tension to overcome the force of gravity. In overcoming gravity, forceless movements tend to have a light feeling. They are most easily expressed in an upward direction because their nature is to defy gravity and express the illusion of weightlessness. Downward light movements present an interesting challenge to dancers because they go against their natural tendency to resist gravity.

In addition to the amount of force being expended in movement, it is also important to consider the manner of exertion. Force can be exerted all at once in sudden movements, or it may be exerted gradually, a little at a time. **Sudden** movements have a sharp, jerky feeling, such as in pulling away after touching a hot surface. **Gradual** or **sustained** movements have a smooth, continuous quality, such as petting a cat or pushing a piano. The polarity of sudden/gradual has a relationship to the time element because the length of time it takes for the force to be exerted helps determine its dynamic quality. But sudden does not necessarily mean fast, nor gradual slow. Sudden movements can be done at a slow pace, resulting in discreet bursts of movement with long pauses in between; and gradual movements can be fast, having an oscillating or rippling quality. The emphasis in the force element is on the quality of the movement as the energy is being expended (either all at once or a little at a time) rather than on how much time there is between movements. Although the distinction between sudden/gradual and fast/slow need not be addressed with beginning or young students, it does provide fruitful material for exploration on an advanced level.

The force of a movement may be directed in a **pinpointed** and **single-focused** manner, or it may be **scattered** and **multifocused.** Planting seeds one at a time is a single-focused use of force, whereas scattering many seeds over an area all at once is multifocused. Single focus involves gathering energy; multifocus involves dispersing energy. This polarity has a spatial aspect because it refers to the use of space where the force is directed. When exploring the focus of movement through the element of force, the emphasis is again on the feeling of the movement and whether it is narrow and condensing or open and spreading.

These sets of opposites (forceful/forceless, sudden/gradual, single focus/multifocus) address the amount of force and its manner of expression. They provide the rhythmic structure for playing with the force element. Different life situations call for combining force attributes in different ways. For example, threading a needle requires pinpointed focus, sustained control, and delicacy of movement. Slashing with a machete involves an opposite use of dynamic polarities—a scattered, sudden, strong use of force. For full artistic range, it is important for dancers to be able to express a wide palette of movement qualities.

Jason's strong/forceful movement occurs suddenly with a pinpointed focus of energy.

❧ Using Force for Accents

In any movement expression, the form is made lively by accenting some parts of the movement more than others. An **accent** occurs when a movement or group of movements receives more stress than others. This requires more force. Accents happen when there is a shift between polar opposites: a strong movement occurring among gentle movements, a fast movement among slow, a big movement among small. The shift in the amount of force produces the accent. The placement of accents within a movement series creates phrases of movement. As students become aware of the accents in a sequence, they begin to recognize rhythmic patterns created by the ebbing and flowing of force.

❧ Dramatic Expression through the Force Element

The element of force connects closely with dramatic expression. Barbara Mettler explained this link by noting that drama involves the interaction of forces (personal communication, Mettler workshop, January–March 1990). Underneath the details of any drama is a tale of forces moving in relation to each other. When conflicting forces meet, the waves and reverberations that constitute the drama of life are set into motion. A tale with a happy ending finds resolution with forces coming into synchrony with each other. A sad ending results when one force dominates the other or opposing forces can find no cooperative resolution. In dance the interplay of forces is generally abstracted beyond a specific situation, whereas in a play the drama (or force element) is generally expressed in the context of a specific situation with specific characters. The force element is present as characters express emotions related to their predicament through the accent patterns of their speech, the strength or weakness of their gestures, and the characteristic rhythm of their movements.

By a subtle interplay of the amount of force, the timing of its exertion, and where it goes in space, all nameable and unnameable emotions can be expressed through dance.

The dynamic quality of this movement is forceless/gentle as well as gradual and somewhat scattered.

The dramatic quality of the movement may be exaggerated in dance beyond its typical expression in everyday life. An emotion may be expressed with the whole body or different parts of the body than those typically used. By working with the force element of movement, dancers and actors create rich, subtly sophisticated dramatic expressions.

❧ *Activity and Receptivity as Interactive Forces in Group Dancing*

When people begin to dance together in groups, the forces of their movements interact in conflict or cooperation with each other. Coordinating the force element among dancers is the most basic skill for group work, especially for group dance improvisation.

A dancer's movement expression can be **active** in relation to others, and it can also be **receptive,** or passive.[3] Active movements express the feeling of being in charge, of making things happen. Activity in group work is supported by the ability to make strong, forceful movements using the instrumental skills of contracting muscles and connecting to the center of gravity. Receptivity means opening up to what is happening in the moment and being influenced by it. It expresses a willingness to be moved, fostered through gentle movements and letting go of muscular tension while connecting to the center of levity. This results in expressing a feeling that is paradoxically loose and light.

Dancers need both these skills for successful group improvisation. If dancers are overly active, they will be unaware of how their actions are affecting the group. This can be frustrating to other dancers because there is a limited basis for relating to each other. If dancers are too receptive or passive, they will glean information from others but lack initiative to contribute material to the group, causing movement themes to languish. In creative dance, students learn to be both active and receptive so that they can respond to any situation presented by the dance, adapting their movements as themes dictate.

CONCEPT SPOTLIGHT 5.2

Activity and Receptivity in Life Interactions

Parallels can be made between active/receptive interactions and effective leadership or any cooperative venture in life. Everyday activities call for judgment about when to forge ahead assertively and when to sit back and take in information. Good leaders need to know when to be assertive and clearly directive, yet they also need to be able to absorb information readily so they know how a group needs to be led. In addition, responsible group members need the ability to be active in order to contribute to their community as needed yet be receptive enough to be cooperative. Dance studies working on activity and receptivity practice the basis of human interactions in movement, without the specific details of an everyday life situation. The expression is dramatic, but the essence of the interaction is abstract.

CONCEPT SPOTLIGHT 5.3

Instrument versus Material versus Relationship Skills

Tight and loose refer to the condition of the instrument.

Forceful and forceless refer to the quality of movement.

Activity and passivity refer to the relationship between the dancers.

Source: (Mettler, 1960/2006)

The force element lives at the core of movement experience: without exertion of force, there would be no movement at all. When focusing on the force element, dancers are working with the most basic aspects of movement material. The amount of force, manner of exertion, accent patterns, and interactive relationships in movement characterize the way individuals and whole cultures communicate emotions and different personalities. See Chapter 14, Interactive Forces, and Chapter 16, Pure Movement Lesson: Strong and Gentle, for lessons that introduce force concepts.

The production of satisfying movement forms in force, time, or space is facilitated by skillful use of the body as an instrument. In addition to general body coordination, specific instrumental skills support work in each element. Therefore, when planning lessons, it is useful for teachers to know which instrumental skills aid expression in each area of dance. A box on instrumental skills (see Box 5.1) is included at the end of Chapters 5, 6, and 7 to supplement the detailed information found in Chapter 4.

Box 5.1

Instrumental Skills Supporting the Force Element

Instrumental skills important for clear expression in the force element include awareness and control of muscular tension through the kinesthetic sense, moving from the center of gravity or center of levity, and coordination of the breath.

Because force is expressed through action of the muscles, skill in changing the tension level in the muscles is needed for clear expression in the force element. Here is where the kinesthetic sense comes into play. Sensory nerves recognize pressure in the muscles, telling dancers how much their muscles are contracting. When dancers sense a lot of pressure in the muscles, they know the muscles are tight. When an absence of pressure is perceived, this indicates looseness in the muscles. Subtle control of muscular contraction and release also supports expression of emotional content because fluctuating tension underlies dramatic expression. As dancers become skilled in monitoring pressure, they can add more tension or relaxation when needed.

Forceful movements involve moving the body's weight with muscular contraction. To maintain control of the body when exerting force, dancers need stability around their center of gravity (or center of weight). This requires engagement of the abdominal muscles and alignment of the pelvis with the rest of the torso, which counteracts the tendency many people have of overarching of the low back. Also, by feeling a connection between the center of weight and the earth (usually through the legs), dancers gain more stability and power because they have a strong base from which to push. Furthermore, efficient effort comes from aligning the base of support, the center of gravity, and the direction of exertion. Students can explore shifting the center of gravity, engaging the abdominal muscles, and planting their feet firmly as they make forceful movements to discover coordinations that feel powerful. This will have a sensation of "putting their weight into the movement." Conversely, students are aided in doing gentle, forceless movements by bringing awareness to the center of levity in the chest. Sensing a connection to this area helps produce a feeling of weightlessness.

Breathing is an instrumental skill that helps with the force element because it coordinates the exertion of force in movement. The beginning of a movement impulse naturally happens at the beginning of an exhalation. Injuries are prevented by breathing out as the force is exerted because the outward breath helps to stabilize the center of gravity as the abdominals contract.

Strong active leadership is instrumentally supported by stabilizing the center of gravity with the abdominal muscles. The receptive partner stays loose and light to express a willingness to be moved.

CHAPTER SUMMARY

- A movement occurs as an impulse of force is exerted in time and space. Force, time, and space constitute the material on which creative dance focuses.
- An impulse is a single wave of activity, beginning and ending in rest. Paying attention to how one movement impulse naturally flows out of the stillness at the end of the preceding movement allows the creation of organic dance forms.
- Polarities within the force element include forceful/forceless, sudden/gradual, and pinpointed/scattered.
- An accent occurs when a movement or group of movements receives more stress than others.
- Interacting forces provide the movement basis of drama.
- Activity and receptivity refer to the interaction of forces between dancers. Successful group dance improvisation requires skill in both modes.
- Instrumental skills that enhance expression of force qualities in movement include awareness and control of muscular tension and relaxation, engagement of the centers of gravity and levity, and coordination of exhalation with the movement impulse.

REVIEW QUESTIONS

1. What elements comprise the material of dance? Why is it advantageous to approach dance material through these elements?
2. How do impulse and creative pause contribute to the creation of organic dance forms?
3. What are the dynamic polarities of the force element? What kinds of movements exemplify each of the force element qualities?
4. How are accents created, and what do they contribute to movement forms?
5. What is the relationship between drama, expression of emotion, and the force element of dance?
6. Why are activity and receptivity necessary for successful group dance improvisation?
7. What instrumental skills especially support expression through the force element?

NOTES

1. In the context of movement analysis, the word *force* does not imply aggression or conflict but simply refers to the exertion required to make something happen. Numerous terms are currently used to denote the force element. Some prefer energy, effort, or dynamics to describe what is involved in producing a movement impulse. Although not entirely interchangeable, any of these labels are appropriate for introducing this material to students. Mettler and H'Doubler both used the term *force* for this element. We like it because it links creative dance expression to the larger world of natural forces.

   Laban Movement Analysis uses the term *Effort* to label the dynamic aspect of movement. Within that system the word *Effort* is a technical term that refers to a person's subjective, inner attitude toward specific movement factors of flow, weight, time, and Space (Dell, 1970; Laban, 1971). Effort is a powerful, far-reaching concept that has been applied to numerous fields including education, therapy, personality assessment, efficiency studies, and choreography. Those familiar with the Laban system will undoubtedly note the parallels between the dynamic polarities identified here and Laban's Effort factors of weight, time, and space. The fluctuation between tension and relaxation identified in the body element can be seen as akin to the Effort factor of "flow." Although these categories show similarities, they are not identical. One of the primary distinctions between Laban's system and the analytical framework we use is that the categories we present are meant to focus the dancer's attention on the objective task of generating an amount of force and/or a manner of exertion, letting the subjective inner states emerge from the movement. This contrasts with Laban's focus on subjective, inner attitudes that are manifested in movement qualities. Although the force element and Laban's Effort system both address the dynamics of movement, they do so from different standpoints. Both approaches are rich in discovery potential and can be used with cross-curricular material. Teachers using the Laban framework can also use the methodology presented here for making curricular links to dance based on a conceptual approach.

2. Finding the exact words to use when teaching the basic polarity of forceful/forceless is difficult because of the positive and negative connotations given to words that are used to describe force. We prefer not to use the polarity strong/weak because of common value judgments associated with those words. Instead, we sometimes use strong/gentle as a polarity. Both have positive connotations. However, there is a difficulty with this pairing in that they are not words generally matched with each other as opposites. Forceful/forceless is the most objective way to describe this polarity, yet these words are not as meaningful as strong and gentle are to very young children. Working within this dilemma, we use action words (such as pound or float) as well as descriptors (such as strong or gentle) to cue students when introducing this polarity. Once students have experienced the movement qualities, it is not difficult for them to grasp the more advanced vocabulary of forceful/forceless. Thus using a constellation of words is often the most useful method for helping students find these qualities.

3. Mettler (1983) used the terms *activity* and *passivity* to describe the polarity of interacting forces. Unfortunately the term *passivity* has negative connotations. If its use is met with resistance, new students may refuse to allow themselves to be moved and thus miss out on developing a vital group skill. Therefore, we use the term *receptivity* but feel that when properly understood *passivity* may indeed be a better term to convey the depth of this concept.

CHAPTER 6

THE MATERIAL OF DANCE

The Time Element

Learning Objectives

1. Recognize basic components of the time element as they relate to time patterns in dance and music.
2. Identify the characteristics of even (steady or regular) and uneven (mixed or irregular) beat patterns.
3. Demonstrate the uses of even and uneven time patterns in the creation of measured and unmeasured rhythmic forms for dance.
4. Explain how sound supports precision in the time element.
5. Describe forms for synchronizing as a group through time patterns.
6. Identify specific instrumental skills that support expression in the time element.

Basic Components of the Time Element

The time element addresses when a movement impulse occurs; that is, the point in time when the greatest amount of force of a movement is exerted. The moment of exertion is felt as a single **beat** at the beginning of a movement. Beats contained within a series of movements produce a **beat pattern,** or **pulse.** Often people feel their movements as "dance-y" when they begin to pay attention to the beat pattern of their movements. When dancers move to music, they are using the time element in a context in which the beat pattern is provided for them. It is not music alone, however, that does this. Beat patterns are inherent in movement, and the time element is shared compatibly by dance and music. Study of the time element centers around the recognition of time patterns in movement and develops the awareness to create interesting, expressive time patterns for dances.

The most important issue when working with the time element is the amount of time between the beginning of one movement (its beat) and the beginning of the next. This interval of time is the **duration** of the movement. The duration includes any pause in action that might occur before the next movement starts. The duration between beats determines the pace of movement. If there is a relatively long time between beats, the **pace** of the movements will be **slow.** If there is a relatively short time between beats, the pace will be **fast.** Even though a single movement may have a feeling of being either fast or slow, this is only meaningful to dancers in the context of a series of movements. One movement does not set a pace. It is the rate of movement impulses in relation to each other that gives any movement sequence its fastness or slowness. The polarities of slow and fast (which in creative dance are identified by feeling rather than by a clock) are so basic that even two-year-olds can follow instructions to create fast and slow movement. With awareness, the basic polarities of slow or fast pace can be combined in an almost endless fashion to create increasingly complex beat patterns.

In this element, the dancer's interest is simply with the time relationship between beats. Qualities from the force and space elements will be present in a movement but

---

6.1 CREATIVE TOOLBOX—TRY THIS!

Fast Movements

The relative pace or speed of movement refers to the frequency of the beats in a series of movements. Students often think they should race across the room when asked to move fast. It is sometimes confusing to them that fast movements do not need to cover great distances. Fast movement means a lot of movement impulses in a short amount of time, not a lot of space covered. To dispel the misconception, try doing fast movements with the feet in place before moving fast through general space.

---

need not affect its timing and are not the focus of time studies. For example, slow paced movements can be gradual (continuing the whole time between beats), or they can be relatively sudden (with a pause between impulses). They can be strong or gentle. Slow movements can travel or stay in one place. The movements can be done with any quality but will still be slow if the beats have a long time between them. Likewise, fast movements can contain any of these qualities, but it is the time between beats that is most important.

Even and Uneven Beat Patterns

The pace of movement impulses may remain **constant** or it may be **changing.** If the pace of the beats is constant, it produces an **even, steady, regular** beat pattern. Walking and jogging are everyday life movements that exemplify a steady beat. The body easily falls into these movements and, under normal circumstances, each step takes approximately the same amount of time.

Sometimes though, the pace of beats changes, producing an **uneven, mixed, irregular** pulse. When the duration between movements changes **abruptly,** slow and fast movements are mixed together. The term mixed beat pattern highlights the change between slow and fast and is especially useful when teaching young children. Speech patterns typically exhibit an uneven or irregular pulse, and many common daily actions employ different durations between movements. Reaching for a jar, trying to unscrew its tight lid, tapping it on the counter, and finally getting it to open creates a series of movement impulses in an uneven or mixed beat pattern. Many kinds of sports (basketball, soccer, boxing) and work movements (cooking, typing, changing tires) also exhibit irregular beat patterns. All these point out the natural intricacy of time patterns in life. A change in duration between movements may also happen **gradually** as it does in acceleration and deceleration. For example, as a bouncing ball dribbles lower and lower to the ground, the beats of its movement get closer together and the pace gradually accelerates. This is a gradually changing beat pattern.

Partners gallop as the rest of the class claps the uneven measured beat pattern of the movement.

Measured and Unmeasured Beat Patterns

When the body experiences a series of beats, it is a natural tendency for the mind to organize and group the beats into patterns. Even when listening to an undifferentiated steady beat, such as a clock ticking, the mind may begin to group beats together by

---

6.2 CREATIVE TOOLBOX—TRY THIS!

Beat Patterns and Speech

Coordinating movement with the beat of speech patterns is a very good way to cultivate uneven pulses, especially with beginners. Pick a sentence from reading material and clap the syllabic beat pattern felt in the words. Then experiment with movements other than clapping to mark the speech pattern. The sound of speech (which reflects the movement of our mouth, throat, and respiratory system) helps students hear the beat pattern, and the exhalation required by speech helps coordinate movement on each syllable.

---

creating accents. This innate grouping of beats is an example of our inherent tendency to make rhythmic forms (H'Doubler, 1932).

Time patterns with an underlying steady beat create rhythmic forms that can be **measured** and analyzed according to how many beats occur between accents. Accents, remember, contain more force and are noticeable and easy to mark. Accents placed at regular intervals will group beats into measures. Typically, a strong accent is placed at the beginning of a measure. If an accent falls in an unexpected place in the measure, it produces **syncopation.** Syncopated time patterns are stimulating forms to play with when students possess a sophisticated sense of timing.

Although the placement of accents can create groupings of 2, 3, 4, 5, or any number of beats, the most basic measure of beats is in groups of 2 or 3. Kinesthetically, 2-beat measures have a very different feel from 3-beat measures. Two-beat measures are active and percussive, as in marching; 3-beat measures feel more passive and swingy, as in waltzing.

In addition to beats being grouped by accents, the interval of time between beats can also be subdivided. For example, a 2-beat measure can be further divided into groupings of 4 or 8. In this case the movements in the 4-beat measure would be twice as fast as in the 2-beat measure; the 8-beat measure would double the speed yet again. Measures of 4 or 8 beats maintain the percussive quality of a 2-beat measure. Beats can also be divided into thirds, creating 6- or 9-beat measures. These variations have the lilt of a 3-beat measure. Groups of other numbers of beats such as 5 or 7 have an uneven quality in movement because they combine both 2- and 3-beat groupings. Although measures of 5 and 7 beats are uncommon in popular dance and music, they do show up in other genres such as Balkan and Middle Eastern dance, jazz, contemporary classical, and "world" music. These relatively complex groupings provide creative challenges for more experienced dancers.

In some movements short uneven patterns are repeated over and over. This creates a pattern of uneven beats within a steady beat. Examples of this are skipping and galloping, wherein one step takes slightly longer than the one next to it. Repeated over and over it creates the pattern of LONG short, LONG short, LONG short. The heartbeat follows this pattern of long and short durations; a less emphasized movement occurs after each major contraction of the heart muscle.

CONCEPT SPOTLIGHT 6.1

Beat Patterns and Rhythm

Rhythm is often seen as synonymous with measured beat patterns. Indeed beat patterns as described here are an important example of rhythmic form. However, rhythm is a much larger concept, encompassing force and space as well as time. Rhythm comes from the interplay of polarities in all the elements. (See Rhythm as an Organizing Principle in Chapter 2.)

CONCEPT SPOTLIGHT 6.2

Dividing Beats in Half

_____ _____ 2-beat measure

_____ _____ _____ _____ 4-beat measure

_____ _____ _____ _____ _____ _____ _____ _____ 8-beat measure

Dividing Beats into Thirds

_____ _____ 2-beat measure

_____ _____ _____ _____ _____ _____ 6-beat measure

_____ _____ _____ 3-beat measure

_____ _____ _____ _____ _____ _____ _____ _____ _____ 9-beat measure

---

Dancers need not always measure the time relationship of beat patterns. **Unmeasured** beat relationships can be explored by playing with the "feel" of the pattern as the duration of movements oscillates freely between long and short. Because of their free, irregular nature, uneven time patterns are not as obvious in their rhythmic form. However, that does not mean that there is no form.

Time work requires a great deal of precision in awareness, which many people feel they do not have. In Western cultures most people have relied so fully on recorded music to set time patterns for them that they are not accustomed to focusing on the rhythms naturally inherent in body movement. Depending on interest, teachers may or may not

---

CONCEPT SPOTLIGHT 6.3

Measured Uneven Pattern

Division of beats can be combined with groupings of beats to create mixed/uneven pulses. These can be measured in relation to an underlying steady beat. Here is an example of an uneven beat pattern within a 4-beat measure.

_____ _____ _____ _____ _____ _____ Uneven beat pattern

_____ _____ _____ _____ Underlying steady beat pattern

CONCEPT SPOTLIGHT 6.4

Galloping, Skipping, and Heartbeat Pattern

_____ _____ _____ _____ _____ _____ _____ _____

LONG   short   LONG   short   LONG   short   LONG   short

This is an example of an irregular pulse that can be measured.

CONCEPT SPOTLIGHT 6.5

Example of an Unmeasured Irregular Time Pattern

—— — — — — — — — — — — — — — — — — ——

Playing claves or other simple instruments while dancing highlights the beat pattern of the movement.

want to go into rigorous analysis of time patterns. However, a basic feeling for beat that does not rely on counting or analysis can be developed quite effectively through creative dance studies. Beyond the basics, advanced students may enjoy the challenge of working with unusual groupings of beats. When beats are grouped together into measures and also subdivided into quick minor impulses, complicated rhythmic patterns evolve. Mathematical in nature, these studies can provide great stimulation in the classroom.

✎ Supporting the Time Element with Sound

Because the body is always moving in some subtle way, it is constantly giving kinesthetic feedback. This can make it hard to tell exactly when the moment of most exertion happens. Sound, on the other hand, has a more distinctive on/off quality. It is easy to distinguish between hearing a sound and not hearing it. The interval of time between impulses is marked by the silence between sounds. Thus sound can help pinpoint the exact moment an impulse happens.

Working with time patterns and creating sound while moving can provide a basis for free creative expression that unites music and dance. Clapping or body percussion, making vocal or breath sounds, and playing simple musical instruments while dancing highlight the beat pattern. Creating music while dancing builds upon the fact that music and dance have a common home in the time element. Teachers with limited experience in keeping a beat may want to use some recorded music as an aid in providing a steady beat for time work. However, overreliance on such aids keeps students from being able to develop their own internal sense of time rhythms, their "inner song." Because prepared music imposes a form on the movement that can limit or alter expression, creative dance in its purest form addresses the time element without recorded music at all.

✎ Synchronizing as a Group

Attention to the time element enables dancers to **synchronize** their movements with each other, creating a feeling of group cohesion. The most obvious way to do this is for everyone to move together on the same steady beat with a **common pulse.** One way to come together on a common pulse is for dancers to begin individually and then adjust to other dancers. Dancers who listen to the impulse patterns of those dancing around them and adapt their movements accordingly will soon be moving together on the same beat, unified in time. This is the process of finding the group body's heartbeat. When students walk or jog among each other with a steady beat, they are beginning to explore this basic experience of synchronizing with others. Once the underlying beat is found by the group, dancers can improvise with subdivisions and grouping of beats as variations within the matrix of the commonly held pulse. An unwavering beat is almost irresistible and builds a sense of community. Through the centuries, dances from many cultures have used the steady beat to unify people and renew a feeling of solidarity.

Beyond moving together within a common pulse, dancers can synchronize in more complex fashions. For example, they can **echo** each other's patterns. In an echo form, short phrases of beat patterns (which can easily be remembered and repeated) are created by one dancer or group, and then repeated by others. Leaders can spontaneously develop echoes as they are repeated with variation three, four, or more times before moving on to

---

6.3 CREATIVE TOOLBOX—TRY THIS!

Sound and Group Synchrony

Adding sound in the form of claps, voice, or simple instruments like drums can turn group time patterns into a spirited rally! See Sensing Time Patterns, in Chapter 14, and Pure Movement Lesson: Measured Time Patterns, in Chapter 17, for lessons that teach time concepts.

---

another phrase. Or patterns can be repeated in an overlapping fashion, with one pattern beginning before the next one ends. This is a **canon** or **round** form.

Another way to synchronize movements in time is for one group of dancers to respond to patterns with a different pattern. An **alternate response** form takes place when dancers answer each other with beat patterns that complement or contrast with each other rather than repeating the same phrase. Even though these phrases may be highly uneven and do not match, they can have a synchronous feeling. This can be witnessed in everyday life if you listen to the rhythmic pattern of a conversation without paying attention to the words. If the participants are communicating well, there will be a synchronous feeling to the irregular back and forth, rhythmic phrases of the beat pattern of their language.

Haji's focus is inward as he exhales from the diaphragm and relaxes into the beat with released knees.

BOX 6.1

Instrumental Skills Supporting the Time Element

To develop confidence in feeling time patterns, the ability to relax into the beat is crucial. When paying attention to beat patterns, dancers become aware of when the movement impulse happens. This requires receptivity and, thus, relaxation. Trying to intellectually count and measure complicated beats can be frustrating because it gets in the way of this receptivity. Rather than actively grasping at a beat, dancers need to learn to be open to the feedback of a movement impulse coming from the muscles and to trust their natural kinesthetic ability to feel the beat without analyzing it.

One way to begin to feel at home with time studies is for dancers to tune in to their own physiological rhythms. The heartbeat and breath are two accessible body rhythms that sensitize a person to time patterns. Lying down and listening to the heart and breath before or after dancing builds skill in sensing the ebbing and flowing rhythms of the body.

Awareness of the breath can also help focus attention on when a movement impulse is happening because the breath coordinates with exertion. This tendency to breathe out when exerting force is what led to the development of work songs in many cultures. By singing while working, the workers exhale from the diaphragm and abdominals on the words of the song. This helps them pinpoint the moment when all their muscles need to coordinate and exert movement to get the job done efficiently. In the same way, purposefully exhaling on the beat while moving can heighten awareness of time. Saying a word, such as now, go, or any other one-syllable word at the beginning of a movement makes that exhalation an audible mark of time (Mettler, 1983).

Gently releasing and bouncing the knees aids in feeling the beat. Bouncing loosens the legs and hips so they can easily mark the cadence of the movement. This can be done in place or while walking. Once dancers can feel the predictable nature of a steady beat (that one beat follows the next after the same amount of time), they can begin to relax with it. The body has a natural response to continue that pattern.

Basic locomotor movements such as walking and jogging can be helpful in feeling a natural regularity of beat because students can easily do these familiar movements without intellectualizing them. Skipping and galloping provide experience working with repetitive irregular beat patterns. The teacher's role is to help students feel the steadiness of these movements. This can be done by accentuating the sound the movements produce naturally or by playing a drum to the beat of their steps.

CHAPTER SUMMARY

- When defining time patterns, the basic components to recognize are beat, duration, and pace. The impulse that begins a movement can be marked by a beat. The duration of time between beats determines the pace of a beat pattern. Relatively long duration produces a slow pace; short duration produces a fast pace.
- Dance and music share the basic concepts of the time element.
- Even, steady, regular pulses have constant durations between beats. Changing durations produce uneven, mixed, irregular pulses.
- An underlying steady pulse of movement can be measured by grouping beats together in a pattern marked by accents. Time patterns in movement can also be kinesthetically felt without being measured.
- The on/off distinction of sound supports dancers' ability to mark beats precisely.
- Synchrony within a common pulse promotes community among a group of dancers. Echo, canon, and alternate response are additional forms through which groups can synchronize.
- Instrumental skills that support work in time include relaxation, awareness of heartbeat and breath rhythms, exhaling on the beat, bouncing with released knees, and sensing the beat of basic locomotor movements.

REVIEW QUESTIONS

1. Name the basic components of the time element and explain how they construct the basis for developing awareness in the time element in music and dance.
2. What defines a steady beat? A mixed beat?
3. How are accents used to create a measured pattern? a syncopated pattern?
4. Show how complicated beat patterns can be created from measuring a steady beat by diagramming different examples than those given in the text for an even measured pattern and an uneven measured pattern.
5. How does one know the form of uneven time patterns that are not measured?
6. How does sound support awareness and precision of beat patterns in movement?
7. What forms can be used by dancers to synchronize as a group within the time element?
8. What instrumental skills especially support expression through the time element?

CHAPTER 7

THE MATERIAL OF DANCE

The Space Element

Learning Objectives

1. Identify the province of the space element of dance and explain how it connects to the visual arts.

2. Differentiate between personal space and general space as an aspect of the range of movement.

3. Discuss the terminology relevant to position of the body.

4. Describe factors of space that are relevant to the direction of movement.

5. Distinguish between one-, two-, and three-dimensional movement.

6. Apply the principle that polarities create rhythmic patterns in movement to the element of space.

7. Recognize spatial forms particularly characteristic of group movement.

8. Identify specific instrumental skills that support expression in the space element.

❧ *The Visual Design of Dance*

The space element focuses on where the movement is happening. It addresses the dancer's relationship to the area in which he or she moves and the spatial patterns created by the dancer's movements. The space element in dance shares many of the concerns and terms of the visual arts because it addresses the same issues of design in space.

Just as with the other elements, the kinesthetic sense plays a major role by relaying vital information to the brain about the body's position and direction of movement. From this information comes all bodily spatial awareness.

❧ *Range or Size of Movement*

In each element of dance a very basic starting point for investigation is to ask the question, "How much?" Just as forceful and forceless refer to the amount of force exerted and slow and fast address how much time is used by each movement, **large** and **small** are the polarities that describe how much space is consumed as the body moves. Large and small describe the size or **range** of movement in space.

Range of motion occurs both in the space immediately around the body, which is called **self-space** (or **personal space**), and in the space of the room or environment, called **shared** or **general space.** Laban (1974) extensively analyzed how the body moves in space. He coined the term **kinesphere,** the sphere of movement, to describe self-space. The outer edges of the kinesphere are determined by the limbs' reach into space. Extending far into space with straight limbs uses the far reach space of the kinesphere. Movements close to the body's surface use the near reach space of the kinesphere. Moving into

Child's drawing of a space bubble. Children like to call the kinesphere the "space bubble."

different reach spaces can also be thought of as changing the size of personal space (Laban, 1971).

When people interact with each other, they expand and contract their boundaries of personal space. Cultural anthropologist Edward T. Hall (1966, 1977) notes that the size of personal space varies between cultures and also is dependent on the situation. Self-space contracts in a confined space (for example, when riding a crowded bus) to maintain a personal boundary near skin level. Large open spaces, on the other hand, invite expansive movements that use a large self-space. Practice in moving with awareness of personal space provides the basis for students to establish appropriate and flexible personal boundaries that can be applied to interactions with people in the rest of life. Good communication relies on being able to find and adjust self-space appropriately for a given situation. This basic skill for human communication can be explored and strengthened in dance.

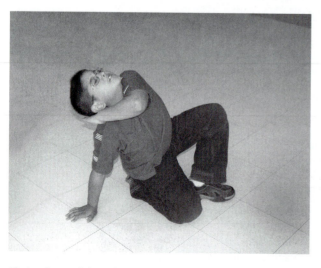

Closing the eyes helps a dancer feel a position.

Position

At any given moment the **position** of the body involves several spatial attributes. These include place, level, facing, and shape. Wherever a kinesphere rests is its **place.** Place is a point directly under the center of gravity of the body. When one moves beyond that point, by taking a step, for instance, the kinesphere moves to a new "place" (Laban, 1974). The concept of place is another of Laban's significant contributions to dance theory. It is central to his system of movement notation (Labanotation) because it provides a reference point for tracking movement through space. Establishing a strong orientation of place is also absolutely

---

7.1 CREATIVE TOOLBOX—TRY THIS!

Safety and the Space Bubble

One of the first skills needed to participate safely in a dance class is the ability to maintain the boundaries of personal space so that no one gets hurt while moving among others. This is developed by students consciously taking their space bubbles with them as they move around the room. If everyone keeps space around them, no one will bump another person or thing. Because establishing the boundaries of personal space is so basic, early lessons often focus on establishing self-space and learning to move within it, both in place and from place to place.

---

essential for managing a dance class. Working with this skill while dancing helps students feel secure and "at home" with what they're doing. Once a strong, in-place orientation has been established, students can begin to leave that spot in the room and travel through shared space.

Level has to do with relationship to the earth. **High, middle,** and **low** are generally recognized as the variables for level, although there can be gradations between these heights. **Facing** refers to the orientation of the front of the body. Where the body is facing can change the feeling of a position even though the shape of the body remains the same. For example, the feeling being expressed by dancers facing each other is very different from that expressed when they face away from each other. In addition, facing is an important aspect of being aware of place for dancers. Perhaps this explains the confusion that sometimes occurs when the "front" of the room is changed or when a dance is moved from a studio to a stage.

The **shape** of the position is determined by the relationship of parts of the body to each other. The proximity of those parts determines the relatively **large** or **small size** of the shape. Size of shape is different from size of movement (range). You can quite easily make small movements while being in a big shape. Traveling through a large amount of space while in a small shape is also theoretically possible, such as an acrobat jumping into the air in a tightly tucked somersault.

In any position, the shape of the body makes a design in space. That design may be relatively **curved, straight,** or **angular.** How the parts of the body are positioned may form namable geometric shapes, such as squares or circles. More commonly, there will be irregular nongeometric configurations. Any shape that the body makes involves space that is occupied, or **filled,** and **empty** space between bodies or parts of the body. When working with design elements, filled and empty space are also referred to as **positive** and **negative** space, respectively. The human body is bilaterally symmetrical; that is, one side

---

7.2 CREATIVE TOOLBOX—TRY THIS!

Cultivating Spatial Awareness

Movement in space can be thought of as a series of ever changing positions. Like a series of snapshots, the position of the body shifts slightly with each frame. To kinesthetically feel (rather than merely see) where they are in space, students usually have to slow down so that they can feel the position of their bodies. Having students occasionally stop, close their eyes, and feel their position in space helps them connect to spatial awareness through the kinesthetic sense.

The straight/angular, symmetrical, low-level position of this pair also creates an interesting design of positive (filled) and negative (empty) space.

of the body is an approximate mirror image of the other. By changing the position of its parts, however, the body may create both **symmetrical** and **asymmetrical** designs. This is true also for groups of dancers. The group shape may be a regular, symmetrical form, or it may be an irregular, asymmetrical shape.

Direction and Pathway

The position of the body is only part of the story when investigating where movement happens. As positions change, dancers create a **direction** of movement that can be **upward, downward, forward, backward, sideward,** or **diagonal** relative to the body.[1] In relation to others, the direction can be **toward, away, over, under, around, between** or **through.**

The direction of movement results in a **pathway.** To get a sense of the pathway of a movement, realize that air is a fluid substance and that the body's movement creates a wake trailing behind it. This is invisible, of course, but actually does happen as air molecules are pushed aside when the body moves through them. Laban (1974) called these trails behind movement "trace-forms" (p. 5). The lines left behind a jet as it streams through the sky or light lingering after the movement of a sparkler at night are visible examples of trace-forms. The changing position of the body and the direction in which it moves create the shape of the movement itself. Movement in personal space shapes a path through the air. Movement through shared space leaves a trace-form both on the floor (or earth) and in the air.

Although the shape of movement pathways is different from the shape of the body itself, some terms that describe them are similar. The pathway of movement may create a design in space that is relatively **curved** or **straight.** The design can be as simple as one straight or curved line, or it may be more complex. Straight pathways that frequently change directions produce angular, zig-zag movements. Pathways that combine many curves produce a squiggly or looping pathway. A dance with primarily curved movements will have a different rhythmic quality than one in which straight or zig-zag lines dominate. Curviness has a flowing, easy feeling that may be meandering and gentle. A jerky, percussive feeling, on the other hand, may tend to produce pathways of straightness and angularity.

Dimension

Pathways and held shapes can be viewed from the perspective of how many **dimensions** they use. Movements that simply rise or sink, go forward or back, or move right and left are **one-dimensional** movements. They create straight **perpendicular lines** and are restricted to movement along the three right-angled **axes** of the body (see Figure 7.1). Also, making single-line shapes with the body produces one-dimensional positions.

Somewhat less restricted are movements that stay within a given **plane.** Here the shape of the pathway and the body's position are flat and **two dimensional.** There are an infinite number of planes along which movement may travel. The three named anatomical planes are the vertical plane, which is positioned like a door and combines up-down with side-side directions (see Figure 7.2); the sagittal plane, which resembles a wheel and combines forward-back with up-down directions (see Figure 7.3); and the horizontal plane, which is like a table, combining side-side with forward-back directions (see Figure 7.4). The descriptive labels of door, wheel, and table are used within the Laban tradition to give a clear image of the anatomical planes (Bartenieff, 1981). In terms of joint action, adduction and abduction dominate in the vertical plane, flexion and extension are emphasized in the sagittal plane, and rotational movement is evoked in the horizontal plane. Because these planes are anatomical (in relation to the body), they are constant no matter what orientation in space the body takes (standing, lying, upside down, etc.). Planes can also be viewed with respect to the environment, in which case the horizontal plane is always positioned parallel to the earth and the vertical and sagittal planes rest perpendicular to it.

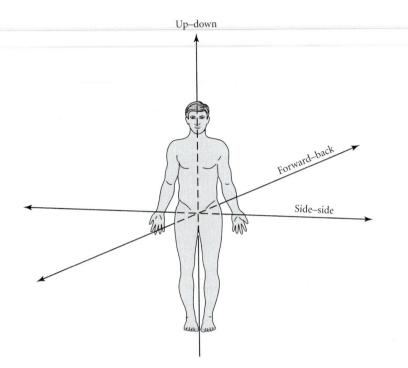

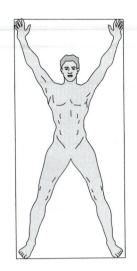

FIGURE 7.1   *Perpendicular Axes in the Body.*

FIGURE 7.2   *The Vertical or Door Plane.*

Three-dimensional movement has a sense of filling or moving a **volume.** This is seen in spiraling movements, which turn while rising or sinking, or in a series of diagonal movements that change direction and traverse through more than one plane. Laban's system of Space Harmony makes it possible to work very specifically with three-dimensional movement by mapping the kinesphere with discrete touch points at the corners of different solid geometric shapes, such as a cube (whose corners are on the periphery of the kinesphere) or an icosahedron (a twenty-sided polyhedron built by connecting the corners of intersecting vertical, sagittal, and horizontal planes). Laban identified many different natural movement sequences that travel three-dimensionally along specific

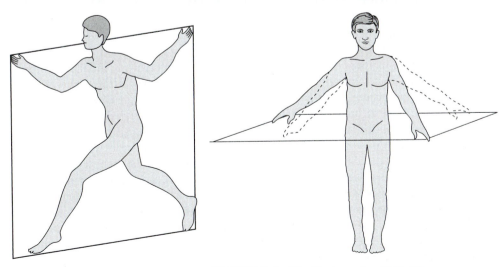

FIGURE 7.3   *The Sagittal or Wheel Plane.*

FIGURE 7.4   *The Horizontal or Table Plane.*

Twisting while descending creates a three-dimensional movement with a feeling of filling a volume. The direction of the curved, spiraling pathway is downward, sideward, and, backward.

trace-forms in relation to points on the icosahedron and other polyhedra. When dancers hold three-dimensional shapes, they produce sculptural designs. Even without the rigorous analysis required by Laban's system, dancers can practice three-dimensional movement by exploring the feeling of pathways and shapes that create volumes.[2]

Spatial Rhythms

Most people are familiar with rhythmic patterns created by durations between beats and accents of force, but the spatial aspect of rhythm is not so commonly considered. However, the polarities within the space element also create rhythmic patterns. The ebbing and flowing of large and small, high and low, curved and straight, create rhythmic designs in space. The spatial scales of movement in the kinesphere that Laban recognized naturally follow a sequence of directions that alternate exertion with recuperative movements (Bartenieff, 1980). These are spatial rhythms. Even though it may seem unusual to represent rhythms with spatial designs, many kinds of graphs and diagrams do exactly that. By creating pictures of information that cannot be seen, they illustrate rhythms of data by showing how one thing relates to another. Consider the electrocardiogram, which makes a spatial record of the rhythm of the heartbeat, or the seismogram, which records the vibrations of an earth tremor. The fleeting visual patterns created by movement are likewise expressions of rhythms.

Group Spatial Forms

With respect to group work, having an obvious **spatial form** allows a group of dancers to function as a single unit. That is, when the dancers are aware of the spatial arrangement of the whole group, it is easier to sense themselves as a group body. This, in turn, clarifies group movement themes because individual dancers not only sense their own movements but also comprehend what the group as a whole is doing.

The most basic spatial formations for groups of dancers are circle, line, clump, and scatter. These spatial forms have parallels in nature. Animals herd together in close clumps for protection. Gnats swarm in billowing scatter formations. Young quail follow their parents in lines. Predators circle their prey. These forms provide structures for social animals to band together for survival. Humans also possess these same instincts for sensing group shapes as structures for coming together and communicating.

The **circle** form provides the strongest sense of group unity. It can be seen in dances in all cultures and is used to help strengthen the bonds of community. When dancers face the center in a circle, everyone can see each other, and there is a sense of equality of position. There is containment in the circle (and other enclosed group shapes such as the square) that promotes a communal feeling of all working together.

Lines are another compelling group formation. People moving in lines are seen in many life situations: grocery store lines, amusement park lines, cafeteria lines, soldiers marching in line, children playing Red Rover. People often dance in lines one behind the other, side by side in lines, or in facing lines such as in the Virginia Reel. Lines show up as a primary form for folk dances, including country line dancing, which became popular in the 1970s. Line formations convey solidarity and establish order and control. That order can either be stifling or deeply satisfying, depending on the context of how a line is used. Overemphasis on moving in lines can be confining and promote pointless competitiveness as students vie for the status of being first in line. However, when lines are used creatively, they can be a welcome container for group participation.

Clump and scatter formations are the least organized group forms. The **clump** is a close, irregular configuration of bodies. Although range of movement may be limited in a clump, there is a strong sense of security in being part of a group. The **scatter** formation is basically a spread out clump with approximately equal amounts of space between dancers. This spatial form is very loose, allowing for more individual freedom than the

An individual dancing in relation to two facing lines.

other group formations. However, because group control is not so defined in a scattered form, it takes more group awareness to maintain equal spacing. As dancers move from place to place, they may break apart into smaller groupings. When this happens, scatter forms with uneven spacing are created. In dances where groupings dissolve and new ones assemble, the relative direction of dancers' movements becomes significant as people move toward, away from, over, under, in front of, behind, around, and between each other.

In group formations dancers discover things they can do that they can't do dancing alone. Perhaps this is what makes group dances so compelling. For example, although one can make a circle with the arms, raise the circle and lower it, that is a very different experience from being part of a circle made of people that rises

Teaching classes in the scatter formation affords maximum individual freedom while also demanding sensitivity to spacing of the group. The students learn to function as creative individuals within a community setting.

 ## Box 7.1

Instrumental Skills Supporting the Space Element

The main instrumental support for focusing on the space element in dance is awareness of the bones. The skeleton (the armature of the body to which the soft tissue is attached) gives the body its spatial form. Without the skeleton, the human form is indistinct. It is the bones that make the shape of the body clear. A good way to prepare for work in the space element is to focus on the bones as they move. When focusing on bones, dancers become aware of the shape of the bones and the relation of bones to each other. This involves an awareness of something concrete, which the dancer can actually see and touch. It prepares the student for the kind of attention needed for sensing abstract spatial designs (such as the trace-forms drawn by the body as it moves through space) that they can't see or touch.

When turning attention toward skeletal movement, less attention is paid to muscular contraction. For the mover, this facilitates a feeling of ease and nonresistance quite different from the vibrant, excited attention stimulated by beat work. Concentration on the bones helps put students into a spatial frame of mind, which is generally quiet and centered. This can be seen in the sometimes whispered discussions that tend to follow intense spatial work. In *Sensing, Feeling and Action* (1993), Bonnie Bainbridge Cohen further explores the relationship of awareness of the bones with spatial awareness in movement.

Because of the way groups of bones flex, extend, and rotate at the joints, the body is able to do both straight and curved movements. Straight movements require several joints to fold and unfold in relation to each other. Movement of the bones around a single joint produces curvy movements. Most beginning students are not ready to make this detailed distinction of how the skeleton moves in creating curved and straight movements. They will find the feeling of the movement more easily by just working with the word cues "curved" and "straight." However, more advanced students can deepen their understanding of straight and curved movements by paying attention to the joint actions required to make those movements.

Muscular strength is needed for every movement skill, but it particularly supports the space element in that strength provides control, enabling the dancer to move with spatial precision and hold clear spatial patterns. If muscles are weak, they will not be able to maintain the spatial design of the body as it moves through space. Abdominal strength is especially important for core stability to ground the body during lifting of limbs and to balance different parts of the body as they form designs in space. Changing levels is a spatial aspect that requires the support of both the joints and the muscles. The joints of the hip, knee, and ankle need to move without restriction in alignment and coordination with each other. The muscles must be strong enough to control the body's weight as it moves with and against gravity.

and sinks, expands and contracts, or rotates. To keep the group spatial configuration clear, dancers must become more interested in the movement of the whole circle than in what their own bodies are doing. Their interest in the individual body is specifically for maintaining the clear spatial form of the group body.

People have been dancing for centuries in group forms as a means of holding themselves together as a community. Typically, communal dances are taught as set forms and may have complicated figures. Yet experience in group dance improvisation reveals that people do not need to be directed into predetermined forms. Once the potential to create group forms has been demonstrated, people have the ability to sense the shape of the group body. One of the most thrilling dance experiences is to be a part of a group that spontaneously creates dances with clear spatial forms. See Lines and Shapes in Space, in Chapter 14, and Pure Movement Lesson: Group Lines and Curricular Lesson: Geometric Planes, in Chapter 18, for lessons that introduce space element concepts.

Chapter Summary

- The space element addresses where movement occurs and shares the realm of spatial design with visual art.
- The personal, self-space kinesphere is a spatial boundary defining the reach of an individual's limbs. General, shared space is the dance environment that belongs to all dancers. The kinesphere moves with the dancer through general space.
- Position of the body and direction of movement provide the basis for all kinesthetic spatial awareness.
- The position of the body includes aspects of place, level, facing, and shape.
- Shape includes characteristics of size, design, positive and negative space, symmetry, and asymmetry.
- The direction of movement defines its pathway in space. Pathways may be curved, straight, or zig-zagged.
- Movement may encompass one, two, or three dimensions.
- Spatial rhythms in dance are created by the flux of exertion and recovery expressed by spatial polarities.
- The most basic spatial formations for dancing in groups are the circle, line, clump, and scatter.
- Instrumental skills that especially support expression in the space element include awareness of the bones and muscular strength.

Review Questions

1. What is the primary focus of the space element of dance?
2. How does the space element connect dance to visual art?
3. How do personal space and general space differ in relation to an individual's range of movement?
4. What are the spatial aspects that figure into a dancer's position? Take a held position with your body and describe it using these position attributes.
5. What factors come into play in determining a movement's pathway? Create a pathway of movement and describe it using these factors.
6. Describe a movement pathway that is one dimensional. Do the same for two- and three-dimensional movement pathways.
7. How are spatial rhythms manifested in dance?
8. Which spatial forms are naturally characteristic of group movement?
9. What instrumental skills especially support expression through the space element?

Notes

1. In Laban's system of space harmony, diagonal movement has the specific meaning of movement along a line running from one corner of a cube through the center to its opposite corner—for example, from the high-front-right corner to the low-back-left corner. We employ the term in its less specific, more common usage. Diagonal movement may be thought of as creating a slanted pathway either along the floor or through personal space.

2. The description of one-, two-, and three-dimensional movement includes only a cursory discussion of these aspects of Laban's system of Space Harmony. See Laban's (1974) *The Language of Movement* and other Laban references in the bibliography for more in-depth study of space harmony.

Elements of Dance
The Body as Instrument

Structure

Head

Torso

      Center of gravity (lower torso)

      Center of levity (upper torso)

      Spine

      Shoulder girdle

      Ribs

      Pelvis

Arms and hands

Legs and feet

Vocal cords

Bones and joints

Whole body

Group Body

Physiological Functions

Kinesthetic sense

Tension and relaxation

Breath

Heartbeat

Alignment

Basic Body Movements

Axial (in place)

      Stretch

      Bend

      Twist

      Turn

      Open and close

      Flop or drop

      Fall

      Shake

      Bounce

      Swing

      Undulate, wave, or ripple

Locomotor (place to place)

      Roll

      Slither

      Crawl

      Walk

      Run

      Jump (on two feet)

      Hop (on one foot)

      Gallop

      Skip

      Leap

The Force Element (How energy is expended to create movement forms)

Impulse/creative pause

Organic form

Dynamic qualities as polarities

      Forceful or strong / Forceless or gentle

      Sudden / Gradual

      Pinpointed or single-focused / Scattered or multifocused

Accent

Group Work

Activity and Receptivity

The Time Element (When the movement happens)

Beat

Duration between beats

      Long / Short

Pace

      Slow / Fast

      Constant / Changing

        Abrupt / Gradual

Beat pattern or pulse

      Even, steady, regular / Uneven, mixed, irregular

      Measured / Unmeasured

      Syncopated

Moving with sound

Group Work

Synchrony

      Common pulse

      Echo

      Canon or round

      Alternate response

The Space Element (Where the movement happens)

Range
    Large / Small
    Personal or self-space, kinesphere / Shared or general space

Position
    Place
    Level
        High, middle, low
    Facing

    Shape
        Size (large to small)
        Curved / Straight, angular
        Symmetrical / Asymmetrical
        Positive space (filled) / Negative
          space (empty)

Direction
    Upward, downward
    Forward, backward, sideward, diagonal
    Pathways
        Curved / Straight

Dimension
    One-dimensional (perpendicular lines or axes)
    Two-dimensional (planes)
    Three-dimensional (volumes)

Group Work
    Group spatial forms
        Scatter
        Clump
        Line
        Circle
        Other polygons
    Directional relationships
        Toward, away, over,
        under, around, between,
        through

Group Forms for All the Elements

Unison
Complement
Contrast

Instrumental Skills That Support Expression of the Material

Instrumental skills that support the force element
    Awareness of muscles: tight and loose
    Moving from centers of gravity and levity
    Breath: exhaling on impulse

Instrumental skills that support the time element
    Relaxation
    Heartbeat
    Breath
    Releasing and bouncing in knees
    Sensing beat of basic locomotor movements

Instrumental skills that support the space element
    Awareness of bones
    Joint actions
    Muscular control

PART III

Linking Dance across the Curriculum

The only source of knowledge is experience.

—Albert Einstein

There are many reasons to dance. When themes are drawn directly from the elements of dance, as described in Part II, the focus is on movement for movement's sake; there is no additional topic. In other words, curved lines are simply curved lines. They do not represent roads, solar systems, whirly-birds, or cursive writing. They can be thick or thin, high or low, or large or small, but they are not meant to be "like" something else. This is abstract art in it purest form. Art, in itself, is reason to dance. The intrinsic value contained in the study of dance enables it to stand on its own as an academic subject.

Movement also shapes knowledge and helps students learn in nontraditional but powerful ways. Through dance, students can deeply embody concepts and basic skills that underlie what they are studying. A pure movement lesson strives to develop kinesthetic vocabulary and expression; the applied dance lesson builds toward additional academic goals. When using dance with other curricular areas, creative dance functions both as an art activity and as a learning tool. This approach honors both the artistic and utilitarian reasons to dance.

Movement can easily be connected to other curricular areas because everything—even a mountain—moves at some level. Movement patterns intrinsically characterize the phenomena that make up the world: relationships of growth, change, action, and reaction. The concepts of dance are probably already familiar to you although you may know them in different contexts. This common ground between movement and other subjects forms the basis for making the link to classroom curriculum. By looking carefully at your curricular subject and using a little bit of imagination, you will discover concepts that link with dance.

The curriculum-related dance lesson uses your abilities to keenly analyze and whimsically free-associate your topic with movement possibilities that are relevant, interesting, and comfortable for you. If two areas at first glance seem to have

---

CONCEPT SPOTLIGHT

Abstract Movement to Concrete Application Using the Space Element

Abstract Movement Theme	Applied Themes
Curved lines	Cursive writing
	Solar system

---

no relation to each other, be open to any associations that pop into your mind. When building your lesson, you can analyze, reject, accept, and order the ideas you have generated.

Representational imagery often plays a significant role when working with cross-curricular subject matter because movement is derived from study topics other than pure dance. However, emphasizing pure movement material before bringing in the imagery of a topic grounds movement expression in a kinesthetic base that will richly enhance the experience. This results in much more meaningful dances than when students are asked to move like butterflies, dinosaurs, clouds, or wind but have no prior experience of the movement qualities related to those images. Instead of stereotypically acting-out topics, students will truly engage their kinesthetic intelligence to help them understand the nature of their subject. When students have a strong base in the elements of movement, expression stimulated by any imagery or curricular subject matter will be richer and more fully realized.

Many teachers already use the sensory experience of movement in the classroom. In the Slingerland method of learning letters, for example, students write large letters in the air or on the back of a partner. This helps to coordinate hands and arms in making the shape of the letter, and it floods the brain with sensory-motor sensations. Another common kinesthetic activity is practicing math concepts with manipulatives. Handling objects that represent mathematical functions solidifies abstract concepts and makes them easier for many students to understand. Experiencing curricula through creative dance combines movement on a larger scale with exploratory problem solving and the creation of expressive forms. It also engages students' feelings through attention to the kinesthetic sense. The combination of these experiences offers the deepest kinesthetic learning, which affects students at many levels. Linking movement to curriculum can be an exciting, stimulating intellectual and creative process that leads ultimately to satisfying rhythmic forms in dance. These memories will not easily fade.

Dance can be integrated with academic themes at any point in a curricular unit. Movement can be used to introduce material or to develop and deepen students' understanding of a topic they are already exploring. Creating dances on a topic to show to others is a satisfying way to culminate an academic unit as well. Dancing a concept demonstrates mastery of a subject as validly as paper and pencil tests, and it is a useful tool for assessment.

Chapters 8 through 10 describe the conceptual process of finding links between dance and specific topics, modes of learning, and cross-cultural studies. Part IV addresses actual lesson planning. The lessons in Part V were constructed using the linking processes discussed in the following chapters.

CHAPTER 8

LINKING INTO THE ELEMENTS OF DANCE

Learning Objectives

1. Understand how dance conceptually links to other areas of study.
2. Link dance to interdisciplinary studies through the body element.
3. Link dance with other topics through the force element.
4. Connect dance to other subjects through the time element.
5. Link dance and interdisciplinary studies through the space element.
6. Connect dance to other topics by linking into more than one element of dance.
7. Understand how to mine curricular material for parts of speech that provide conceptual material with which to construct a lesson.

❧ *Moving from the Conceptual to the Concrete*

Movement is made up of force, time, and space, and so is everything else in the world. This insight is the key to making a link between curricular topics and the elements of dance. Any topic can be explored through movement because all topics are related to at least one of these elements. Once you understand the analytical framework of movement presented in Part II, you can use this knowledge to create a variety of movement problems for students to explore. Parallels between a subject and one particular element of dance often are obvious: for example, the relationship of counting beats to the time element. When several elements come into play, one connection is often stronger than the others. Identifying that strongest relationship between an element of dance and a topic is the first step in making meaningful interdisciplinary connections for your students.

To start the linking process, think of a curricular topic you would like to explore with movement and take a moment to consider its nature, especially in relation to the dance vocabulary in Part II. If your topic conjures up visual pictures or designs, you may want to refer to the element of space as a base of instruction (Figure 8.1). If it drums up emotions or forces of nature, consider aspects of the force element as common ground. If numbers, beat patterns, or sequences come to your mind, the time element may serve as your link. If nameable movements are paramount, connect your topic to the body element. Once you have identified your link to an element of dance, you can build your lesson primarily within the context of that element. Concentrate on the simple and objective movement experience. From that, let imagery flow to generate details for a movement lesson.

The following sections examine each element of dance separately, analyzing relationships between curricular subjects and movement. Themes developed by linking with the elements of dance exemplify what you can do with your own topics of study. Ideas from several lessons in Part V are used in this chapter to illustrate the conceptual process described, and worksheets and brainstorming lists provide guides to the linking process.

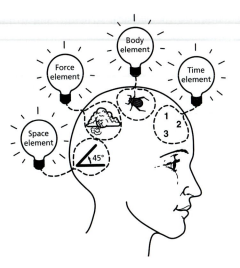

FIGURE 8.1 *Making Connections between Curricular Topics and Movement Elements.*

✑ *The Body Link*

It is easy to find direct links to the body element because physical form is so tangible. For those new to teaching creative dance, this is a good place to start. If a curricular topic has a body or any physical form, the body element can come into play. For links to the body element, look at the subject's prominent actions and how its form is configured. Ask yourself these questions:

- What are the interesting parts of the subject's structure?
- How many of each part does it have?
- How do the parts fit together and coordinate with each other? Do the parts move separately or all as one unit?
- Do parts or the whole form typically perform nameable actions?
- Do actions occur in a natural or predictable order?
- How can individuals or groups express these body structures and actions?
- What material or foundation lessons should precede this lesson?

The Physical Form of Objects

Tangible subjects such as animals, modes of transportation, and machinery have physical forms that link easily with the body element. Let's explore some of these links using the topic of animals. Many animals have structural parts similar to those in the human body; others require creative treatment. For example, snakes and fish have no arms or legs, so dancers must accentuate spinal movement. Some animals have more than two legs or have trunks, tails, or protective shells. To show this, students can let an arm or a leg represent these parts. Another way to solve the problem is to imagine those nonhuman parts (a tail, trunk, shell, or wings) and move the body as if those parts were present. Emphasizing one aspect of a physical form, such as a fly's huge multifaceted eyes, an elephant's soft foot pads, a bird's claws, or a kangaroo's pouch, adds specificity to students' movements. Encourage students to research the facts and couple them with the power of imagination to change their movements in expressive ways.

Students can also work in groups, making one animal form out of two or more people. There will be many variations in how groups solve the problem of a six-legged insect, for example. Each is acceptable as long as their "insect" has six legs and is performed safely. Students absorb and retain concrete knowledge of their study topics through this kind of attention to the physical structure and to movement. Encourage groups to share their solutions with the whole class.

Inanimate objects can also be portrayed when working from a body perspective. Students can easily represent simple machines such as screws and levers. A few people moving together as a group body can express the different parts of more complex machines and show how the movement of one part affects another. For example, circular groups of people can move in gearlike fashion, or a single student can rise and sink inside a small group of surrounding students to represent the movement of a piston inside the cylinder of an internal combustion engine. Many objects (airplanes, washing machines, clocks, blenders) have parts that move. Analyzing how these parts work together provides a wealth of material for individual and group exploration.

Characteristic Movements of a Topic

Another aspect of the body element that provides linkage to the curriculum is the whole gamut of basic body movements. Have students give names to typical animal movements: monkeys swing, snakes slither, turkey vultures swoop and soar. Inanimate objects may move as well: bulldozers push, clouds float, planets rotate and revolve. Can your students move their bodies in similar ways? Have students investigate whether the movement travels from place to place or remains stationary. Ask students to consider the order of several actions. For example, a cat crouches, wiggles, then stills before it pounces. Does one movement naturally follow another to create cycles, sequences, or patterns? Examining these factors can help give form to movement studies.

You may need to address specific physical and safety skills that are required to accurately experience and express movements from your topic. Flamingos stand on one leg, cats creep silently, kangaroos propel themselves great distances in a single bound. Technical skills, such as how to balance on one foot, walk softly, and land safely from jumps, should be addressed if your topic calls for it. The skills themselves are fun to play with, and the fact that they are characteristic of your topic can provide incentive for your students to master them. One important skill to practice is stillness. Remaining motionless for even one minute helps students gain perspective on animal behaviors such as metamorphosis and hibernation. Working with characteristic physical skills like these gives students kinesthetic empathy for their subject. The technical challenges of many of these skills build respect for the capabilities of animals and a realistic understanding of the limitations of the human body. Allow time for students to develop technical abilities that will increase safety factors and self-control as well as artistic craftsmanship.

The Spiders lesson worksheet in Box 8.1 demonstrates an obvious connection to the body element. By paying attention to the use of the characteristic body parts and movements, there is less tendency to dramatize the spider's scariness or other less-appealing attributes. The focus is grounded on concrete scientific observations. Students kinesthetically absorb this knowledge and use it in their creative process of making the dance.

Health and the Human Body

It is fun for students to move as they study human anatomy and physiology in science lessons. Moving a part of the skeleton with awareness of that part's structure is also a great way to study the skeletal system itself. It is possible to use the proper names of bones (femur, vertebrae, and so forth) even with the youngest kids. All

Individuals connect extremities with others' in a nursery web design on the floor.

Box 8.1

Body Link Worksheet: Spiders

What are the interesting parts of the subject's structure?

Jointed legs, eyes

How many of each part does it have?

8 legs, 8 eyes

How do the parts of the subject fit together and coordinate with each other?

Legs extend radially out from a center and move with sequential joint actions
Eyes move all around, sets of eyes move independently from each other
Whole body movements also used

Do parts or the whole form typically perform nameable actions?

Legs: spread, reach, crawl, creep, wander, leap, wrap
Eyes: look around, roam
Whole body: spin webs, lay eggs, hatch from eggs, knit nursery webs, sail (balloon)

Do actions occur in a natural or predictable order?

Hatch, nursery web, balloon, look around and crawl, spin web, wrap prey, lay eggs

How can individuals or groups express these body structures and actions?

Individual: spread and reach arms and legs crawling close to floor
Partners: combine two bodies to make one spider
Group: connect extremities with others in web design on floor or midlevel

What material or foundation lessons should precede this lesson?

The Moving Body
Lines and Shapes in Space

See Curricular Lesson: Spiders in Chapter 15 for a lesson constructed from this process.

---

ages are fascinated by their human skeletons and seem to love moving as if they were made only of bones.

Health lessons may include awareness of more subtle body functions such as breath and heartbeat. In analyzing body systems, remember that the parts of the body—even the lungs, the heart, the nerves—all have characteristic actions that can be abstracted into creative movement ideas. The movement of breathing can be exaggerated as whole bodies or whole groups enlarge and shrink to express the idea of lungs expanding and contracting. A human body lesson about the circulatory system could have one group of students form the heart and another group represent the red blood cells, which can be "pumped" through the body as they gallop to the rhythm of the heartbeat. To dance the nervous system, students can form a matrix of "nerve cells" stretching toward each other on the floor, with points of contact or near contact representing synapses. The cells vibrate messages to each other through touch. Material from these explorations can be combined in a dance that demonstrates an understanding of how the physiological systems function.

The senses of sight, hearing, touch, taste, and smell are common topics in many classrooms. Because the kinesthetic sense is the basis for the other senses, movement provides a fertile arena for studying the senses.

Framing an area increases awareness of the visual field by blocking out competing stimuli.

When studying the sense of sight, the experience of moving with eyes closed can be contrasted with moving with eyes open. Visual awareness will be heightened if students close their eyes and then, upon opening them, look at an object through a "frame" either made by their hands or an actual picture frame. With this heightened visual perception, students then move in response to the lines and shapes they see in front of them. They might move as if tracing the shape of an object or by filling in the negative space around it. This activity works well with paintings and sculptures as well as with natural objects such as flowers, shells, and branches.

Just as a class can work with both sight and no sight, moving with attention to both sound and silence heightens awareness of hearing. Auditory stimulation, whether actual or imagined, can be a great starting point for creative dance. Sounds such as scrape, bonk, twang, and rumble evoke natural responses that cause a person to move in a related way. A scraping sound could make the body cringe; a bonk could elicit a jerky jump. The natural responses to sounds can be objectively observed, named, exaggerated, and varied as dance material. Hiccoughs and yawns can be explored in movements that accompany their audible sounds. After exaggerating both of these to a somewhat dramatic effect, remove the sound. What remains is a notable example of movement expression in silence.

Touch, smell, and taste can also produce sensory awareness that stimulates dance. For example, in a unit on baking bread, students could perform the actions of making bread and include movement studies showing the kinesthetic response to the smell of baking bread, its taste, and the texture of dough at different stages in the process. Whether you are studying each sense as a topic in itself or linking it to other subject matter, keep your explorations grounded in the kinesthetic sense. It is the birthplace for the other senses and connects them to dance expression.

For lessons that link with the body element see Chapter 15.

The Force Link

Linking with the force element opens a wide palette of descriptive movement qualities that can be used to express concepts across the curriculum. When creating a movement lesson that links with the force element, ask yourself these questions:

- What qualities or emotions are inherent in the topic?
- In the range of forceless to forceful, what degree of force does the subject use?
- Are movements sudden or sustained?
- Does energy converge or scatter?
- What interactions of force take place between parts of the topic? Does the movement of one thing affect that of another?
- What kinds of movements could express the emotional qualities and dramatic interactions involved?
- What material or foundation lessons should precede this lesson?

Qualities of Movement in a Topic

Natural phenomena are a good starting place for demonstrating how the force element can link to curricular topics because connections are often obvious. For example, in a study of weather systems, students can research the characteristics of each part of a storm. This could result in the following exploration of material. The wind moves with varying

BOX 8.2

Brainstorming List: Volcanoes

Linking element

Force

Qualities of materials

Magma: fluid, heavy, strong
Hot gases: light, airy
Volcanic rocks ("bombs"): heavy
Gas-filled rocks (pumice): light
Ash: very light, easily moved
Hot molten lava: heavy but fluid, thick
Cooling lava: gradual, heavy, congealed

Qualities of actions

Quaking, trembling (of the earth): sudden and strong
Pushing (of magma under the earth's surface): sustained, converging
Erupting: sudden, strong
Bursting (of boiling lava): scattered, strong
Spewing (of ash): light, scattered
Flowing, undulating (of lava): strong and gradual
Congealing (of lava): gradually becoming still
Controlling and releasing energy: both sudden and gradual in different phases

Precede this lesson with

Interactive Forces (Chapter 14)
Strong and Gentle (Chapter 16)

See Curricular Lesson: Volcanoes in Chapter 16 for a lesson constructed from this process.

---

degrees of energy: whirling gusts, strong hard blows, or easy soft breezes. Rain can fall with varying degrees of force from a light mist to a strong downpour. Rain tends to fall in a pinpointed and direct pattern, whereas precipitation in the form of snow has a scattered quality. The dance will express the feeling of each kind of wind or precipitation with a different use of force.

The Curricular Lesson: Rain Dance (Chapter 16) studies the range between opposites of the force element. It starts out very gently, with the image of a light breeze and billowing clouds. As a storm begins to build, so does the dancers' energy. Raindrops begin to fall, first sporadically, then as sprinkles, light rain, hard rain, and, finally, cats-and-dogs rain. Thunder and lightning mark the climax of the dance, then all begins to gradually subside. The change of energy is reversed in order until only drips are left. The dance ends as gently as it began with lightness lingering as the dancers express images of rainbows and puddles.

Descriptive qualities of natural phenomena are found in both their actions and the substances involved. Unexpected links to the force element can sometimes be revealed by this method of looking at qualities of a topic. For example, in the story *The Three Little Pigs,* the differences in the quality of building materials is key to the unfolding story. These differences can be expressed in movement. Straw is light and easily scattered. Sticks are stiff and maintain that quality when blown down. Bricks are strong, solid, and immovable. In a dance, each building material evokes movements with different feelings. A lesson plan on this topic could include preparatory exploration of force concepts before

Dancers express the eruption of volcanic rock with forceful jumping.

working with the nature of the straw, sticks, and bricks. This primes students' sensitivity for the quality of movement and helps them clearly express the differences between the three materials. (See Curricular Lesson: The Three Little Pigs in Chapter 19.)

The interplay of opposites occurs in all the elements but is particularly prominent in the force element. The simple need of the body for both activity and rest leads dancers to balance cycles of forceful and forceless movement. This creates a natural rhythm that directly relates to other cycles of waxing and waning energy. Day follows night. Growth becomes decay, which in turn supports new life. History, political science, and even economics demonstrate cycles of rise and fall that can be expressed in movement. For example, the force qualities used to express a "Bull market" would be very different from those of a "Bear market." It is not difficult to depict these fluctuations of force if students have had prior experience with the polar opposites of the force element. By working with clear opposites first, your students' expressive vocabulary will be broadened, laying the groundwork for distinguishing the subtle gradients between opposites.

Emotions and Dramatic Characters

There is ample opportunity to work with emotions and dramatic characterizations in academic curriculum. This is useful for understanding characters in stories, people involved in historic events, and issues addressed in social studies.

Dancers express emotions by modulating the strength of their movements, which involves controlling or releasing energy. Calmness can be expressed through sustained, light movement. Boredom also has a sustained quality but releases into heaviness. Frustration is expressed as a strong force that is held back either through tight solidity or with small vibratory movements. Very different emotions may have similar attributes. Happiness and agitation may both be light and quick. Jubilation and anger both involve strong movements. An emotion such as anger can combine force qualities in a variety of ways. Anger may be expressed in either a sudden or gradual manner, and it can be direct or scattered in focus. A blind rage is multifocused and sudden, whereas obsessive anger is sustained and concentrates its energy narrowly. Different people may use different movement qualities to express the same named emotion. For one, happiness may be light, sustained, and scattered. For another it may be the opposite, as when happiness is expressed with a strong, sudden, direct "Yes!" The more force attributes a dancer combines in movement, the more intense the expression of emotional feeling. Young children can identify with many emotions, but they tend to act out stories, pretending to be the characters. Guide them instead into objective expression of the strong and weak emotions by having them sense the appropriate amount of force needed to express the emotion.

Human interactions are commonly expressed through the use of force. Think of different ways two people could approach each other and use degrees of energy to communicate meaning. A stealthy creep could cause goose bumps; a direct, face-to-face encounter means business; and a swingy skip seems friendly. Dancers can

Laughing is expressed by these students with different degrees of energy.

Box 8.3

Force Link Worksheet: The Lion and the Rat

What qualities or emotions are inherent in the topic?

Fear, relief, gratitude, worry, patience (rat)
Strength, pride, arrogance, ridicule, frustration, anger, helplessness (lion)
Compassion, jubilation, freedom (both)

What degrees of force are used?

Strong (lion) and weak (rat)
Forceful: fear, pride, anger, frustration
Forceless: relief, helplessness
Either (individual's preference): compassion, freedom

Are movements sudden or sustained?

Sudden: lion's rage; rat's worrying
Sustained: lion's stalking; rat's gnawing

Does energy converge or does it scatter?

Scatter: lion's rage
Converge: rat's focus and determination on chewing through the net to free the lion

What interactions of force take place between parts of the topic? Does the movement of one thing affect that of another?

Lion's kindly letting rat go gives him freedom
Net restrains lion
Lion struggles against net
Rat's sustained gentle gnawing causes net to fray apart
Rat creates freedom for lion
Compassionate symbiotic ending with two opposites coming together as friends

What kinds of movements could express the emotional qualities and dramatic interactions involved?

Lion letting rat go free: compassionate releasing movements
Rat being thankful: exaggerate thanking gestures to use whole body
Lion ridiculing rat: exaggerate laughing gestures to use whole body
Lion falling into trap: express rage and struggle with strong resisting moves
Kind and patient help of the rat to free lion: gentle friendly movements
Friendship and respect: gentle unison movement

What material or foundation lessons should precede this lesson?

The Moving Body
Rhythmic Opposites
Interactive Forces

See Curricular Lesson: The Lion and the Rat in Chapter 19 for a lesson constructed from this process.

---

relate to each other by responding to the other's force in a cooperative or conflicting manner. This is discussed more fully in the next section.

Addressing emotionally charged material can be difficult because it is so personal. In dance, the dramatic interplay in everyday expression is abstracted by working with the movement characteristics of the emotions involved. Characters from stories and their actions can then be analyzed for their emotional qualities. Who did what to whom? What emotions triggered or resulted from the action? What combination of force qualities might be used to express these emotions? Have students tune in to the feeling of strong, gentle, sudden, gradual, direct, and scattered movements to examine emotional material from an objective standpoint. This abstract approach provides a degree of objectivity that helps students break through inhibitions. Such a process helps prevent expression from being dominated by the face, and it leads to a deeper embodiment of the emotions found in a story.

Your goals, coupled with the age and interest of your students, will determine how you explore the conscious relationship between force attributes and emotions. You can break down emotions into their component force element attributes, or you can simply use the abstract polarities of the force element at the beginning of a lesson to prepare students for expressing emotions in a direct, intuitive way. The goal is to develop awareness and the ability of students to express emotion in movement.

Dramatic Interactions in Social Studies, Literature, and Science

Dramatic themes often involve two or more forces interacting. History is full of disagreements and resolutions between peoples. Dramatic conflicts and their impact on politics, economics, or society are clearly the force element at work. Rebelling against slavery or struggling to settle new territories are dramatic themes that tie in to social studies or history topics. There is even drama in themes such as persevering in research for disease cures. Students can express the dogged, patient, focused qualities needed by dedicated research scientists; the excitement and elation when discoveries are made; and the disappointments when experiments fail. Throughout history empires have been conquered and lost, kings and governments have toppled, and cultures have flourished and changed. The emotional aspects of these and other historical developments can be expressed in dance.

As with The Lion and the Rat, the initial tendency of students may be to act out these stories. By considering aspects of the force element of dance, students can be encouraged to express the interactive relationships between people or powers. By using forceful or forceless movements, sudden or sustained actions, and single-focused or scattered patterns, one group can affect the movement of another.

This is a perfect place for group work that builds on studies of activity and receptivity. (See Interactive Forces in Chapter 14 for more on this.) In a given situation, one character may be in the active role, the others in a more passive role. When a dictator or charismatic leader influences a mass of people, he is in the active role and the people are passive or "movable." Some situations may involve two active forces working in conflict: warring countries, daily life "turf wars" in the workplace, or peer competition at school. Forces may also work cooperatively with each other. When hunters and bird watchers join together to save a wetland, their forces harmonize. If all aspects of a situation are passive, stagnation may ensue. By experiencing these different force relationships in movement prior to discussing the dynamics of a social situation, students have a vivid physical knowledge on which to base their analysis of social studies topics. Exploring activity and receptivity in movement can provide the basis for understanding social and psychological topics over a whole school year.

To illustrate how to use abstractions to transform playacting into dance, let's walk through a historical event with suggestions for how it could be danced. During the American colonial period in the 1700s, the British government was challenged by New World colonists who did not want to continue paying British taxes or to be governed by her rules without representation. Demonstrations of British power could be expressed through active movements such as directive gestures or "taking" movements. These would be expressed in conflict with sustained, determined and steady movements of resistance by colonists. Forceful, sustained steps moving forward or blocking movements may be appropriate here. These early attempts to work things out peacefully with Britain were unsuccessful and, in time, the resistance grew into frustration. This could be expressed by increased force in both inward and outward directions. Eventually colonial and British interactions became explosive and troops clashed in armed confrontation. American forces gradually gained strength and numbers with their allies from France, Spain, and the Netherlands. The British surrendered, and the American War of Independence had been won. In the dance, the group representing the colonists and their allies would now be larger and express the stronger, more active role. The dance could end with the defeated group actually retreating from the space. The fighting dances described in the Pure Movement Lesson: Strong and Gentle (Chapter 16) demonstrate how these strong conflicting actions can be danced without harm.

One student is safely expressing an angry punch while her partner expresses the effect of the action. If partners maintain space between themselves, these "fighting dances" provide a healthy structure for dramatic interactions.

An interesting subplot within the American Revolution is the war to win the allegiance of different factions within the colonies. People struggled with joining the revolution or remaining loyal to the British Crown. The underlying exchange between these warring forces can be danced by three students: a Patriot, a Loyalist, and a person whose affiliation is Undecided. The first two characters would make active movements to influence the third, who would waffle back and forth. Eventually the Undecided person would join one of the sides.

Not all historical power struggles ended with division. The Edo Period in Japan brought a long period of stability and unity after a series of civil wars. Dancing this historical period would begin with conflicting movements and with one group dominating the other. As these relationships change over a period of time and events, more receptive interactions are emphasized in movement. When harmony is achieved, dancers could express peace with the cooperative use of force or unison movements.

This point of view is also valuable in finding the meaning and structure behind dramatic literature. Interactive forces are at the heart of an interesting development in the widely read *Lord of the Flies,* by William Golding. Right from the start, unspoken active and passive roles are established between two of the main characters, Ralph and Piggy. Another active force, Jack, soon enters the story. A sort of symbiotic balance of power works for quite a while, but the stress of the boys' situation builds to a conflict between the two active forces. Interactions change dramatically as power shifts among the boys on the island. Although dance movements themselves may come from verbs or abstracted images from the story, the force element is the basis for the energy expressed in these movements. Emotions from the survival quest and the power struggle of the two leaders combine to fill this piece of literature with ideas that can be expressed in movement through linking with the force element of dance.

Interacting forces from any realm can be readily expressed by a group of two or more dancers working with the force element. The wind and a kite, a bulldozer and earth, and the sea and a sailboat are all examples of active moving forces being met with a willingness to be moved. Many natural forces fit this same pattern: gravity holds satellites in orbit, the forces of wind and water erode mountains, magnets repel each other and pull passive materials toward them. These scenarios of cause and effect make wonderful partner dances, especially if a lesson begins with abstract force interactions. Nature also provides ample opportunity to explore the notably different relationship of conflicting forces. Continental plates push toward each other to cause earthquakes, weather systems come together and create storms, and chemicals react in explosive combinations. When opposing natural forces actively converge, the result is analogous to conflicting forces in human affairs. As a basis for movement material, the force aspects of these natural interactions are much the same as those in dramatic literature and in the daily challenges of human relationships.

The ability to express degrees or qualities of force helps students develop a fine-tuned kinesthetic vocabulary. Students learn to empathize with the qualities of natural and living things by forming movements that express their essence. The force element also provides dances with rhythmic dynamics that make them exciting for both dancer and audience. By focusing on movement sensations as human and nonhuman phenomena are expressed, dance studies illustrate a deep understanding of the dynamic forces that move our earth, our universe, and our lives.

For lessons that link with the force element, see Chapter 16.

❧ *The Time Link*

Time studies help dancers recognize and control the beat patterns that characterize movement. Patterns in language and mathematics can be studied by linking them to movement beat patterns. As with the other movement elements, sets of polarities such as fast and slow or even and uneven can be explored. These qualities, which naturally occur when anything moves, can be helpful in structuring movement explorations that connect to curricular topics. Turtles move slowly, jaguars run fast, clocks tick with an even or steady beat, speech emerges unevenly. Such time patterns can be explored as simple individual forms or combined into complex sequences.

When looking for a link between the time element and a topic, consider these questions:

- How is time used by this subject? Look for characteristics such as pace (slowness or quickness), how long things take, beat sequences, and the regularity or irregularity with which they occur.
- Is there a steady pace or a change of speed?
- Are there interesting changes in time patterns? Do they happen suddenly or gradually?
- Can beat patterns be measured?
- Do alternations of fast and slow occur in regular phases?
- Do patterns repeat themselves?
- How can these patterns be expressed with movement?
- Which material or foundation lessons should precede this lesson?

All of these contribute to the identification of time patterns that supply material for movement explorations. Have dancers express these patterns by moving different body parts or by concentrating on movements that stay in place or travel. By investigating these questions, students will improve their attention and listening skills and discover a deep feeling for the rhythmic life of the topics they are studying.

Beat Patterns and Language

The language arts provide a lucrative connection with the time element. Spoken language has a beat, so this is one way to combine movement with curriculum. Poetic patterns such as nursery rhymes, limericks, and iambic pentameter tend to order language into measured beat patterns. Our everyday language, however, does not; it combines words with relatively unpredictable, irregular timing. When people talk, they generally do not give each syllable of a word the same time value. If they did, they would sound like robots. The irregular beat patterns of normal speech and more cadenced patterns in poetry, song lyrics, or chants can all be used as structures for movement. Look for beat patterns created by syllables in speech and move in time with those patterns. Seek a feeling for the rhythmic time patterns of conversation, prose, free verse, or highly structured patterns of poetry. Because each language has its own characteristic beat patterns, students studying any language will kinesthetically absorb its "feel" and flow by moving to syllabic beat patterns.

Repeated refrains from a story or song can be used as chants to mark the beats of movement. One example of this are the well-known refrains in *The Three Little Pigs*: "Let me come in," "Chinny chin chin," and "Huff and puff". Young children can use these phrases as chants to mark the beats of movements. In the phrase, "Little pig, little pig, let me come in," you may suggest movements to do on specific syllables—such as tip-toeing on "Little pig, little pig" and stomping on each syllable of "Let me come in." Or let students explore the beat pattern to create their own movement phrases. These can be individually danced or taught to the class as a whole. A variation of the chant itself can create new patterns to be danced such as "Little Pig, let me come in. Let me, let me, let me come In, In ininin." Many stories, especially fairy tales, contain chants that can provide a basis for movement with connections to the time element. Older students can dance lines from literature or plays they are studying.

Words from any topic can be put into patterns in a way that highlights the number of syllables, their relative durations, and accents. In a class discussion, have students generate lists of vocabulary words on a given topic and group them according to the number of syllables in the words. Or create this list yourself—complete with pictures of each word if you wish. Here is a short list with words related to insects:

1 syllable	2 syllables	3 syllables	4 syllables
ant	beetle	dragonfly	praying mantis
egg	larva	butterfly	caterpillar
legs	stinger	antennae	pollen basket

Before patterning these words, have the children freely explore each word and its beat pattern in movement. Watch the children's investigations and use ideas from their explorations to create a movement phrase of a few words that the whole class can learn in unison.

The sequences created from such a list provide time patterns for the students' dances. One possible pattern could be to choose a word from each list and say each word four times while accentuating and moving to the syllabic pattern. Here is a pattern using words about butterflies in a sequence related to their life cycle:

Egg, egg, egg, egg.
Larva, larva, larva, larva.
Caterpillar, caterpillar, caterpillar, caterpillar.
Butterfly, butterfly, butterfly, butterfly.

A simpler structure for beginners could be to work with two words that have a different number of syllables, such as the following:

Praying mantis, ant.
Praying mantis, ant.
Praying mantis, praying mantis, praying mantis, ant.

This syllable pattern can be transcribed into numbers: 4 1, 4 1, 4 4 4 1. Students can then be asked to use this numerical pattern with other words from their lists. Here is one pattern students might try from our insects list:

Caterpillar, egg.
Caterpillar, egg.
Caterpillar, caterpillar, caterpillar, egg.

A more complex variation based on the same structure can be created with a four-word sequence that uses one word from each syllable list. These can be done in a 1 2 3 4 order:

Ant, beetle, dragonfly, praying mantis.
Ant, beetle, dragonfly, praying mantis.

For more challenge, reorder the words into nonsequential patterns such as 2 4 3 1:

Beetle, praying mantis, dragonfly, ant.
Beetle, praying mantis, dragonfly, ant.

Syllables provide time patterns for students' dances.

Movement combinations resulting from simple syllabic links can provide material for variation and development into lengthy compositions. Curricular Lesson: Word Rhythms with African Animals (Chapter 17) uses pictures of animals to generate words that are then combined into sequences. This lesson format can be adapted to any vocabulary list.

More advanced students may work with irregular rhythms in less rigid but no less demanding ways. In using a free verse poem, such as Robert Frost's "Fire and Ice," students move as the poem is read, responding kinesthetically to the irregular pattern of the language. They will not necessarily match each syllable exactly as in the previous examples, but they can respond to the overall pattern of the poem with a pattern of their own.

Mathematical Patterns

As the structures for counting syllables demonstrate, math can be applied to time studies. Lessons that link movement with number concepts often emphasize steady beats. Have you ever noticed the steady cadence children use when they count? Each beat in their counting indicates a regular measurement of time, which represents a distinct unit, an integer. Such chanting is a subliminal reinforcement for forming units that are all the same size. The ability to sense equivalent units is a basic skill for math comprehension.

Another building block in mathematics is understanding the notion of "sets" of integers. Grouping beats into sets is a way to use movement to devise math problems. Multiplication, fractions, division, and algebra link with these kinds of time structures. For example, Curricular Lesson: Multiplication (Chapter 17) starts with clapping an undifferentiated steady beat. As soon as counts are added to the beats, there is a tendency to begin grouping the beats into phrases. It is natural to make the first beat of the phrase stronger by accenting it with more force like this:

$$\textbf{1}\ 2\ 3\ 4,\ \textbf{1}\ 2\ 3\ 4,\ \textbf{1}\ 2\ 3\ 4$$

If the accent is shifted to the last beat of the phrase, the beat pattern marks sets of that number. This becomes a "factor" in a multiplication problem. For example:

$$1\ 2\ 3\ \textbf{4},\ 1\ 2\ 3\ \textbf{4},\ 1\ 2\ 3\ \textbf{4}$$

If the count keeps going rather than starting over on 1 with each new set, the accent will mark numbers that are multiples of the factor—in this case, multiples of four:

$$1\ 2\ 3\ \textbf{4},\ 5\ 6\ 7\ \textbf{8},\ 9\ 10\ 11\ \textbf{12},\ 13\ 14\ 15\ \textbf{16}$$

When students mark accents with movement (beyond just marking them in sound with clapping), the pattern becomes a dance form. For instance, students may stand or walk on the first three beats of the set and then make a large movement such as a jump or a large shape on the accented counts 4, 8, 12, and 16. If you give your students a total of sixteen counts, and their accents fall on every fourth beat, they will perform the series four times since $4 \times 4 = 16$.

Groupings of four are easy to start with because people are used to dancing to music with four-beat measures. If the class is new to time studies and has difficulty controlling these patterns, insert a pause after each set. This can help curb the excitement that is sometimes generated by time patterns. The pattern looks like this:

$$1\ 2\ 3\ \textbf{4}\ (\text{pause}),\ 5\ 6\ 7\ \textbf{8}\ (\text{pause}),\ 9\ 10\ 11\ \textbf{12}\ (\text{pause}),\ 13\ 14\ 15\ \textbf{16}$$

Working with other groupings, such as sets of 2, 3, 5, 6, and so on, will expand students' number sense and will also increase their rhythmic acuity beyond the limits of standard four-beat measures. Other groupings produce distinct patterns of their own:

$$1\ \textbf{2},\ 3\ \textbf{4},\ 5\ \textbf{6}$$
$$1\ 2\ \textbf{3},\ 4\ 5\ \textbf{6},\ 7\ 8\ \textbf{9}$$
$$1\ 2\ 3\ 4\ \textbf{5},\ 6\ 7\ 8\ 9\ \textbf{10},\ 11\ 12\ 13\ 14\ \textbf{15}$$
$$1\ 2\ 3\ 4\ 5\ \textbf{6},\ 7\ 8\ 9\ 10\ 11\ \textbf{12},\ 13\ 14\ 15\ 16\ 17\ \textbf{18}$$

Box 8.4

Time Link Worksheet: Multiplication

How is time used? Notice pace (slowness or quickness), how long things take, beat sequences, and the regularity or irregularity with which they occur.

> *Regular, steady beats of counting*
> *Group beats into sets*

Is there a steady pace or a change of speed?

> *Keep pace steady throughout*

Are there interesting changes in time patterns? Do they happen suddenly, or gradually?

> *Mark sets (measures) of beats with accents at end of set*

Can beat patterns be measured?

> *Measure sets of beats with accents that mark the factor being worked with*

Do alternations of fast and slow occur in regular phases?

> *No alterations, beats stay steady*
> *Add pauses between sets if needed*

Do patterns repeat themselves?

> *The measured set of counts / beats repeats itself as many times as the multiplications problem dictates (4 × 5 = sets of four beats repeated five times)*

How can these patterns be expressed with movement?

> *Use movement opposites; the stronger of the two opposite qualities is used as the accent movement that identifies the factor; e.g., factor of 4 is shown by three small movements followed by the large accented movement on the 4th count of the set*
> *Many sets of opposites could be used as ideas*

Which material or foundation lessons should precede this lesson?

> *Sensing Time Patterns*
> *Rhythmic Opposites*
> *Strong and Gentle*
> *Finding Unison*

See Curricular Lesson: Multiplication in Chapter 17 for a lesson constructed from this process.

When working with fractions, an opposite process takes place. Instead of grouping sets of beats together, the time interval between beats is divided. For example, the Fractions lesson adaptation (Chapter 17) begins with a slow pulse and then has the class divide the time between beats. Dividing beats into halves, fourths, or thirds builds up kinesthetic skills for sensing, marking, and manipulating beats. These skills are introduced in the foundation lesson Sensing Time Patterns (Chapter 14) and in the Pure Movement Lesson: Measured Time Patterns: (Chapter 17). Whether a class groups beats together or divides the time between them, exploring time patterns is fertile ground for working with math functions.

Telling Time, Relative Duration, and Pace

Measuring time using seconds, minutes, hours, days, and weeks is easily explored with beat and duration dance studies. Groups of students can demonstrate the relationship between seconds and minutes. In real time one group counts seconds and moves one movement per second and another group moves one movement per minute. A vestige of the lesson could be extended throughout the whole day with students making a movement to mark each passing hour. To show the relative duration of longer periods of time (for example, hours in a day or months in a year), use a similar structure without marking the exact amount of time between movements. Ratios could be created by older students to determine how this would be done.

A less obvious link to the time element uses a variation on the idea of relative duration. Historical time lines compare the duration of different periods of time. How long did the Egyptian, Greek, and Roman civilizations last when compared with each other? Movements that take a long or short time relative to each other can demonstrate this. Did one civilization start before the other ended? Different groups representing each civilization can begin and end their movements at different times to show this historical relationship. Duration and pacing of natural phenomena can also be expressed. Consider such topics as the growth rates of different trees; the comparative life spans of an ant, an elephant, and a human; or the orbit of different planets. Comparative time studies take skill and concentration, but students often step up to the challenge successfully.

Changeable Time Patterns

Many real-life and natural occurrences do not continue at a steady pace. The pace of your subject may gradually speed up or slow down. Ask students to identify these changes in time patterns. In *The Little Engine That Could* the train is a classic example of this pattern. Other examples include the increasing and decreasing rotations per minute in an automobile engine or the speeding up and slowing down of a pump. When working with time, try to feel the inherent beat pattern and express it in movement. In these studies it is vital to have an ending structure. The beat pattern must eventually either slow down to a stop or accelerate into a chaotic frenzy. Although a frenzy might be one choice for an ending, it should be used with discretion appropriate to your group.

Many phenomena do not demonstrate such distinct or predictable time patterns as those described so far. Sometimes changes are subtle or highly irregular. The often irregular beat patterns exhibited by sounds in nature are one example. Listen to nature sounds to gain a deeper appreciation for their rhythm. Once the authors danced outside in the desert to beat patterns produced by songbirds. It took an immense amount of concentration to identify separate songs, to exactly mark a song's pattern, and to switch from one song to another in the dance. The delight of moving to these recognizable "musical" patterns was unforgettable. In this case, the pattern was provided by sound. Often, however, the beat pattern is not audible. To have no sound does not mean that a time pattern does not exist. A fluttering leaf moved by a light breeze produces a silent, irregular time pattern that can be danced.

For lessons that link to the time element, see Chapter 17.

❧ *The Space Link*

Classrooms are generally alive with visual stimuli, and material for linking to the space element is readily available. What a topic looks like provides a simple link to movement; visual imagery plays easily into space connections with dance. The simplest way to begin linking with the space element is to create body positions that describe the shape and size of an object. But lessons built solely on replicating shapes of objects often become static. Deeper, more satisfying explorations extend into pathways on the floor and through the air. Focusing on pathways helps keep spatial studies alive as dancers feel the transition from one shape into the next. The spatial links that follow engage the kinesthetic sense as they build on abstract spatial concepts to link to curricular areas.

When planning a lesson based on the space element, ask yourself these questions:

- What is the physical shape and size of your subject? Do straight or curved designs predominate? Does the shape or size change?
- How can still shapes be abstracted into movement? Could they be expressed in pathways or be moved through space?
- Are there recognizable directions or pathways of movement: straight or curved, up and down, backward or forward, side to side, spirals, or zigzags?
- Are there level changes?
- What spatial planes are prominent? Is there a transfer from one plane to another, creating three-dimensional movement?
- How are empty and full space incorporated?
- What spatial relationships exist between objects?
- How can these spatial characteristics be expressed by groups of dancers?
- Which material or foundation lessons should precede this lesson?

Learning Readiness

Orientation in space is a skill so vital to academic performance that it is addressed as a topic in early childhood education. Recognition of simple geometric shapes and basic spatial relationships—large, small, inside, outside, in front, behind, toward, away, high, low, left, right—are taught as preparation for math and reading. Therefore, even a pure movement spatial lesson such as Lines and Shapes in Space (Chapter 14) provides support for the academic curriculum. The positive developmental effect of these lessons happens on its own if you provide students with a wide spectrum of opportunities for using the body with spatial awareness. Students gain experience from exploring spatial relationships that are encountered in everyday situations, and this material is fabulous for building vocabulary for youngsters or for those just learning English.

Lines and Shapes in Writing

When you write numbers, letters, or any other symbol, you are employing the spatial aspects of a topic. This provides an easy link to dance. Both children and adults enjoy moving in a way that replicates numbers or letters and words from their daily math or spelling lessons. These can be explored both as still shapes and as lines through space. To begin, emphasize abstract characteristics: curved, straight, large, small. By making straight and curved lines before introducing a specific symbol's image, students explore those ideas at a formative level and internalize a feeling for the curviness and straightness of letters and numbers. With a kinesthetic awareness that straight lines feel different from curved lines, dancers will be able to express the differences in shapes more clearly, and their letter or number shapes will come alive. Kinesthetically feeling the roundness of an O, the angularity of a Z, and the combination of both qualities in an R are integral experiences for anyone dancing these letters. Making the shape, holding the shape, transforming that shape into another, and moving the shape can all create beautiful dances. This kind of movement experience is much more meaningful to dancers than assuming a posed shape and holding it or just writing letters in the air with their hands. Backed by kinesthetic knowing, dancers will use the whole body for a much richer and more exciting learning experience.

Size and Number Sense

Spatial studies are excellent groundwork for math. Attention to the size of movements and shapes helps students develop number sense through such elementary concepts as greater than, less than, and equal to. Students can work individually, in pairs, or in small

Box 8.5

Space Link Worksheet: Cursive Writing

What is the physical shape and size of your subject? Do straight or curved designs predominate? Does the shape or size change?

Curved lines
Letters vary in shape and size

How can still shapes be abstracted into movement? Could they be expressed in pathways?

Make curved shapes of letters
Draw in the air or on the floor with different body parts
Write words or names as culmination

Are there recognizable directions or pathways such as straight or curved, up and down, backward or forward, side to side, spirals, zigzags?

Continuous curvy pathways move from left to right
Shapes of individual letters loop forward and backward

Are there level changes?

Yes, placement of letters on lines:
  High level = top of space or "headline"
  Midlevel = middle or "beltline"
  Low level = "footline" or below the line

What spatial planes are prominent? Is there a transfer from one plane to another, creating three-dimensional movement?

All on one plane, usually vertical, but could be other
Could spiral the writing to be three-dimensional

What spatial relationships exist between objects?

Letters relate to each other in sequences when spelling words

How can these spatial characteristics be expressed by groups of dancers?

Keep as individual studies for sharing

Which material or foundation lessons should precede this lesson?

Lines and Shapes in Space (curved shapes and pathways)
Geometric Planes

See the lesson adaptation Cursive Writing in Lines and Shapes in Space in Chapter 14 for a lesson constructed from this process.

groups and compare the size of steps, the size of arm movements, or the size of their body positions. A walking dance study that explores relative size would first establish the polar opposites of very large steps and very small steps and then find a middle-sized step. Students can make a dance that begins with small steps and gradually increase the size of the steps until they are as large as possible, then gradually diminish the size of the steps until they are very small. Each incremental change in the size of steps can be made with a voice or rhythm instrument signal from the teacher. By adding and taking away space from the walking steps, students are physically experiencing the meaning of addition and subtraction.

Number facts of addition and subtraction can be danced by moving along a line for a specified distance:

Addition	**Subtraction**
4 steps forward	6 steps forward
+ 2 steps forward	− 2 steps backward
6 steps forward	4 steps forward

The distance traveled forward or backward (measured by the number of steps) creates a spatial link to addition and subtraction. When using distance in this way, each movement should cover as close to the same amount of space as possible. You can use a large number line on the floor as an aid, or if your floor has them, linoleum tiles can be used as a measurement guide. Skips, jumps, and leaps can be used instead of walking to measure distances. A locomotor movement can serve as a basic unit to measure furniture or distances in the room.

Geometry

The body's geometrical use of space is fascinating and beautiful, and pure movement studies link to geometry with little adaptation. The foundation lesson Lines and Shapes in Space (Chapter 14) provides the basis for geometric concepts such as lines, planes, angles, polygons, and three-dimensional forms.

When studying basic shapes and polygons, individual studies include drawing those shapes in the air with different body parts and moving from place to place along pathways of those shapes on the floor. This is easiest to do when walking but can also be done by jumping, crawling, skipping, and so forth. Groups of students can form squares, triangles, hexagons, and circles with or without physical contact. By dancing in geometric formations and discovering what movements the group can make while maintaining these spatial configurations, students get a vivid body experience in the nature of that geometric shape.

A lesson that works precisely with angles formed by intersecting lines can be adapted from the straight and bent line explorations in Lines and Shapes in Space (Chapter 14). As individuals, students can form different kinds of angles by placing body parts in different positions. The apex of the angle can occur at any joint. Ask students to show a right angle with their arms, legs, arms and legs, or the torso bent at the hip joint (Figure 8.2). If you give students free choice to use any of these, you will see many different solutions. The activity can be repeated asking for acute or obtuse angles. In this

FIGURE 8.2   *The apex of the right angle can occur at several joints.*

Box 8.6

Brainstorming List: Native American Pottery Design

Visual aid:

> *Picture Book, When Clay Sings by Byrd Baylor*

Use of shape and size

> *Work from pottery designs in book*
> *Curved, hollow shape of pot (empty space)*
> *Shapes used in designs:*
> > *Abstract: curved and zig-zag*
> > *Representational forms of animal and flute player*
> > *Repeated shapes*

Movement ideas

> *Build up a "pot" in personal space*
> *Decorate pot with curved and straight lines; use all levels*
> *Hold shapes on "pot" then leave pot*
> *For abstract designs, dance pathways of designs from place to place*
> *For representational designs: shapes "come to life" leaving the pot, dancing as that animal and coming back to pot*
> *Return to same body designs created on the pot (challenge focus and kinesthetic memory)*

Culminating forms

> *Share individual or partner "pot" dances*
> *Groups of students make designs on one pot*

Preparatory material

> *The Moving Body*
> *Lines and Shapes in Space*

See Lines and Shapes in Space lesson adaptation Southwest Native American Pottery Design in Chapter 14 for the complete lesson constructed from this process.

---

students look at pictures of different landscapes to help them generate words that describe characteristics of mountains, buttes, canyons, and mesas. Words such as *pointed, tall, curved, bumpy,* and *flat* become stimuli for movement and shape studies that kinesthetically describe the different land forms. Students then work individually and in groups, changing their shapes to show the effects of erosion. Again, movement material from the foundation lesson Lines and Shapes in Space (Chapter 14) provides a good lead-in for these topics.

Any topic that can be represented visually can be explored in a manner similar to that for dancing shapes and pathways of letters and numbers. Identifying the prominent spatial aspect of a topic and building a lesson from that movement base also works well with pictures and books. For example, Eric Carle's picture book, *The Very Busy Spider,* chronicles the building of a web through story and pictures. Begin by establishing a feeling for straight line movement from place to place. Apply that experience to the creation of a spider web from straight line pathways. A group can also become the whole web shape, with dancers interconnecting their straight lines.

Dancing with Objects

Physical objects can be associated with many topics, and dancing with them evokes an intimate connection with the subject matter. It is rewarding to dance with leaves when studying seasonal changes in trees or with cloth to represent water. Dancing with objects from nature is especially satisfying and can promote reverence for natural beauty.

Object dances can be done while holding the object or relating to its shape as it rests on the floor. Look on such objects as an extension of the dancer rather than as props to dance with. Although some objects can make sounds and the quality of the object will influence the dynamics of the movement, moving with an object is primarily a study in visual design. This approach provides a link between dance and visual art related to a topic of study. Holding a flower, a rock, or a leaf changes the shape of the body. Moving with the object creates designs in space. Prepare the class for working with objects as you would any work in space: tune in to the movement of bones and explore pure movement themes such as lines and shapes. With this preparation, the dancers' bodies will be more fully engaged in expressing the object's spatial characteristics.

For lessons linking with the element of space see Chapter 18.

The dancers and their held objects unite as visual design.

Crossovers: Linking with More Than One Element of Dance

So far we have described linking with a single element of dance. Working within the limits of one element gathers ideas into a contained body of material and offers valuable structure for linking to curriculum. It is also possible to step outside the confines of the single-element approach and link with more than one element. When exploring many curricular subjects, two or more elements can often be combined as a strong movement base. Crossover links employing more than one element can be incorporated in one lesson or in a series of lessons. It is important that you clearly identify the elements you will use as links.

A thorough look at any topic can reveal less-than-obvious connections to various elements. For example, Curricular Lesson: Volcanoes (Chapter 16) exhibits a dominant element of force. This is evident in the pressure that builds toward the volcano's eruption and the changing amount of exertion as materials spew from earth's caldron. But time and space aspects are also present. The conical shape, the streams of lava, and the arching spray of ash and pumice are spatial links. The time element can be incorporated by emphasizing the beat pattern of the eruption. Curricular Lesson: Rain Dance (Chapter 16) can also be taught in a way that addresses several elements. Again, the force element is dominant. But the increasing and decreasing frequency of raindrops links to time, and the body element is evoked when students use basic body movements to express the falling rain, pushing wind, and rolling clouds.

Middle school students collaborate on a machine dance that incorporates all three elements: force, time, and space.

8.2 CREATIVE TOOLBOX—TRY THIS!

Machines: Crossing Over the Elements

Body	Parts of the machine
Force	Dynamic power of the machine
Time	Beat of the movement (its pace) and sound effects
Space	Pathway, positions of individuals, interrelated shapes

All elements combine in culminating dance of a machine in full action.

 BOX 8.7

Crossovers Brainstorming List: Dinosaurs

Lesson I: Space, Force, and Time Qualities

Space

Large: Diplodocus, Allosaurus, Triceratops, Pteranodon
Small: Fabrosaurus, Coelophysis

Force

Strong: Tyrannosaurus Rex
Light: Pteranodon

Time

Slow: Diplodocus
Fast: Fabrosaurus

Combining space, force, and time qualities

Strong, Fast, and Large: Allosaurus
Strong, Slow, and Large: Triceratops
Light, Fast, and Small: Coelophysis
Light, Slow, and Large: Pteranodon

Preceding Foundation Lesson

Rhythmic Opposites

Lesson II: Space Element

Adapt Human Sculptures format to create predator / prey statues in pairs relating to each other

Preceding Foundation Lesson

Lines and Shapes in Space

Lesson III: Time Element

Dance beat pattern of dinosaurs' names

Preceding foundation lesson

Sensing Time Patterns

Another way to use crossovers is to teach a series of lessons about a single curricular topic with each lesson featuring a different element or combination of elements. In the Curricular Lesson: The Three Little Pigs (Chapter 19) this series is broken down into three parts: the body element for the actions of the wolf, the force element for the quality of the building materials, and the time element for the chants of the wolf and pigs. Different explorations focus on each element. These kinds of lesson series work best if the elements used have been introduced in foundation lessons so that students have a grasp of the elemental concepts in their pure form. With that background, students can adapt their knowledge to inquiries regarding the crossover topic. Explorations and culminating forms from the foundation lessons can often be adapted to suit development of classroom studies. See Box 8.7 for how this might be conceptualized.

Approaching a topic through many dance elements allows students to delve deeply into their topic and explore many facets of a given subject through movement. It also provides an opportunity for the comfort and success of students who are not equally skilled in all the elements.

For lessons that crossover more than one element see Chapter 19.

❧ The Linguistic Analogy: Generating Dance Material from Parts of Speech

Language is an area of strength for many teachers, and it can make an excellent starting place for generating conceptual material to use in classroom movement lessons. The linguistic analogy is a simple and highly successful method that uses the structure of grammar to help people see the structure of movement. In this method, the different aspects of movement are categorized in terms of parts of speech and are explored from this angle as a means to movement expression. The curricular topic is analyzed for grammatical structures by finding nouns, verbs, adjectives, adverbs, and prepositions that have a relationship to movement. By keeping these linguistic categories in mind, teachers can extend their strengths into teaching curricula through movement.

Let's look at how you can generate movement material using this method. The nameable body movements of dance are all action verbs: stretch, flop, shake, skip, and so forth. The body and its parts are all nouns: head, torso, feet, hands, and so on. In fact, anything that moves is a noun. Adjectives and adverbs describe how, or with what quality, movements can be done: slow, fast, high, low, strong, gentle. Relationships between parts of the body, or the body and other objects, are described by prepositions that focus on relative positions: toward, away from, into, under, and over. If you let your imagination run freely, you can use these parallels between movement and grammar to quickly find links to your curriculum and organize movement material into logical lesson strategies.

Verbs as a Source of Movement Investigations

Because dance requires action, the most obvious place to begin is with verbs related to your subject matter. Stories, dramatic historical events, science, nature, and character studies are easily mined for action verbs. Even if you are not using written materials, you or your students can list and try out actions that relate to a topic. If you are studying cats, list and explore all of the actions a cat does: pounce, stalk, lick, crouch, swipe, frisk, turn, chase, and so on. Actions can be arranged in their natural order to form a logical movement combination, or they can be ordered by kinesthetic feeling.

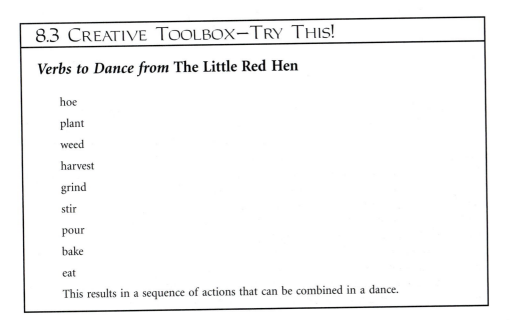

8.3 CREATIVE TOOLBOX—TRY THIS!

Verbs to Dance from The Little Red Hen

hoe

plant

weed

harvest

grind

stir

pour

bake

eat

This results in a sequence of actions that can be combined in a dance.

Nature often exhibits itself through action, and science books are full of verbs. Wind blows; rain pours, sprinkles, and splatters; volcanoes erupt, lava flows, ash settles. Plants reach and climb, water evaporates, planets rotate and revolve. Human events in history and social studies often reflect actions performed by groups. Explorers sail, armed forces march, nations unite or divide, activists parade. Pioneers trudge, farmers till. Each verb can be a stimulus for guided exploration.

You can use action verbs in many ways to vary and develop movement investigations:

- Use the whole body or individual parts.
- Exaggerate the movement and feel the sensations of doing that action.
- Find the natural pace or try others for a challenge.
- Do the actions in different places or on different levels.
- Try the actions with different force qualities: suddenly, gradually, with a lot of or very little energy.
- Work in groups to discover interesting relationships and formations.

In these explorations students are not "acting out" an event literally but are discovering and experiencing the abstract essence of the action verb. The movement experience yields feelings that can be expressed by that verb. This provides an understanding of the verb beyond the specific circumstances and makes the activity a dance study rather than a drama. Furthermore, abstract exploration of a verb adds depth of meaning to the specific context of a curricular topic.

Nouns: Things That Move

Working with verbs naturally brings in another part of speech: nouns. A fruitful way to use nouns with movement is to recognize that parts of the body are nouns. Body parts can be combined with verbs from your topic in unusual ways to increase your students' movement vocabulary and break away from monotony.

8.4 CREATIVE TOOLBOX—TRY THIS!

Nouns to Dance from **The Little Red Hen**

She can stir with her:

    arms and hands

    head

    shoulders

    knee

    belly

The result will be a very interesting "stirring" dance.

If animals are part of your topic, notice the differences in their body parts when compared with those of humans. Discover how the human body can be used to express the body structure and movement patterns of animals. Claws, wings, tails, or hooves each move in characteristic ways. Actions that are not typical of human movement (such as soar and wag) may arise from working with these nouns.

Simply listing nouns from a topic and exploring how these things move is a very direct strategy for approaching movement of both animate and inanimate topics. Students can do dances of wind, birds, animals, lava, or insects. These nouns often evoke beautifully free, expressive dances. However, students with limited experience might be at a loss as to how to use these nouns as a springboard, resulting in stereotypical or stiff

Students "stir" with their bellies as part of an exploration combining nouns and verbs from *The Little Red Hen.*

movement. To avoid this problem and stimulate movement imagination, combine other parts of speech with nouns. For example, begin by having students make the shape of a thing and then use verbs to show what that noun does. Ultimately, add adjectives and adverbs to describe the noun and its movement.

Adjectives and Adverbs as Descriptive Qualities of Movement

Verbs or nouns can be examined by the manner in which they move; that is, by the quality of their movement. Adjectives and adverbs describe a subject or its actions and can be used to add variations to the subject's movement. Look for adverbs related to your topic that describe how a movement can be done: lazily, hurriedly, painfully, nervously, exuberantly. Find adjectives that both describe the nouns in your topic and evoke movement expression: pointed, curved, enormous, microscopic. Ask students to examine a story or subject to discover inherent adjectives and adverbs. From the story of *Jack and the Beanstalk,* they might generate descriptors of the giant such as big, strong, mean, slow, or heavy. Adjectives describing Jack could include light, little, fast, and clever. Try moving in these ways, comparing different qualities.

8.5 CREATIVE TOOLBOX—TRY THIS!

Descriptors to Dance from The Little Red Hen

The Little Red Hen can stir:

    quickly

    slowly

    with large movements

    with small movements

    with a lot of energy

    with a little energy

A variety of qualities results in a dynamic exploration of stirring.

Natural phenomena can be studied for their qualities of movement too. The noun *hurricane* can be described as strong and fast, a breeze as gentle and slow. Clouds can be light and loose, thunderheads are heavy and tight. A volcanic eruption could be sudden and scattered, but flowing lava is thick and slow. List words like these from class material to use for exploration in a movement lesson.

Prepositions as Spatial Relationships

Prepositions pertain to relationships. Exploring prepositions in movement is simple and enjoyable for dancers of all levels. Prepositional movement studies can provide an opening for thinking about relationships and finding ways to express them in movement. With young children and English language learners this is important basic vocabulary for daily life. Prepositions often describe a spatial relationship—toward, away, above, behind, over, or under—that can be explored in movement by the relationship of two or more people, body parts, or objects. The meaning of the words is solidified by the movement experience.

Your curricular topic may include objects that come toward or go away from each other, as when the colonists sailed away from Europe and toward the New World. Or one thing may be inside or outside of something else, as cities, counties, states, and nations are arranged. There may be hierarchical relationships involved, with subjects figuratively positioned above or below each other. For example, the laws of the federal government are above those of the state. Classrooms can brainstorm ideas to generate flow charts, webs, maps or models. The spatial relationships indicated by these layouts show relationships between ideas. These can be expressed as a sequence of movements or as part of a more developed dance.

8.6 CREATIVE TOOLBOX—TRY THIS!

***Prepositional Phrases from* The Little Red Hen**

The hen can do her stirring:

> in a bowl
>
> on the floor
>
> over her head
>
> around the room

Adding spatial relationships to the movement creates interesting pathways.

Combining Parts of Speech

A single part of speech can be the focus of a topical movement lesson, as previously described, or parts of speech can be combined into one period of study. Here the power of the linguistic analogy method is demonstrated as it provides structures for in-depth exploration of a topic. For example, a movement study can revolve around one verb and then add an appropriate noun, descriptor, and prepositional phrase. If desired, you can even create a short dance based on a full sentence using all the words. Use this format to organize your lesson plan or let students generate the words and accompanying movements. Such investigation is great fun and opens doors to creative learning in action.

8.7 CREATIVE TOOLBOX—TRY THIS!

***Combining Parts of Speech to Dance from* The Little Red Hen**

> She
>
> > stirred   (verb)
>
> with her
>
> > legs   (noun)
> >
> > slowly   (descriptor)
> >
> > around the inside of the bowl. (prepositional phrase)

Students can combine ideas into their own movement sequence, or the whole class can create movements together.

The linguistic analogy is presented as a way of thinking about an unfamiliar topic (movement) in terms of a familiar one (language). By using the grammatical categories of language, you will have many options for approaching your curricular topic through movement. This approach is also a great way to light up a grammar lesson. Studies on parts of speech are superb vocabulary builders, both physically and verbally. They encourage and direct creative freedom and are popular with teachers and students alike.

For examples that use the linguistic analogy as a method of linking, see the lesson adaptation Varying Curricular Material in the Rhythmic Opposites lesson (Chapter 14).

Using the elements of dance as a matrix for linking to academic curricula provides a strong foundation for lesson planning. The examples given are intended to stimulate your imagination for discovering your own links. As you work with elemental dance concepts, you will discover many interesting relationships between movement and the multifaceted characteristics of your subject matter. Review the descriptions of the elements in Part II to familiarize yourself with movement concepts. The Elements of Dance chart on pages 60–61 is a quick reference for this vocabulary. Be sure to explore these vocabulary words in movement on your own to get a feel for how they translate into actual experience. The Interdisciplinary Links to the Elements of Dance and Linking Lessons chart on pages 94–100 will help you to quickly find movement links for subjects you study.

CHAPTER SUMMARY

- Curricular connections to dance are found by analyzing the common ground between dance elements and classroom subject matter.
- Dance links with other topics through the body element when there is a physical form involved or when specific, named movements can be identified.
- The force element provides a link between dance and other subjects by examining the way a subject uses energy, generates descriptive qualities, and elicits emotional associations that can be expressed in movement.
- Dance links to topics of study through the time element when attention is focused on the natural time patterns exhibited by a subject such as the beat patterns of language and groupings of numbers in math.
- Connections between dance and other subjects rely on the space element when visual designs are dominant.
- Crossover links employ more than one element of dance to express the nature of a topic.
- Parts of speech relating to any topic can be explored as movement material because action verbs are movements, things that move are nouns, the descriptors are qualities of movement, and prepositional phrases describe spatial relationships.

REVIEW QUESTIONS

1. How do you determine the dominant element to use as a link between dance and another topic? Pick a topic and explain how you would decide which element to use as a link.
2. Name several ways dance can be connected to other subjects by linking with the body element. For each, mention specific common areas between the two subjects that could become the focus of movement studies.
3. How can the force element be used as a link between dance and another subject? Pick one method and give examples of movement ideas that come to mind.
4. Explain how emotions can be used as a link between topics and the force element of dance.
5. Explain how both language and math link with the time element.
6. Why are dance studies linked with the space element helpful in developmental learning?
7. Pick one subject area and explain which links can be found with the space element for guiding movement studies.
8. Using one of the examples provided for crossover links, explain how the topic draws material from more than one element.
9. Using the linguistic analogy approach, pick a topic and list related verbs, nouns, descriptors, and prepositions that stimulate movement investigation.
10. Using the topic you chose in Question 1, construct a worksheet or brainstorming list that organizes the conceptual connections between dance and that topic.

Interdisciplinary Links to the Elements of Dance and Linking Lessons

	Body Element	Force Element	Time Element	Space Element	Lessons and Lesson Adaptations
Language	Nouns: how body parts or parts of anything are used Verbs: actions from a story or curricular topic	Opposites Adjectives and adverbs: quality of movement or physical characteristics Plot development Expressive qualities and emotions of literary characters Dramatic interactions in literature	Beat patterns in language • Syllables and word rhythms • Poetic forms and chants • Speech patterns of conversation or prose	Reading readiness Lines and shapes in writing • Symbols, number and letter shapes, spelling • Cursive writing Prepositions Visual imagery from literature and picture books	The Moving Body • Movement Similes • Verb Sequences: "I go." • Verb Sequences: Occupational, Sports, Historical Rhythmic Opposites • Adjectives and Adverbs • Synonyms and Antonyms • *Exactly the Opposite*, by Tana Hoban • *The Little Red Hen* Lines and Shapes in Space • Letter and Number Shapes • Prepositions • Cursive Writing Sensing Time Patterns • Sports Movement and Verb Beat Patterns • Nursery Rhymes, Poetry, and Chants Finding Unison • Sports, Occupational Movements, Vocabulary/Verbs Body Parts • Prepositions • Creatures, Nouns, and Fantasy Stories Word Rhythms with African Animals Sound and Movement • Phonetic Sounds • Sounds and Movements Derived from Familiar Things or Actions The Three Little Pigs The Lion and the Rat

					The Moving Body Lines and Shapes in Space • Letter and Number Shapes • Geometry (lines and angles) • Geometry (perpendicular and parallel lines) Sensing Time Patterns • Addition and Subtraction Finding Unison • Symmetry and Asymmetry Measured Time Patterns • Fractions Word Rhythms with African Animals Multiplication • Rhythmic Accents • Skip Counting Group Lines • Geometry • Geometric Planes • Geometric Motions
Math	Counting or measuring with basic movements or steps Addition and subtraction	Counting to a beat Sequences and patterns Sets, multiplication Fractions, division Relative time	Spatial orientation Size and number sense Measurement Addition and subtraction Counting or measuring with basic movements or steps Fractions, division Geometry: lines, shapes and polygons, angles, symmetry and asymmetry, planes dimensions Mapping and navigation		
Science	Animals, machines, transportation, or anything with characteristic movements Health and the human body • Body awareness • Anatomy and physiology • Body systems and functions Senses	Forces in nature: weather, volcanoes, earthquakes, erosion Qualities of substances Interactive forces • Physics: action and reaction, magnets, gravity • Chemical reactions • Dramatic interactions in scientific research	Acceleration and deceleration Time patterns in nature	Skeleton Geography, land formation, erosion Layers: habitat, atmospheric Astronomy: solar system, constellations Architectural construction Objects in nature Mapping and navigation Ecosystems and environments	The Moving Body • Developmental Movements/Evolution Interactive Forces • Wind: Weather, Seasons, and Sailing Lines and Shapes in Space • Predator/Prey Sensing Time Patterns • Animal Beat Patterns Body Parts • The Skeletal System • Creatures, Nouns, and Fantasy Stories

(Continued)

Interdisciplinary Links to the Elements of Dance and Linking Lessons   (*Continued*)

	Body Element	Force Element	Time Element	Space Element	Lessons and Lesson Adaptations
The Arts (*Continued*)					• Verb Sequences: Occupational, Sports, Historical Rhythmic Opposites • Adjectives and Adverbs • *Exactly the Opposite*, by Tana Hoban • Varying Curricular Material (occupational movements) Interactive Forces • Political Forces • Sports Interactions Lines and Shapes in Space • Predator/Prey • Human Sculptures "Diorama" Body Parts • Creatures, Nouns, and Fantasy Stories Strong and Gentle • Fighting and Friendly Sound and Movement • Sounds and Movements Derived from Familiar Things or Actions The Three Little Pigs The Lion and the Rat *Music* Sensing Time Patterns Finding Unison • Your Own Folk Dance Strong and Gentle Measured Time Patterns Word Rhythms with African Animals Multiplication

- Rhythmic Accents

Sound and Movement

- Sounds and Movements Derived from Familiar Things or Actions

Dancing with Objects

- Dancing with Found and Traditional Rhythm Instruments

Visual Arts

Lines and Shapes in Space

- Geometry (lines and angles)
- Geometry (perpendicular and parallel lines)
- Human Sculptures

"Diorama"

- Southwest Native American Pottery Design

Finding Unison

- Symmetry and Asymmetry

Body Parts

- The Skeletal System

Group Lines

Geometry (planes)

Dancing with Objects

(*Continued*)

Interdisciplinary Links to the Elements of Dance and Linking Lessons *(Continued)*

	Body Element	Force Element	Time Element	Space Element	Lessons and Lesson Adaptations
Personal and Social Development	Attentiveness Appreciation of uniqueness and diversity	Human interrelationships • Conflict/cooperation • Assertiveness and responsibility Emotions	Synchronizing with others	Safety Boundaries (awareness of personal space) Group spatial awareness	The Moving Body • Developmental Movements/Evolution Rhythmic Opposites • Varying Curricular Material (occupational movements) Interactive Forces • Political Forces • Sports Interactions Lines and Shapes in Space • Predator/Prey • Human Sculptures "Diorama" Sensing Time Patterns Finding Unison • "Ice-Breaker" Unison at Tables • Symmetry and Asymmetry • Your Own Folk Dance • Sports, Occupational Movements, Vocabulary/Verbs Body Parts Strong and Gentle • Fighting and Friendly Group Lines Sound and Movement The Lion and the Rat

CHAPTER 9

CONNECTING TO
WORLD CULTURES

Learning Objectives

1. Tie into world cultures as a basis for both traditional dance and creative dance studies.

2. Recognize the importance of and potential resources for authentic representation of cultural studies.

3. Analyze movement of different cultures by conceptual characteristics related to the elements of dance.

4. Draw from a variety of cultural materials to provide bases for creative dance studies.

5. Acknowledge dance as a means to build cross-cultural community.

Investigating World Cultures as a Basis for Dance

All societies dance. Traditional dance offers a direct way for students to experience the choreography of a culture and gain insight into the values and beliefs of another culture. Creative dance, with its emphasis on inquiry and problem solving, is also an excellent vehicle for studying and comparing cultures from around the world. Learning traditional dances can dovetail beautifully with creative dance studies to provide rich cultural experiences. Several resources on cultural dance are provided in Appendix F. In this chapter we explore cultural material using the movement problem-solving strategies presented in Chapter 8 for linking across the curriculum through the elements of dance.

Authentic Representation of Cultures

When teaching material from a culture different from your own, it is critical to research reliable ethnographic sources for information. Most libraries have a wealth of material on folktales and myths, customs, daily life, history, values, and art forms of people all over the world. Use this research—done by either the teacher or students, depending on grade level—as the source for generating movement problems. Authentic music that is truly representative of the geographical region can play an important role and add immeasurably to the students' understanding of the culture being studied. Although it does not need to be included with every study, music provides rich sensory communication that conveys the feeling for a culture. Recorded music need not be the only source of sound accompaniment for cultural-based dance lessons. Accompanying movement with traditional instruments such as drums, mbiras (finger pianos), rainsticks, shakers, and rattles greatly enriches a lesson. Singing songs from a region can also provide structure for creating dances. The meaning of words and the rhythm of the song are good themes for exploration and dance making. The teacher can sing the song as students work on discovering movements. If the song is simple, students can sing while dancing, or half the class can sing while the other half dances.

Photographs provide information about the customs, movement styles, and costumes of a culture that can be the basis for movement exploration. Pictures reveal answers to questions such as these: What are some daily life and ceremonial activities? What are some typical postures? Is the weight lifted into the center of levity or sinking with a low center of gravity? What is the relationship of the feet to the floor? How do clothing and type of foot covering affect movement? Conveying feelings from photographs and starting dance explorations in positions taken from such pictures helps students begin to appreciate the culture. Videotapes of scenes from a culture and its dancing are also immensely worthwhile.

Check community resources for people with connections to cultures you are studying. In addition to providing information on which to base creative dance lessons, they can guide you away from inadvertently violating cultural taboos. Ethnic restaurants and churches are often good local resources. In multicultural classrooms there are often parents or even grandparents who would love to come in and share dances, music, language, stories, and objects or clothing from home. Creative movement lessons based on these presentations can follow.

✎ Relating Cultural Studies to the Elements of Dance

The strategies described in Chapter 8 can be used to develop dance lessons using cultural material as themes. Analyzing cultural material through the elements of dance can alert students to common cross-cultural traits.

The Body Element

All actions involve the body, whose structure is common to all people. Basic body movements permeate people's daily lives and dancing around the world. The body is often used in characteristic ways, which can be explored in the lesson's tune-up. For instance, a lesson on an African folktale can be introduced by moving with a flexible torso, bending the knees to lower the center of gravity, and firmly connecting the feet to the earth when stepping. This movement pattern and others isolating different parts of the body are typical in many West African dances. An Irish folktale lesson could be preceded with work that emphasizes rising up onto the balls of the feet, straightening the spine, and lifting from the center of levity. In Irish dance the emphasis is on the footwork while the rest of the body remains still.

Work movements and daily life tasks offer insightful windows into a culture. Creative dance gives students an opportunity to explore and make forms with the movements of planting, harvesting, hunting, fishing, food preparation, washing, building, traveling, and more. Different cultures accomplish these life-sustaining tasks in various ways. Whole regions may share a common connection to a staple crop and the movements characteristic in its production. For example, rice planting and harvesting movements are common to all of Asia. Cultivation of corn, along with the grinding and pounding movement of its preparation, was seen in native societies across the Americas. Appropriate daily life movements pertaining to basic necessities in a culture can influence a patterned sequence of movements.

CONCEPT SPOTLIGHT 9.1

Links between the Elements of Dance and Movement from Different Cultures

Body Element

Links to characteristic uses of the body
Links to basic movements of work and daily tasks

Force, Time, and Space Elements

Link to qualities found in dance and movement styles
Link to comparative analysis within or between cultural dance and movement styles

Force, Time, and Space

Movement from any culture combines force, time, and space factors. Some aspects of a culture will lend themselves more to one element than another; however, a lesson can also be built upon several elements. Drawing from polarities in force, time, and space, analyze the qualities found in the movement style or traditions of a culture and incorporate them in the lesson. Once identified, qualities can be explored separately and then in combination, possibly to music from the region. Movement qualities can also provide a basis of comparison between different dances. In Japanese Kabuki theater, for example, the female "cloud walk," which is relatively forceless, gradual, multifocused, small, slow, and curving, contrasts with the male "Samurai" walk, which is forceful, large, sudden, single-focused, somewhat fast, and straight. Cross-cultural comparison of qualities can also be made, such as in the contrast between classic Flamenco's sudden, forceful actions of the legs and feet and classic Hula's gradual, relatively forceless use of those same parts.

In the culture-based creative dance activities mentioned here, students are not expected to replicate specific steps or master techniques for which their bodies are likely unprepared. They are simply being made aware of stylistic differences and offered the opportunity to experience them. As a problem-solving methodology, the emphasis is on getting the feeling and essence of the style rather than duplicating traditional forms. Emphasizing movement qualities of dances, as opposed to replicating steps, gives students a sense of the sentiments embodied within the dances.

✍ *Using Cultural Materials to Instigate Dance Studies*

Folktales and Myths

Traditional folktales and myths are good anchors for working with cultural material. Look for age appropriate themes in the stories you choose. A section of *Creative Storytelling,* by Jack Maguire, lists specific cultural examples of stories that are appropriate for different ages. The strategy for using a folktale to inspire creative dance is the same as working with any story. Investigate the characters, setting, and moods of the story, looking for descriptive words that can guide movement studies. Extract the most prominent action words from the story and explore them. Look for interesting beat patterns of words or repeated phrases to use as a basis for movement timing. The African tale *Bringing the Rain to Kapiti Plain,* retold by Verna Aardema, or the English classic *The House That Jack Built* have beat patterns that are staples of a genre that builds the tone of the story around repeated compelling refrains. Children enjoy developing dances around these familiar tales. Older students can extract events or themes from the story that call for explorations in a given element. For example, in the Chinese folktale *The Seven Chinese Brothers,* each brother has his own qualities and role in the story. The emperor's army is swept away by the seventh brother's copious ocean of tears. This can be shown through group movement by working with the force element skills of moving as an active force and being passively moved by another force. The active ocean waves move the passive helpless soldiers.

Forceful striding expresses the strength of the third brother from *The Seven Chinese Brothers.*

Significant Animals

Animals may play an important role in the life of a culture, and they are often characters in folktales. Sometimes an animal is revered for its majesty, like the quetzal bird in Central America. Some animals identify clan groups and provide symbolic protection such as the Eagle, Raven, Wolf, Beaver, and Bear clans of Native Americans of the Pacific Northwest. An animal that is a primary source of food may also be revered as the salmon is in this same region. Creating animal dances is a favorite of dancers of all ages. To find material for detailed movement exploration, analyze the animal's distinctive body size and shape, characteristic actions, adjectives and adverbs that describe it, beat patterns of locomotion, and typical sounds. The dances can be further influenced by stylized visual art depictions of the animal.

Visual Arts and Meaningful Objects

Visual arts and cultural symbols can be explored in movement. The Native American Pottery Design lesson (Chapter 14) illustrates one way to study the visual arts style of a culture through dance. Any visual arts form—sculpture, painting, pottery, crafts, or architecture—can be approached through the space element. The principle is the same as with other spatial links: work with basic design elements in movement to embody the style of that culture's visual arts.

Dancing with characteristic objects from a culture gives an immediate, nonverbal connection to its traditions. Dance lessons can complement the study of customs associated with that object. For example, handheld fans developed in early civilizations of Egypt, Rome, Greece, and China and have spread throughout the world. In Japan the stylized use of the fan became codified into gestures that express feelings. Women in Spain, England, and the United States also took up this custom. To create fan dances that express specific feelings, students may use traditional fans or make their own or even use their hands as fans. Working with an object like this that is found in several cultures is a good focus for cross-cultural comparisons.

The ribbon and wand dances that have been a part of Chinese culture for many centuries inspire beautiful pathway explorations. Crepe paper streamers or strips of fabric can be procured for this purpose in the five colors prominent in Chinese mythology: yellow, black, red, blue, and white. The symbolic meanings of color in different cultures make good themes for exploration as dancers move colored streamers or cloth in ways that express their meaning.

Masks are also important in the lore of many cultures. Mask making and dancing while wearing or holding a mask adds a dramatic element. Byrd Baylor's *They Put on Masks* includes examples of authentic mask designs from many cultures. Moving with an object from a different culture bridges a gap between two worlds and brings greater appreciation for that culture.

The totem pole comes to life as students dance the movement qualities of the animals their masks represent.

Ecosystems and Spatial Environments

Through research you may discover how dance reflects the influence that geography, climate, and the ecosystem have on people's experience. Dances of storms, rain, snow, dryness, heat, and cold as well as geographical influences such as mountains, rivers, the sea, forests, or plains are all expressions of the environment within which the culture operates. Mitten dances are common all along the Arctic region of North America. Students can create their own mitten dances alone, with a partner, or in groups. Have dancers don mittens they have decorated and use them as a theme for improvisations. Oven mitts, which resemble the large mittens of the northern region, are readily available and a good choice for this use.

The spatial environment of a culture can also be investigated through creative dance. In Japan people live in close proximity to each other and learn to maintain personal space in close quarters. In the Navajo Nation neighbors live far apart in a vast landscape. Explore different population densities with simple structures that relate dancers to each other from near and far. Compare the feeling of many people moving in a small space to a few people moving in a large space.

Culture-based Personal Space

Very strict but often unwritten or unconscious cultural rules govern the comfortable and appropriate use of space when people relate to each other (Hall, 1966, 1977). The typical size of a person's self-space varies between cultures or subcultures within a larger society. The culture of a work environment may call for larger personal spaces than the culture within a family. Comfortable spacing can also vary across genders and age groups. Exploring partner and group dances with different sized space bubbles and discussing how different cultures use space teaches cultural sensitivity, bringing to the surface cultural understandings that often are deeply buried. Knowing how to adjust the size of space between yourself and others in different situations is powerful knowledge. It can go a long way in helping people bridge problems by pinpointing differences that may seem huge but, once identified, can be negotiated.

Building Cultural Community through Dance

In cultures around the world, dance brings the community together and builds bonds between people. Culminating forms for culture-based dance lessons can serve that same function in the classroom community as students dance their own creations inspired by cultural knowledge. Group spatial forms such as circles and single or facing lines appear in dances around the world. These provide good unifying structures for final dances in a lesson. Some cultures emphasize one group form over others, such as in the Balkan line dances. If this is so, use that characteristic when pulling together the explorations into a culminating form.

Some cultures, like the Northwest Coast communities of Canada and Alaska, make ceremonial gifts of dances, songs, and stories. Understanding the custom of these Potlatch ceremonies can add meaning to the sharing of dances at the end of dance sessions. It can encourage students to sing, tell, and perform their gifts for family and friends as well. This is a good alternative for children who don't have the resources to give material gifts.

A fun way to acknowledge commonalities within a classroom community is to have students make up their own folk dance. Ask students to identify demographics or characteristics that are shared by the whole class or that describe the community culture of which they are a part. As with studying other cultures, local traditions and pastimes, the climate, population density, geography, historical events, industries, and the arts can all supply material around which dancers can create movement forms. After exploring these ideas freely, specific movements can be performed in unison in a circle or line formation. See the lesson adaptation titled Your Own Folk Dance in the Finding Unison lesson (Chapter 14) for an example of this.

Working with cultural material through dance will help students learn about new and different ways of solving life's challenges. Different customs, music, and ways of moving may seem strange and even cause discomfort at first among students. Students may giggle to cover that discomfort. It is important to acknowledge differences and model respectful regard for the material. Be sensitive to aspects of another culture that would be uncomfortable for your students. First, offer movement problems and challenges that will not cause uneasiness. Once students are engaged, you may find a more receptive audience for new and different ways of moving. Creating dances inspired by different cultures helps students appreciate the diverse ways that human customs evolve from basic common roots. Mettler (1988) eloquently addresses the potential of creative dance to build bridges between diverse peoples:

> My work in different countries has made me realize that people everywhere are the same in their natural ability to dance when given an opportunity to create their own movements, and in their joy of communicating with one another in the language of movement. I believe that if this language, practiced as a creative art activity, were recognized for its universality and power it would be widely used to break down barriers between people who speak different tongues. Creative dance is a new kind of folk dance which can unite a group as no other activity can. It can become a factor in furthering international good will. (p. 8)

Appendix F lists some cultural resources that celebrate human diversity.

CHAPTER SUMMARY

- In addition to learning traditional folk dances, the problem-solving methodology can be used to integrate cultural studies with creative dance.
- Representational studies of different cultures should be based on authentic, reliable information. Music from the region, library materials, and community members are accessible resources for such information.
- Movement of different cultures can be analyzed according to conceptual characteristics that relate to the body, force, time, and space elements of dance.
- A variety of ethnographic materials can be drawn from for creative dance studies. These include folktales and myths, significant animals, visual arts, meaningful objects, ecosystems, spatial environments, and cultural mores.
- When practiced as a creative art activity, dance bonds people through movement experience.

REVIEW QUESTIONS

1. How can cultural studies be connected to creative dance using a problem-solving methodology?
2. What resources provide authentic representation of a culture's movement patterns? Explain how each might be used as a basis for creative dance studies.
3. How can the elements of dance provide connections to cultural inquiries?
4. What kinds of cultural materials can provide stimulus for creative dance?
5. Do you believe creative dance experience can build community among different peoples? Develop your own point of view and explain your position.

CHAPTER 10

❦

ENGAGING MULTIPLE INTELLIGENCES

Learning Objective

Understand the relationship between movement/dance and each of the eight multiple intelligences delineated by Howard Gardner:

1. Bodily-kinesthetic intelligence
2. Intrapersonal intelligence
3. Interpersonal intelligence
4. Musical intelligence
5. Spatial intelligence
6. Linguistic intelligence
7. Logical-mathematical intelligence
8. Naturalist intelligence

The human race has evolved a variety of ways to perceive, respond, express, and create. Theories about diverse thinking strategies have been labeled as modalities, sign systems, multiple intelligences, multisensory learning, systems of knowing, and learning styles. Each theory has its own terminology and way of looking at things, but all seem to agree that when a topic is explored through more than one mode, students have a greater opportunity to learn successfully. Teaching through different modalities taps into more of the brain's potential by developing diverse intellectual paths. Recognizing that people assimilate, order, and communicate information in different ways helps teachers notice and build on what students can do instead of what they cannot. By using students' strengths as a bridge to areas of weakness, we can tap students' interests and motivate the learner.

A useful and well-known structure for thinking about the many ways people use their minds productively is provided by the work of Howard Gardner (1983/2004) in his theory of multiple intelligences. Gardner outlines a broad framework for planning and instruction that encourages active learning—including integration of the arts into the classroom—supports individuality, and offers means for potentially engaging all students. Describing intelligence, Gardner says, "To my mind, human intellectual competence must entail a set of skills of problem solving—enabling the individual *to resolve genuine problems or difficulties* that he or she encounters and, when appropriate, to create an effective product—and must also entail the potential for *finding or creating problems*—thereby laying the groundwork for the acquisition of new knowledge" (pp. 60–61). Gardner identifies and describes eight modes of intelligence: bodily-kinesthetic, intrapersonal, interpersonal, musical, spatial, linguistic, logical-mathematical, and naturalist.

Each person is a unique blend of intelligences. Although Gardner identified separate intelligences, they also function in concert. Rather than just addressing one intelligence at a time, teaching through varied modes of learning develops and integrates intelligences. By acknowledging the very existence of bodily-kinesthetic intelligence, Gardner has given credence to what dance educators have been saying for almost a century: movement is an essential mode for learning and expression. His category of bodily-kinesthetic intelligence has piqued the interest of educators to find ways to bring movement into the classroom. Creative dance highlights bodily-kinesthetic intelligence, but more important, it stimulates many intelligences at once. Consequently, it can involve the whole person and can be used as a link from one intelligence to another. Let's discuss each intelligence in turn to see how creative dance applies to Gardner's theory.

Bodily-Kinesthetic Intelligence

People with a facility in bodily-kinesthetic intelligence have skill and interest in doing large and fine motor tasks. They are dancers, athletes, actors, carpenters, surgeons, and craftspeople who easily settle into the natural synchrony of body and mind. Bodily-kinesthetic intelligence involves "thinking" through the movement of the body. It requires the ability to use awareness of movement as a guide in decision making and as a means of expression.

Examples of using bodily-kinesthetic intelligence outside the field of creative dance include using the physical movement of writing to help organize thoughts, manipulating objects while pondering their relationship, taking a walk to help sort out a problem, noticing the physical sensations in the body to help determine an authentic response to a situation, and using gestures and body alignment to aid communication. People do these activities all the time; however, they are often done unconsciously and with little attempt to cultivate the intelligence behind them. By heightening awareness of movement through the kinesthetic sense and approaching movement from a problem-solving standpoint, creative dance truly activates the bodily-kinesthetic intelligence.

Humans begin their lives using movements of the body to take in information and express themselves. Infants and young children discover who they are and explore the world through pushing, reaching, rolling, grasping, mouthing, and touching. Their explorations are total body explorations. Their expressions of need—hunger, discomfort, pleasure, restfulness—are also total body movements. Greeting and exploring the world through movement enables the child to develop the complex neuromuscular patterns that are required not only in everyday tasks but in developing emotional stability and higher level thinking skills (Cohen, 1993; Hannaford, 1995). Creative dance study approaches problems with the same sense of awe and urge for discovery that starts the infant on his or her developmental pathway. As students focus on movement problems, they cultivate innate bodily-kinesthetic intelligence and find meaningful and satisfying movements to express their solutions.

The kinesthetic intelligence can also be used to develop the other intelligences. If a child is talented in bodily-kinesthetic ways of knowing but has trouble in another area, such as language, he or she can use skills in movement problem solving to engage other intelligences. For example, dancing the meaning of words or the ideas from a story will stimulate verbal intelligence. It is true as well that creative dance can be a tool for opening the world of movement for students who are not very comfortable kinesthetically but are at home in another intelligence. Those students can use their strength in, say, verbal imagination to create word images with which to move freely. The excitement stimulated through their linguistic intelligence will spill over to their movements, helping them use their body with newly discovered imagination.

Intrapersonal Intelligence

Intrapersonal intelligence is the ability of people to attend to their feelings, sense what they want, and make decisions based on that self-reflection. The functioning of this intelligence relates very closely to the way the mind makes associations and choices as part of the kinesthetic sensory loop (see Chapter 2). When a mover turns his or her attention inward, the mind interprets objective movement sensations by remembering similar sensations, making emotional associations, and finding meaning in those associations. This internal awareness becomes the basis for further action. The process can happen in an instant or it can extend over a long period of time, repeating the loop over and over as one "feels through" alternative solutions for a problem. This is intrapersonal intelligence at work.

When people attend to the kinesthetic sense to make sequential movement choices, they are integrating bodily-kinesthetic and intrapersonal intelligences. When these two intelligences are working well together, decision making has a very different quality from weighing alternatives and making a logical choice. In this mode movements are discovered by the body and emerge through awareness of what the body wants rather than through manipulation or contrivance. This experience can be an important step in self-knowledge. When this kinesthetic way of working is used for art making, the result is an intuitively generated creation that Mettler (1960/2006) called "organic form." (See Chapter 5 for more about organic dance form.)

Another way to engage intrapersonal intelligence through creative dance is by the self-knowledge you acquire by becoming familiar with your own movement preferences. Not only can you explore preferences between simple polarities such as sudden versus gradual, but you can investigate emotional responses to the many subtle distinctions in movement. For example, you might discover a preference for strong/sudden/pinpointed movements over strong/gradual/pinpointed movements. Taking time for reflection after a dance lesson through journal writing, drawing, sculpting, or making collages about the dance experience can further develop intrapersonal intelligence. These introspective activities, along with discussion, help students digest the artistry of their dance experiences and integrate them into their perception of self. This knowledge of self prepares them for understanding and relating to others.

❧ *Interpersonal Intelligence*

The ability to help people get along and promote harmonious group interaction is the province of interpersonal intelligence. For Gardner (1983/2004), "the core capacity here [of interpersonal intelligence] is the *ability to notice and make distinctions among other individuals* and, in particular, among their moods, temperaments, motivations and intentions" (p. 239). Thus interpersonal intelligence involves skill in the interplay of perception and response. People who apply their interpersonal intelligence tend to work well with others. They are good leaders and facilitators in groups because they can sense the needs of others and communicate effectively. People with strong interpersonal skills learn easiest in group situations in which they can benefit from relating, interacting, and cooperating with others. Their thinking processes are stimulated by brainstorming with others, and they enjoy group problem solving.

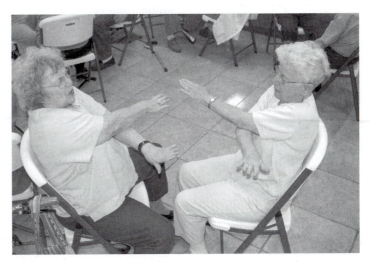

Unison movement by partners calls upon interpersonal skills.

Group dance improvisation is a naturally supportive environment for those at home with interpersonal intelligence. It can also be a haven for those with less developed interpersonal skills. Creative dance actually teaches the skills needed for functioning in a group. Many shy students have blossomed through creatively dancing with groups. This may be because the group work in creative dance is done at a very primary, preverbal level. Establishing rapport through movement without words can facilitate verbal communication outside of the dance experience.

Through collaborative studies in force, time, and space, dancers practice the skills they need to function in a group. In the force element, group themes teach students to modulate their energy in relation to others. In studies on interacting forces, students learn the very basis of a cooperative group endeavor—the ability to sense what is going on in a situation and make a contribution to it. Through time studies, dancers learn to synchronize with each other when they dance together within a steady beat structure. Using the space element to establish a kinesphere, students become aware of personal boundaries, which is so important to mutual respect and group studies that explore relationships between people.

Creative dance also builds interpersonal intelligence as lessons follow a progression from individual, to partner, to small group, and then larger group studies. The dynamic of constantly working with thematic material in both individual and group explorations builds a student's confidence in knowing how to function both as a strong individual and as a productive group member. These community building skills are fundamental to life in society. To dance as a cooperatively functioning group is the kind of experience that supports the healthy development of interpersonal intelligence.

❧ Musical Intelligence

Musical intelligence involves the organization of sound into meaningful forms. As such, it includes sensitivity to qualities of sounds and a sense of their rhythmic relationship. A person with an affinity for musical intelligence has a keen ear for all kinds of sounds and enjoys distinguishing and playing with subtle differences in pitch and timbre. Being able to feel and manipulate beat patterns is also a hallmark of musical intelligence. The beat patterns of music highlight the time element that dance and music share. Creative dance engages musical intelligence when the dancers focus on the time patterns created by their movements.

Sound requires movement. It is easy to coordinate sound making and the beat of movement because they are not separate at all but are created in the same moment. Making a vocal sound requires coordination of the breath and vocal cords; a percussive sound requires movement of a part of the body to strike something; playing a wind instrument requires integration of the breath with movement of the fingers. In all these instances, it is movement that produces the sound. Furthermore, skilled sensitive production of sound depends on skilled sensitive movements. Guided by this knowledge, creative dancers often make music by speaking, singing, clapping, stomping, or playing rhythm instruments as they dance. When music is created along with movement, it stays close to its kinesthetic roots.

Dancers do not have to make audible sound, however, to engage musical intelligence. The rhythmic time pattern of a movement can be sensed internally without being produced externally. When dancers improvise and attend to the kinesthetically felt rhythmic pattern of movement impulses or internally sensed melodies, they are attending to their musical intelligence. Each is moving to the beat of his or her own "internal drummer." This also happens in group dances when the group works with a common pulse, sensing and responding to the beat of their "communal drummer."

❧ Spatial Intelligence

Spatial intelligence involves perceiving, creating, recalling, and manipulating information that has a spatial pattern. Although most often associated with visual perception, it can be keenly developed in people without sight as they use the tactile sense to gauge spatial relationships (Gardner, 1983/2004). People with strong spatial intelligence are often very aware of visual stimuli and describe things in terms of shape, color, and size. They tend to be able to easily see mental images. People use spatial intelligence in the visual arts and in the design and organization of living spaces. Map reading, finding the way around a locality (with or without a map), and demonstrating awareness of the boundaries of personal space are areas where spatial and bodily-kinesthetic intelligences interact.

Playing the drum while dancing unites kinesthetic and musical intelligence.

FIGURE 10.1   *Moving color creates a visible record of movement feeling.*

Dance is first a kinetic art, but it is also a visual art. All of the dance studies that use space element attributes such as size, shape, direction, position, quality of line, level, or plane engage spatial intelligence. Students with a poor sense of spatial awareness can develop this intelligence by exploring movement problems from the space element that heighten awareness of where they are, where they are going, and the pathway that their movement takes.

Spatial intelligence is also engaged when dance lessons are followed by a visual arts activity. A simple way to record movement feeling visually is to move a crayon, chalk, or a paint brush across a paper or other art surface while paying close attention to the kinesthetic feeling of that action. The mark left on that surface records the spatial trail left by the movement of the hand and arm (Figure 10.1). A. A. Leath coined the term "moving color" to describe this activity (personal communication, 1984). Barbara Mettler (1960/2006) often used a similar approach as part of her lessons on space. She also suggested working in other media such as clay or wire to produce sculptures reflective of the dancer's movement experience. Working with visual art materials after dancing provides a tangible artifact that documents the student's expression of both bodily-kinesthetic and spatial intelligence.

ɔ Linguistic Intelligence

Linguistic intelligence refers to the use of verbal language for expression, communication, and learning. People with high linguistic aptitude excel at storytelling, writing, reading, debate, and word games. Linguistic skill begins to develop at an early age. It is truly amazing how most children absorb the rudiments of a language's sounds, meanings, and organization within their first few years. As they enter school, many children are fascinated with word play and books. They enjoy the power of communication that verbal language affords them. Creative dance activities can develop linguistic intelligence and sustain the love of language by linking the child's natural desire to move with the desire to communicate and learn through language.

Four widely accepted components of language are semantics, phonology, syntax, and function (Gardner, 1983/2004). The first three components combine to fulfill the fourth aspect of language, its function—be it to explain, excite, convince, describe, record, or reflect upon itself. Creative dance lessons help develop all four areas of linguistic intelligence.

The teaching methodology of creative dance is intimately connected with *semantics* (the meaning of words). In creative dance lessons, words are often used to name the aspects of movement being explored. From the very first lesson when students move to the meaning of words such as *stretch* and *shake*, linguistic and kinesthetic experiences are united. This verbal approach can be used throughout dance study. Over and over, creative dance methodology employs words that can be used to succinctly delineate the parameters of movement problems. The meanings of words such as *meander, rotate, rapid, gigantic, angular,* or *spiral* become very clear when they are experienced through movement. Curricular vocabulary as diverse and unusual as *cumulus, prickly, oblique, unification,* and *palindrome* can be moved with attention to their meanings. Because of the verbal emphasis in creative dance, dance classes can also help teach any second language. By providing opportunities to move the meaning of words, as in "Shake your hands above your partner's head," movement experience builds vocabulary that deepens understanding of a student's native language and clarifies semantics for students just learning a new language.

Creative dance lessons can also focus on *phonology* (the sound of words), emphasizing letter sounds, the beat of syllables, or both. Effective movement-based phonics lessons can be built around saying and moving related words such as *go, gallop,* and *goat; slide, glide,* and *ride;* or *skate, shake,* and *snake.* Movement words like these can be gathered to exemplify any phonics concept. They may be explored as single words or as chants that create patterns of word sounds. The beat patterns of syllables can also be explored to create rhythmic patterns students will long remember.

It is fun and easy to teach grammar through movement. In Chapter 8, the linguistic analogy was employed to explain how the *syntax* (grammatical structure) of language can be used to discover and organize the movement material of a topic. It can also, of course, be used to teach nouns, verbs, adjectives, adverbs, and prepositions themselves by working intentionally with words in each of these categories. Part V includes several lesson adaptations on parts of speech. Thinking about movement in this way is a handy tool for teaching language skills in combination with other curricular material. See the lesson adaptations for The Moving Body and Rhythmic Opposites in Chapter 14 for some examples.

The content of stories, articles, and essays also provides material to be danced. Using the elements of dance or the linguistic analogy links, material ranging from the Three Bears' return from a walk, to Dr. Zhivago's wintry trek, to scientific articles on the migration of monarch butterflies can be expressed in movement. Dancing the content of a reading assignment increases comprehension of its *function* (purpose) through embodiment of that material. It allows students to digest the written material through another intellectual mode.

The process of writing is similar to that of dance making. The traits sought after in good writing are almost identical to those combined in dance composition because both seek to communicate effectively albeit in different mediums. Succinct phrases, attention to descriptive detail, transitions, and efficiency in communication are ingredients of both expressive forms. Dance and written composition both engage an understanding of meaningful and logical sequence. Authors and choreographers alike work to find the appropriate style or voice to serve their purpose. Learning to kinesthetically sense the structure and flow of a dance composition can help students develop appreciation for the fluency in language composition as well.

Having students discuss and write about their creative dance lessons tills fertile ground for engaging linguistic intelligence and serves as a way to reflect upon and assimilate movement material. Movement experiences, particularly explorations introduced through words, tend to stimulate imaginative, sensitive use of language. In everyday communication, verbal and kinesthetic language intermingle and support each other constantly. Gestures and postures underscore—and at times contradict—the meaning of words. Thus teaching that links bodily-kinesthetic and linguistic intelligences can be quite powerful.

Logical-Mathematical Intelligence

Logical-mathematical intelligence includes the ability to classify phenomena into sets, see patterns, understand relationships, and manipulate ideas. A strong number sense is also an important facility for this mode of thinking. Gardner (1983/2004) bases his understanding of this intelligence on the work of Jean Piaget. While disagreeing with Piaget's emphasis on approaching other aspects of intelligence primarily in terms of a logical mathematical model, Gardner reaffirms Piaget's understanding that the ability to think in logical-mathematical abstraction develops from "one's actions upon the world" (p. 129). Specifically this begins with a child's handling and sorting of physical objects. In creative dance the "objects" students manipulate are their bodies. The importance of sensory-motor experiences for the development of logical-mathematical intelligence is a key factor in linking it to creative dance. Creative dance engages logical-mathematical intelligence when it builds patterned sequences and works with relationships. When students use the movement of their bodies to inquire into patterns and relationship, they are concretely developing skills for abstract thinking.

Because recognizable patterns occur in all areas of dance, each of the movement elements stimulates this intelligence. In the time element, working with metric beat patterns solidifies the notion of sets. This, in turn, strengthens students' intuitive number sense as they group beats together or divide beats into halves, thirds, quarters, fifths, and so forth. Similarly, space element studies develop and reinforce number sense via simple comparisons of size and quantity. They also concretely address geometric forms as they work with the positioning of the body in relation to lines, shapes, planes, and angles. Spatial forms of movement can be analyzed simply in terms of the geometric shapes created by movement of individuals or group bodies. Movement elements can also be plotted in three dimensions and described with great complexity, as demonstrated by Rudolf Laban's (1974) analysis of the pathways that movement naturally follows within one's kinesphere.

From the body element, locomotor movements provide an excellent format for students to develop analytic and observational skills. They can identify and count skips, walks, and leaps, and different kinds of human locomotion can be analyzed and compared for similarities and differences. For example, a skip and a gallop have the same beat pattern but different foot patterns, whereas a gallop and a run have the same foot pattern but different beat patterns. (See Chapter 4 for analytical descriptions of different locomotor movements.) In the area of force, students can analyze their movements in terms of the movement qualities they use and how more than one aspect of force can be combined to express a feeling or emotion.

In any artistic endeavor, we do not recommend attempting to create and analyze at the same time. Therefore, in creative dance, students are steered away from thinking analytically about their movements while they are doing them. Their focus needs to be on the experience as a whole without the distraction of analysis. However, bracketing movement experience with logical-mathematical thinking provides an intellectual container for the dance experience.

❧ *Naturalist Intelligence*

Naturalists have a deep connection to the natural world and an understanding of its intrinsic patterns. With a keen eye for detail, they are readily able to classify flora and fauna and to recognize how living organisms relate to and influence each other. Naturalist intelligence helps a person become aware of an environment, the relationship between its parts, and its overall gestalt. Like logical-mathematical intelligence, naturalist intelligence relies on the ability to observe and discriminate. In contrast to the logical-mathematical analysis, which operates from a place of separation, naturalist intelligence involves a sensitivity to and communion with the environment. Whether that environment is indoors or outside, naturalists are at home in their world.

Creative dance requires careful observation of natural movement forms through the kinesthetic sense. When moving the individual body, naturalist intelligence can be evoked as a dancer assesses the relationship of the parts of the body to the whole body, the quality of the movement, and the development of movement themes in relation to the whole dance. Here, the individual moving body and the space around it comprise the environment of which the dancer is most keenly aware. The practice of creative dance is about exploring natural human expression beyond the focus of one's individual personality. As a person becomes more skilled in using creative dance as an art medium, naturalist intelligence is evoked because the world of nature includes human nature. Cultivating a deeper identification with human nature can result in a fuller identification with all of nature.

Naturalist intelligence also strongly comes into play in group dancing. It is the faculty that enables an individual to experience the reality of a group body. In workshops Barbara Mettler would often use the directive "Get your antenna out" to describe how to attend to what was happening in a group body. This process of being aware of how an environment is functioning, while at the same time being a part of that environment and contributing to the function of that environment, requires naturalist intelligence. In group dance improvisation, the environment is the group body. The functioning of that body is the unfolding and evolving of movement themes. Awareness in group dance goes beyond personal interactions to identification with a larger whole. By operating within a group, the dancers sense both the movement of the group as a whole and the interrelationship of all the parts.

When dancers work with nature themes as topics, a connection is made to the essence of those themes. By asking students to pay attention to the details of a theme from nature, they absorb the skills of observation needed to make the classifications and distinctions that characterize the work of naturalist intelligence. Themes may be general such as a bird, a flower, or a creature, or they may be as specific as a flamingo, an orchid, or a desert tortoise. Either way, students can express details that make the specimen what it is. If dancers unite their nature with the nature of the subject of their dance through movement, the dancers' sensitivity to detail will be expressed in clear qualities of movement derived from the subject.

Sometimes the focus in creative dance is to move with awareness of the environment, whether indoors or out. Dancing outdoors has a very different feeling from dancing inside, and it goes a long way toward helping dancers feel free in their movements and as one with nature. Whether working kinesthetically with individual or group pure movement themes, or focusing on themes derived from nature or an environment, creative dancers use their naturalist intelligence to more fully experience their own nature as expressive movers and as an integral part of all nature.

Because creative dance addresses all of the multiple intelligences, it can benefit all types of learners and feeds the ability of each student's mind to use all of its intelligences. Dance provides a means to build from strength to help students grow. Because creative dance combines many intelligences, it can also be a meeting ground for people to bring together their different talents and gifts. Working on movement problems together can be a way for people with different intellectual strengths to find a common meeting place within a creative project.

CHAPTER SUMMARY

- Because creative dance addresses all the intelligences, it benefits every type of learner.
- Creative dance engages bodily-kinesthetic intelligence through creative problem solving in movement.
- Creative dance highlights internal awareness and intrapersonal intelligence through use of the kinesthetic sense, discovery of personal movement preferences, and reflection after dancing.
- Creative dance evokes the interpersonal intelligence in group dancing.
- Creative dance uses musical intelligence in time beat studies and in exploring the relationship between sound and movement.
- Creative dance studies that focus on the space element highlight spatial intelligence.
- Creative dance studies address all four aspects of language identified by Gardner, thus stimulating linguistic intelligence.

- Creative dance engages logical-mathematical intelligence by working with patterns and making abstract analytic concepts concrete.
- Creative dance evokes naturalist intelligence by uniting the dancers with their own nature and through studying themes of nature and the environment.

REVIEW QUESTIONS

1. Describe the advantages of offering learning challenges that reach different kinds of learners.
2. For each intelligence, give an example of a creative dance activity that stimulates learning in that modality.

PART IV

BUILDING MOVEMENT LESSONS

Students learn . . . the meaning of rhythm by experiencing the rhythmic progression of the study program. In the art of body movement the teacher must be an artist in the organization and presentation of the study material. A dedicated teacher-artist may find creative fulfillment in the making of every study period a dance.

—Barbara Mettler (1980b, p. 52)

CHAPTER 11

THE LESSON PLANNING PROCESS

Learning Objectives

1. Recognize that the creative process is central to planning and teaching creative dance lessons.
2. Identify principles of progression that indicate a logical pathway for lesson development and interdisciplinary linking.
3. Recognize helpful steps in guiding the lesson planning process.
4. Distinguish important parts of a creative dance lesson.
5. Adapt creative dance to different needs, abilities, and situations.

꩜ The Creative Art of Teaching

Creative dance requires creative teaching. From planning a lesson that guides student learning to managing a room full of moving bodies, the creative dance teacher's job is full of challenges. How creative dance lessons are taught has a huge effect on how dance is perceived by students. A genuine eagerness to teach movement, careful consideration of the material, and an orderly presentation set the stage for a creative learning experience. Ask yourself what the group needs. How can you best communicate your own excitement and enthusiasm for teaching this lesson? How can you build on students' interests and their current topics of study? What are students' strengths, and how can you capitalize on them? What barriers prevent students from fully participating in creative dance? How can you as a teacher overcome those barriers? How can you draw creativity and expression from your students so they can experience the making of art?

Although creative dance forms rely on improvisation, the lesson planning process is structured and concrete. Careful planning is critical to success in teaching any creative art. First, be clear about your objectives and their meaning in the context of larger learning goals. Whether your focus is on pure movement activity or integration with another subject, know what you want to accomplish. Then assess your students' needs in relation to your goals. Does your class need experience with basic creative dance concepts such as instrumental skills, spatial awareness, or group work? Maybe you want to work on patterning for math or vocabulary for writing. All these things may be included in any one lesson, but focusing on the primary goal drives your lesson plan.

꩜ Principles of Progression

The material selected for a lesson does not always make the activity successful. If the material is presented in the wrong order or an important step is missed, a lesson can fall flat. Conversely, insightfully ordering a series of progressive studies can bring a welcome "aha" to previously opaque concepts. Teaching progressions give logical form to a series of movement studies and guide students step-by-step through exploration, skill building, and finding satisfaction in a cohesive conclusion. Let's look at some principles of progression that guide the order of the lesson.

Simple to Complex

The principle of moving from **simple to complex** can be used several ways when organizing lesson material, including progressions from individual to group work, from personal space to general space, from an intrapersonal focus to interpersonal focus, from general to specific movement problems, and from part to whole.

Progressing from **individual to large group** is a mainstay for organizing creative dance lessons. When introducing a movement theme, it is generally useful to explore the nature of that theme individually first, so dancers can pay attention to their own kinesthetic sense before relating their movements to others. Individual studies provide the safety of working in self-space as material is introduced. Dancers can achieve personal success in this part of the lesson as they explore movements according to their own abilities and needs. Students need time to find their own way of working with the material presented, both to understand the concept and to determine its physical possibilities.

By working with a theme alone and then as part of different groupings, dancers experience the same material in progressively more complex settings. Different facets of the material are revealed through each different format. Group work generally begins in partner relationships. Dancing in duets provides a relatively uncomplicated environment and often supplies support and confidence, which will facilitate transition into larger group work, especially when less confident students are placed with appropriate partners to boost their success. Improvisations can then be done in groups of three to five. In small groups, each size group offers different possibilities for group forms. Very often a lesson (or lesson series) culminates with a dance for the whole class. Spatial forms gain new dimension, elements of force create exciting dynamics, and time patterns become more powerful in larger groups. In general, as the group gets larger, dancers must be aware of more information and address more complexity in making movement choices. This progression is demonstrated in the Lines and Shapes in Space lesson (Chapter 14) as it builds toward the group variations of Human Sculptures.

Group relationships in dances follow several established formats. Group formations include lines, circles, scatter, and clump. Dancers can make the same movements in unison or successively, one after another, as in an echo. They can also move successively or simultaneously with different movements that have a complementary or contrasting relationship. Appendix C lists group work formats and provides examples of where they occur in the foundation lessons.

Even though the general suggestion is to start individually and build to larger groups throughout the lesson, there are exceptions to this sequence. These exceptions primarily have to do with motivation and social ease. Sometimes working with a partner can help dancers kinesthetically experience a movement more easily than working alone.

By working with a theme alone first, and then in groups, dancers experience material in progressively more complex settings.

An example of this is the Equal Pushing activity near the beginning of the Strong and Gentle lesson (Chapter 16). Simple studies of counterbalance and limited weight-sharing can be fun for students and bring them out of their shells into trusting dance relationships. Teens may prefer to break the ice with a simple whole group dance; a satisfying group experience will motivate them to explore a concept individually. After having a good group or partner dance, these otherwise hesitant students may be willing to experience a movement theme on their own. However, if students are willing to turn their attention inward, it is generally wiser to give individuals their own time to awaken movement feeling before progressing to group work.

Lessons also build in complexity by first working with material in **personal space** and then doing the movements through **general space.** For the most part it is easier to explore a movement idea in one place before adding the challenge of shifting weight in locomotion and having to be aware of other bodies while moving from place to place. Studies in Rhythmic Opposites (Chapter 14) follow this route. Margaret H'Doubler's teaching progressions built from exploring single-joint actions while lying on the floor blindfolded in personal space, to exploring how that action functions while standing, and eventually to exploring it while traveling through general space. (Of course, the blindfolds came off along the way.) This progression ensured that the kinesthetic sense was primed before the body took on more challenge.

Working from self-space to general space and from individual to group work both involve going from an **intrapersonal focus,** which is inner-directed, to an **interpersonal focus,** which is outer-directed. When building lessons this way, the inner-directed experiences provide a base for the students to bring self-awareness into their interactions with others. The relaxation studies at the beginning of Interactive Forces (Chapter 14) use intrapersonal awareness as a basis for developing receptivity, which is crucial for the interpersonal dance work that culminates the lesson. Often it is effective and satisfying to close a lesson by returning to an intrapersonal focus, tuning back into the kinesthetic sensation in the body.

Another way to progress from simple to complex is to work from **general to specific** movement problems. The foundation lesson Sensing Time Patterns (Chapter 14) is a good example of becoming more specific step-by-step:

- The lesson begins by simply moving parts of the body slowly and quickly.
- Directives become more specific, asking that movement of those parts happens at an exact moment and be marked with a sound.
- These relatively simple tasks are then combined into the slightly more complicated task of making a slow or fast beat pattern.
- Further specificity is applied as students mix slow and fast movements to make uneven beat patterns.

This sequence also involves the progression guideline of working from **parts to whole.** Time problems are explored with isolated parts of the body before working with the whole body. Working with single body parts keeps a movement problem simple and gives students a narrow focus. It is a good way of providing a limiting structure as students explore other aspects of movement freely. A variation on this progression is to begin working very generally with the whole body in an undifferentiated way, then working with each part of the body, and concluding the exploration with the whole body again. The middle exploration with body parts makes the whole body movement at the end of the progression richer and more skilled. Establishing a group body for dance also progresses from parts to whole, beginning with individual dancers (the parts) and, through group awareness, unifying them into a functioning group. The Body Parts lesson (Chapter 15) exemplifies this kind of progression.

A different way to follow this progression is to explore the component parts of a movement one at a time and build up to a whole. This is what H'Doubler's students call the "sneaky approach" because she would sneakily teach a complex movement by introducing its component parts separately (Brehm, 1988). For example, the complex movement of skipping can be developed from simple movements by progressing from walking, to bouncing on two feet, to bouncing on one foot. The instrumental skills involved in each of these movements are the basis for being able to skip. The class can then emphasize upward movement with a springy walking step until it turns into a skip. Finally, the time element is brought in so that all dancers skip on the same beat. In this sequence the parts to whole principle does not involve physical body parts but the component skills of a movement. As each separate skill is easily assimilated, students gain confidence. By focusing on the skills one at a time, the movement ultimately becomes more integrated.

The principle of working from parts to whole can also be seen in lessons that explore the different aspects of a theme separately before combining them into a whole. Sometimes it is helpful to decide on a culminating form first and build the lesson backward. Make a list of the component parts of the culmination and put them into the lesson progression. In the foundation lesson on Lines and Shapes in Space (Chapter 14), the culminating form Sculpture Garden involves the skills of moving through general space and making shapes with a partner. In the lesson students explore those experiences separately before putting them together. Without the progression of building through those steps, the culmination could be a shallow, even dangerous, experience for students.

Some situations, such as a tightly structured teaching schedule or the teacher's inexperience in leading longer movement sessions, do not lend themselves to teaching a progression of movement problems in a single study period. In these instances, start with bite-sized movement studies and build the progression over several days, adding a little each day. Bringing little bits of movement into the school day allows teachers and students to gradually become comfortable with movement before attempting fully developed lesson plans. Most lessons in this book can easily be broken up into pieces that could be taught in sequence over several sessions. Appendix E lists short movement activities that can begin this process.

Thematic Progressions

A general progressive principle is to build lessons that start with **instrumental preparation** as a base for proceeding into **movement material.** Instrumental work involves moving the body while attending to the kinesthetic sensations produced by that movement. Choose instrumental studies that prepare the body for work in the movement element you will be emphasizing. On the Elements of Dance chart (pp. 60–61) some instrumental skills are noted that support work with different movement material. For example, knowing that spatial studies are helped by awareness of the skeletal frame, you can begin lessons in the space element by tuning in to movement of the bones. Thinking of the body and movement as separate categories is a useful analytical tool for generating dance lesson progressions and for providing a clear focus for the content of creative dance studies.

Curricular themes have a basis in the way things move and dictate a progression of working from **movement material to curricular application.** This progression applies to both single and series lessons. Pure movement exploration helps students understand concepts on a basic kinesthetic level and guides their awareness in making connections with specific curricular themes. When introducing movement to a new group, devote at least one lesson (better yet several) to laying a kinesthetic base by teaching pure movement concepts before diving into academic themes. The foundation lessons in Chapter 14 provide good introductions to pure movement concepts and sensory awareness, and the material is readily adaptable to curricular applications. When teaching topics across the curriculum through dance, identify the most basic movement components of a theme and explore them near the beginning of a curricular lesson or unit. By working from kinesthetic feeling and making meaningful forms out of explorations, students will have an art experience that provides a vivid, satisfying understanding of their curricular material. Many examples of this progression are provided in Chapter 8.

CONCEPT SPOTLIGHT 11.1

Progression Guidelines

Simple to Complex
Individual to partners to small groups to large groups
Self-space to general space
Intrapersonal focus to interpersonal focus
General to specific
Parts to whole

Thematic Progressions
Instrumental preparation to movement material
Movement material to curricular application

From Freedom to Awareness to Control

Although building from movement material to curricular application is a general principle of progression, in some situations you may want students to begin by exploring representational themes, such as familiar animal movements. Young children love representation, and this works especially well if they have had some previous experience of pure movement exploration. After an introduction of representational exploration, the class can abstract these themes by delving into the specific aspects of each animal's movement such as their speed, size, and quality. This will enrich the representation immensely. The progression here is to begin with the concrete topical material (moving like a turtle) and deepen it with abstract movement qualities (low, slow, steady). Consciously adapting and playing with progressions in this way demands full knowledge of dance elements and an appreciation for the subtlety of lesson planning.

From Freedom to Awareness to Control

In her teaching, Mettler (1980b) used the principle of working from **freedom** in using the body as it is guided by kinesthetic sensation, to **awareness** of movement expression, to **control** of the movement form. With greater control, dancers have greater freedom of expression, and a cycle of freedom, awareness, control begins again. Careful structuring is needed to allow as much freedom as possible, knowing full well that too much freedom may not give enough guidance for children and beginners as they focus on movement studies. Learning how to construct movement problems with the right balance between freedom and control is a skill worth developing. The challenge is to be able to gauge from your knowledge of the class exactly how much freedom students can handle at each point in the lesson.

The progression guidelines presented here augment each other, and activities in a lesson often follow several progressions at the same time. In addition, completing a progression calls forth its repetition at ever higher skill levels. Lessons taught with a progressive teaching methodology do not develop in a linear fashion but circle into spirals of increasing understanding. Just as increased control of movement allows for increased freedom of expression, the ability to perform a complex movement brings about the desire to analyze the movement and explore its simplified component parts with greater awareness, increasing the skill level when the movement is resynthesized. Likewise, a satisfying group experience gives rise anew to the need for more individual work. These examples show that as the end of a progression is fulfilled there is a need to return to the beginning in subsequent lessons. In this way the progressions are rhythmic, with opposite poles of the progression evoking each other.

❧ *Steps in Planning*

When approaching any lesson or curricular unit, be it dance or another topic, goals or objectives drive the choices throughout the planning process. In some instances, lessons may address official standards for learning in dance and other disciplines. In other situations, a lesson's goal may be generated by the specific needs of the class or may be simply to explore and learn more about a topic of interest. Before beginning the process, it is crucial to think about your objectives or reason for teaching the lesson. As you plan, you may be surprised that your lesson addresses many more objectives than you had considered at the beginning of the planning process. The following steps in planning a dance/movement lesson work well for most learning objectives.

Gather Information about Your Thematic Topic

Do a little research on your topic. If the lesson is pure movement, list concepts you want to cover. The terms listed on the Elements of Dance chart (pp. 60–61) will guide you in selecting material that is conceptually interconnected. The pure movement lessons presented in this book and in the creative movement books listed in the Bibliography provide plenty of ideas for movement material. Your own body is also a good reference for exploring pure movement concepts. Try some ideas out yourself to see what feels right. If you are teaching other topics through movement, draw upon resources of the classroom, library, computer programs, and the Internet. Jot down notes on any ideas that click with you as you read. Also, use your students as a resource to research and brainstorm ideas. Notice themes of interest or areas that need to be reinforced. From all of this, you can begin to sculpt the lesson to fit your situation and to address your learning objectives.

If Integrating Another Subject, Find the Link to Movement

As you scan information about a selected topic, zero in on connections to movement. (Part III worksheets provide some examples of linking dance across the curriculum.) One avenue of linking is not necessarily better than another. Start in your comfort zone—just don't get stuck there. Keep in mind that your topic may relate to many areas of movement. Determine the route you'll take to make curricular connections, and consciously build from a movement base into your topic.

Narrow the Material Down to a Manageable Lesson

Presenting too much material leads to lack of depth and ineffectual results. Identify the essence of your topic and material that supports the lesson's goal, and eliminate material that doesn't pivot around your focus. In many cases you will have more material to work with than can be neatly packaged into one lesson, in which case the material can be separated into two or more lessons.

Within each lesson, narrow material down to specific selected concepts from the elements of dance. For example, a lesson on space does not need to cover every aspect of that element. Choose only material that supports your topic. For example, the Cursive Writing lesson adaptation (Chapter 14) works exclusively with curved lines; there is no reason to explore straight lines and shapes in preparation for this lesson. If the class has experienced concepts previously in pure movement lessons, you will only need to touch on them briefly in the lessons that apply to integrated studies.

Build a Progression

The aim in a lesson is not only to have a good final product but to engage students with a sense of discovery and aesthetic experience throughout the lesson. The craft of ordering parts of a lesson deserves a teacher's full attention because it will affect the receptivity of students and the outcome of the lesson. Use the principles of progression as you layer one movement study upon another to draw students toward your goals, which will be expressed in the last part of the lesson.

Consider the Use of Music, Sound, or Silence

Music can be used as a container for movement in the same way verbal structures can provide limitations for students. Moving in silence offers the most undiluted relationship with one's kinesthetic sensations, but people do naturally respond to the energy of music. It is one way to motivate students. Here are some guidelines for using music, sound, or silence as support for movement studies.

Music can help to give a sense that the movements students are doing are different from the movements they do in everyday life. In this way music can help prime students to turn inward and provide a barrier between them and the distraction of peers. Very young children, whose linguistic skills are not yet highly developed, respond well to the support of music because it reaches them on a preverbal level. Using music that is familiar to your students can help them dive into the unfamiliar territory of movement expression with less trepidation. This may be especially important for teens. You may even allow students to bring in their own music, subject to your approval. Once they are "hooked" on movement, try different kinds of music, sound created as a group, and opportunities to move in silence.

Sound is a way to help people to move with defined qualities. This is especially true in evoking qualities that are not their preference. Playing simple rhythm instruments can help your students find different qualities of movement. You may play these instruments as accompaniment or teach students to play and move with the instruments (see lesson adaptation Dancing with Found and Traditional Rhythm Instruments, Chapter 19).

Different kinds of music lend themselves to different movement elements. Music with clear accents, or strong emphasis on certain beats, can help students feel the dynamic flow of movement patterns. Force studies are often based on a contrast of strong and gentle, qualities that are easy to identify in music. Because music is so powerful in creating a mood, it is good for dramatic and emotional force studies. Be sure to choose music that matches the quality you are asking your students to express.

Music is commonly used with dance to establish beat patterns, and it can be an aid for those who have trouble in the area of time. Music with a strong unwavering pulse can help students relax and feel the predictability of an ongoing steady beat. Choose music with an obvious and simple beat that is easy to follow. Music that has complicated internal rhythms or accelerates and decelerates, such as West African drumming, will likely be too difficult for beginners to follow. You will be doing your students a great service by also giving them the opportunity to create steady beat patterns without the aid of music. The foundation lesson Sensing Time Patterns (Chapter 14) provides a progression for this.

Each of these instruments evokes a different quality of sound for accompaniment. Clockwise from top: claves, very sudden; hand drum, strong and sudden; triangle, gentle, gradual, or sudden; shakers and jinglebells, gentle, fast, and loose; gong, gradual sustained; rasp, tight.

Music is generally metered; be mindful of the number of beats in each measure of the music you use. If you want a driving, active quality, choose music with a four-beat measure, the most common meter in modern popular music. For lilting or lyrical movement, find music with the three-beat measure of a waltz. Counting, grouping, and subdividing the beats of music can be an aid in mathematics study as described in The Time Link section of Chapter 8. However, using music with time studies generally limits dancers to three or four beat time patterns. Although measures of five and seven beats are uncommon in popular dance and music, they do show up in Balkan and Middle Eastern dance, jazz, contemporary classical, and "world" music. For students more

---

CONCEPT SPOTLIGHT 11.2

Steps in Planning

1. Gather information about your thematic topic.
2. Find conceptual links between movement and a curricular topic.
3. Narrow the material down to a focused and manageable lesson.
4. Build a progression that meets your objectives.
5. Consider use of music, sound, or silence.

---

advanced in beat work, these less common measures can provide stimulating and rewarding study and can readily be done with voice, body percussion, or rhythm instrument accompaniment. Avant garde music without a steady beat (such as that of John Cage) and free verse poetry may be helpful in illustrating uneven time patterns. Moving in response to these works is difficult because of the unpredictability of the time pattern. The movement will always be slightly after the sound. It is much easier for musicians to watch and follow the movements of the dancer, using their kinesthetic empathy to match sound with movement in the same moment.

Spatial work lends itself to complete silence. The space element emphasizes visual design, and as such it is not concerned with beat patterns. However, your students may not be ready for the concentration required to maintain clear spatial focus with no sound accompaniment. Music can be used to delineate the dance container. When using music for spatial studies, it's best to choose selections that deemphasize the beat. Ambient and environmental sounds, Native American flute music, or New Age music may set the right tone. If you use music with a beat pattern, the quality expressed by sharp twos and fours may suit angular movements, whereas threes have a more curvy feeling. If you cannot find music that suits your needs, students can employ their own vocal sounds to express spatial qualities, making curvy feeling sounds while doing curved movement, and straight feeling sounds while making straight movements.

Music can also be used effectively in the culminating form of the lesson. First, allow students to explore concepts freely and discover their relationship to the movement material without musical accompaniment. Then use a carefully chosen piece of music that supports the quality of the dance during the culmination. This will help provide a sense of form as the lesson concludes.

✍ *Lesson Template*

Now let's turn to the structure of the lesson itself. The following lesson template is a handy guide that works well with the progressions just described. Lesson plans in Part V all use this format. Throughout this discussion, a lesson on volcanoes will provide examples of appropriate activities for each part of the lesson. See Curricular Lesson: Volcanoes (Chapter 16) for the complete lesson template.

Introduce the Concept

Prepare students with a brief verbal introduction to the upcoming lesson: refer to previously learned concepts and skills, demonstrate movement basics, and review rules for safe conduct and appropriate behavior. Thoughtful consideration of your words and movement can make a big difference in the success of a lesson. Connecting the lesson's concepts to a life situation with which students can identify will make it easier to understand. You can also elicit ideas from students that connect movement to cross-curricular topics. For example, students could brainstorm important aspects of a volcano that can be used as vocabulary for movement exploration later in the lesson. Remember that your words are in service of evoking kinesthetic experience. Explain or discuss only enough to set the stage for movement.

The introduction is also important for gathering focus, which aids management and success of the lesson. Sitting in a small circle or close group gives the lesson a clear beginning and sets a communicative tone. You may wish to take a few minutes to guide students' focus before you get moving. Having students attend to their breathing or lie down and close their eyes are useful centering directions if the class needs to settle down.

Kinesthetic Tune-Up

Before delving into the material of the lesson, students need to make a shift from every-day movement and awareness to using themselves as expressive instruments for art making. Mettler called this process of awakening movement feeling the "instrumental tune-up" (personal communication, 1997). Beyond a mere physical warm-up of the body, the tune-up summons expressive sensitivity. It doesn't take long to activate the body and sharpen attention to movement sensations. Begin the class with simple movement activities, directing students to tune in to the kinesthetic sense and let movement feeling dictate their actions (closing eyes when possible will help here). Activating the kinesthetic sense at the beginning of the lesson sets the stage for its prominence in the whole lesson and is essential for true kinesthetic learning. This is a time of preparation, but it is more than that. The kinesthetic tune-up can be a deeply personal experience for each individual, a time to notice and acknowledge the entry into creative work. This process is not a mere mechanical warm-up of the muscles but more a waking-up of the senses and a kinesthetic tuning-up of the body as an instrument of expression. For safety's sake, always reestablish the concept of self-space in relation to shared space. Claiming a spot, painting space bubbles with body parts, and filling the bubble with named movements are excellent activities for the early part of the lesson.

To choose material for the tune-up, look at your lesson content and decide what movement elements will predominate. Then think about the instrumental skills that will support full expression of those movement concepts (see the Elements of Dance chart, pages 60–61).

Although creative dance lessons do not emphasize the perfection of instrumental technique, the mechanics and coordination of movement are very important for safety and efficiency as well as for effectiveness in expression. Lack of coordination can stand in the way of the creative art form and may inhibit less agile students. The early part of a lesson is a good time to work on movement skills that will be called for in your day's session. Spend a few minutes introducing, reviewing, or polishing those skills. Empowering your students with basic movement techniques will facilitate their success as dancers and also as athletes.

The Volcanoes lesson links to the force element, and students prepare instrumentally with studies in tight and loose movement. This gets them ready for the expression of the different combinations of force qualities involved in the volcanic eruption. Also, attention to the center of lightness and center of gravity aids students in working with varying qualities of force. Practicing engagement of the abdominal muscles in coordination with an exhalation is good preparation for making strong, forceful volcano movements.

Exploration

This is the heart of the lesson and deserves the greatest percentage of time. By definition, creative movement is about exploration. It is the method dancers use to generate freedom and awareness of movement. During movement exploration, freedom is encouraged as students gather kinesthetic information and make discoveries about the concepts they are studying. Exploratory activities should be guided yet provide for personal interpretation in many ways. This simultaneously opens doors of diversity and success for all

Strong "volcano movements" call for preparing the instrument by finding a tight feeling in the muscles.

students. If this is a curricular lesson, the exploration section should build from pure elemental movement studies that link to the topic, enabling students to fully express the topical themes that will follow. When aspects of the topic come from more than one element, explore them separately before putting them together into a form that combines elements.

Manipulating the material of any art form takes craft, which requires practice. Don't hesitate to review material from previous lessons. This is often welcomed with open arms. It gives you an opportunity to improve your presentation and lets students hone their expressiveness too. Repetition is especially valuable for early grades when it is a big part of developing learning skills. In addition to repetition, movement themes can be expanded, varied, contrasted, or developed into more complex forms.

In planning the exploration section, use the progression guidelines discussed earlier in this chapter to arrange a series of creative movement problems. Begin exploration with individual studies of pure abstract movement experience. The Volcanoes lesson uses force studies in strong and gentle, gradual and sudden, as well as combinations of these qualities. Continuing to curricular application, students would express the qualities of magma as it presses against the earth's crust, earthquakes, and material erupting from the volcano. The individual exploration enables students to embody the volcano movements of the lesson. Then move on to partner or small group studies on qualities of material erupting from volcanoes.

The exploratory part of class is a living storehouse of ideas for development. Ideas may emerge that can be used as themes for future lessons. It is also a perfect time to observe your students. As they research ideas and possibilities through the progression of movement studies, students deeply engage the kinesthetic sense in the process of making choices. This is where new experience, artistic ideas, and choreography are born. Polished form is not the goal during the exploratory part of the lesson, but movements from the explorations may be selected individually, collectively, or by the instructor to become part of a culminating form. In many ways, exploration is the richest part of a lesson. Take time to enjoy it; the creative process is unfolding before you.

Culminating Form

Throughout the lesson, movement progressions build toward a connected finale. Students gain a sense of satisfaction and completion by putting the fruits of their explorations into a final form. Teachers usually lay out the culminating form as a creative problem to solve, but students can create their own final assignments too. Ideas drawn from explorations earlier in class should be the basis for a culminating structure. It is critical that you connect the dots between these two parts of the lesson. Students become confused and frustrated when a teacher leaps from free explorations to a complex form that doesn't originate in earlier studies. In a well-constructed culminating form, students demonstrate their understanding of dance concepts, work cooperatively with each other, and learn to appreciate each other's efforts. The culminating form is one place to assess your students' learning.

Any number of individual or group structures can work as culminating forms, but provide clear and simple instructions. The complexity of the culminating form should balance with the amount of time spent in exploration. Less time spent exploring generally indicates the need for simpler culminating forms. More complex culminations will need additional explanation and practice time to be satisfying. Many variations of final form dances are suggested in the lessons in this book. They are containers that different thematic material can be "poured" into. Generally this does not mean creating set choreography, nor is the final dance something that students will need to practice over and over. Rather, it is a cohesive movement form that pulls together the material of the lesson. Some of these structures may become favorites, adaptable in many ways to serve and solidify the material explored in your lessons.

The structure of a culminating form may be as basic as a beginning shape, thematic content, and a set ending. For example, a form to culminate a spatial lesson could (1) begin in a curved shape, (2) draw curved lines individually in space and then come together as a group to create circular forms, and (3) end in a circle. A simple dance like this could be explained and performed in a matter of minutes. A more challenging problem to solve would be for students to create a short dance sequence derived from several of the explorations of the lesson. Either way, the material of the dance should demonstrate a thematic idea. No matter how specific or free the culminating dance theme, it is crucial with inexperienced students to set clear goals and provide beginnings and endings. More experienced students will be able to create dances with loose structures. Very experienced groups can improvise a dance together with only the simplest of directions.

A culminating volcano dance pulls the explorations from that lesson together into a group dance. The entire class could decide on the form and sequence of the dance, which might look something like this:

- Begin with a group-expressed earthquake at a low level.
- Individuals with specifically assigned roles of different materials move as if erupting from a volcano.
- End with the group creating the volcano's cone in a final shape together.

This form provides free choice of movement with a clear guide of beginning, middle, and end. The dance can be improvised by the whole group, by half the class at a time, or by small groups. Group members work out the sequence cooperatively and show it to the rest of the class.

Even if material will be carried forward to the next lesson, allow time for a culmination to connect ideas from the lesson. A lesson that is not tied together conceptually is like a smorgasbord on a limited time schedule—frustrating and unsatisfying. In contrast, well-conceived culminating forms unify concepts and offer the satisfaction of a fully realized creative art experience.

Closure

Always save at least a few minutes to finish each session with a kinesthetic closure. There are many ways to go about this time to cool off, settle down, and return to mindful introspection. Stretching upward and then dropping one segment of the arms at a time (bit-by-bit relaxation) or rounding the spine are simple and quick ways to give a good feeling of closure. With the body warmed up, this is a safe time to stretch large muscles. Pay attention to which part of the body is feeling stretched, relaxed, or especially active and alive. Maybe your students are tired and need to calmly rest. If they lie on their backs, you can go around to briefly jiggle each student's two arms as in the "floppy test." Students may also wish to rest in "hook-up" position. When you have time, these longer closures are luxuriously conducive to relaxation and reflection. These closures are described in more detail in Box 11.1.

Creative dance or any art activity can leave a person very full of stimuli and in need of time for assimilation. Guiding a reflection about the dance class is one way to begin this. An excellent assimilation procedure called "memory integration" originated with psychologists Eugene and Juanita Sagan and was further developed by A. A. Leath (Sagan, Sagan, Leath, and Graham, 1967). Memory integrations are times when students contemplate their experiences in a relaxed setting. Rather than being a time to focus on *information* that they have learned, it is a time for students to become conscious of their *emotional response* to their dance studies. During this time students do not interact; they follow your guidance internally.

To do memory integration as the closure for class, direct students to lie or sit quietly and comfortably. Invite them to turn their attention inward, possibly closing their eyes. They can listen to their heartbeat or breath and relax their muscles. Verbally list

Box 11.1

Lesson Closures

Bit-by-bit relaxation. Stretch the arms upward. Drop both hands from the wrist, giving into gravity. Next drop the arms, but only from the elbows; then drop the whole arm from the shoulder joint. Each dropping of a section of the arm is accompanied by an exhale and *slight* release of the knees. The arms finish hanging loosely. Repeat this sequence if desired. This can be done sitting or standing.

Rounding the spine or "taking a bow." Stand with weight on both feet, bend knees slightly, slowly curve the spine forward, beginning with tilting the head forward. Return to standing, uncurling the spine slowly with the head hanging and coming up last. This can also be done sitting on the floor or in a chair turned away from a desk (Figure 11.1).

Whole body opening and closing. Move from high to low level, ending closed on floor.

Standing calf stretches. Place one leg behind the other in a lunge position and hold, lengthening the back side of the leg. Add simple upper body gestures such as slow big arm circles or pushing on an imaginary wall.

Sitting stretches. On the floor or in a chair, round the spine forward and sideward with each of these leg positions: soles of feet together, straight out in front, and open at a comfortable angle.

Lying leg stretches. While lying on the back, bend knees and plant feet on the floor. Lift one leg, bringing the knee toward the chest. Then extend the leg upward, pushing the heel toward the ceiling. Hold for at least 30 seconds. Bend the knee and plant the foot back on the floor. Repeat with other leg. Now try both legs stretching upward together. Finish by hugging knees to the chest (Figure 11.2).

Shake, fling, flop, and drop. Do a series of loosening, letting go movements using the whole body or parts of the body. End in a relaxed position.

Resting or relaxation. Lie down in a loose position and consciously allow the body to relax. (See Chapter 12 for suggestions on guiding students to relax.)

Floppy test. Lie down on the back and relax. The teacher briefly goes to each student and lifts both arms, holding them at the wrist, and gently shakes the arms to release tension. The arms are then gently placed on the floor or laid over the belly (Figure 11.3).

Hook-up. Sit or lie down. Cross one ankle over the other. To put the arms into the hook-up position, place the palms on the chest with arms crossed (one wrist on top of the other); maintaining that crossed configuration, turn the palms toward each other and interlace fingers. Relax, close the eyes, and listen to breathing or the heartbeat. To come out of this position, uncross the arms and legs and place the fingertips together, making a ball shape.

(Continued)

FIGURE 11.1 *Rounding the spine gives a feeling of closure to a lesson.*

FIGURE 11.2 *Lying leg stretches.*

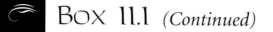

Box 11.1 *(Continued)*

FIGURE 11.3 *Gently jiggling the arms in the "floppy test" helps students relax at the end of class.*

FIGURE 11.4 *The hook-up.*

Hold this for a few moments. An alternative way to come into hook-up is to extend both arms in front of the chest with palms outward, thumbs down. Cross one arm over the other and interlace fingers. Bend the elbows. This will loop the hands toward the chest (Dennison and Dennison, 1994). It is sometimes difficult for students to learn the position. You may need to physically guide them into it with a gentle touch. Mastering this complex movement task helps connect both sides of the brain and enables focus (Figure 11.4).

Memory integration. Relax (sitting or lying) and listen while the teacher briefly recalls activities from the current or a previous lesson. (See Creative Toolbox 11.1.)

some activities from the dance class for them to remember, or pose a few questions for them to think about. Have students recall how they felt during each activity. What did they like about it? What did they dislike? Were they comfortable or uncomfortable? What movement sensations do they remember? What emotional reactions did they have? All of these questions have to do with evaluating their own experience rather than demonstrating knowledge of facts or understanding concepts.

Proceed with your verbal guidance at a slow pace. Leave a bit of time between each item to allow students to relive the experience briefly. If you go too fast, students will not have time to recall the study, relive its movement sensations, and evaluate how they felt about it. Watch your students to judge whether you are going too fast or too slow. The length of a memory integration varies depending on the age and needs of your students. It can be quite short, directing students to think of one or two studies from dance class, or it can be a whole session in itself conducted at a later time. Memory integrations are different from other kinds of review approaches in that nothing is demanded of students other than that they not disturb the process. If they daydream or simply rest during the guiding, that's all right. However, you may be amazed at the clarity of students' responses after a restful chance to assimilate a lesson's content.

Centering the class to close the dance session allows students to finish with composure rather than with scattered hurriedness or exhaustion. This will make a big difference in their transition to whatever activity comes next. Some teachers use the same closure for every dance session, building a routine that physically signals to students that the lesson is finished. Or you can individualize each closure from the dictates of the lesson and the needs of the group on that day.

11.1 CREATIVE TOOLBOX—TRY THIS!

Memory Integration: Volcanoes

Here is an example of a short memory integration used as closure.

> Lie down, close your eyes and rest comfortably. Let yourself relax. [*Pause*] Think back to the volcano movements you have done today. I'm going to list materials that erupt from a volcano. As I say each one, see if you can remember how it felt as you moved like it. [*Pause between each item*]
>
> > Hot gasses
> > Ash
> > Heavy rocks or bombs
> > Pumice
> > Hot lava
> > Cool lava
>
> Which one did you like the least? [*Pause*] Which one of these was your favorite? [*Pause*] Now turn your attention back to your body and slowly sit up.

After the memory integration the class can discuss, write about, or draw images of their volcano dance experiences.

Follow-Up Activities

Follow-up activities anchor and extend the dance material. The class can discuss the content of the class, problems and successes, and how the material relates to life in other situations or to school subjects. Vocabulary can be added to spelling lists or a word bank for help in writing about dance experiences. This makes a natural transition to journal writing. Think up your own questions or refer to the section in Chapter 13 on Self-Assessment and Peer Assessment for ideas.

Use discussion topics or vocabulary to lead into follow-up arts activities that address the same concepts as your movement lesson. Let students reflect on what they have just learned or experienced by freely drawing, painting, making collages, or sculpting with clay, wire, foil, or cardboard. Perhaps they could create poems or songs based on their movement studies. Assignments in different expressive mediums engage different intelligences, further integrate the dance work, and solidify understanding of the lesson's material. You will find several follow-up activities listed at the end of each foundation lesson in Chapter 14.

CONCEPT SPOTLIGHT 11.3

Parts of a Creative Dance Lesson

1. **Introduce the Concept:** explain the body of material to be explored and how it most basically relates to the elements of dance.
2. **Kinesthetic Tune-Up:** prepare the body as the instrument of dance.
3. **Exploration:** investigate lesson material through progressions of guided improvisation. This is the heart of the lesson.
4. **Culminating Form:** structure the findings from explorations into a finished form.
5. **Closure:** return to inward kinesthetic experience to relax and prepare for transition into students' next activity.
6. **Follow-Up Activities:** anchor and extend material of the lesson through guided discussions, writing assignments, or art projects.

Box 11.2

Lesson Template Worksheet: Volcanoes

1. Introduce the concept
   Brainstorm important aspects of a volcano as vocabulary for movement exploration
2. Kinesthetic tune-up
   a. *Tight and loose*
   b. *Center of gravity, center of levity*
   c. *Engagement of abdominals with exhale*
3. Exploration
   Individual studies
   a. *Pure movement: strong / gentle; gradual / sudden; combinations of these qualities*
   b. *Applied to curricular topic: magma pressing against earth's crust; earthquakes; eruption of materials from volcano*
   Partner or small group studies
   c. *Choose a quality of material that erupts from a volcano.*
      Briefly improvise on that theme, freely relating to each other.
4. Culminating form
   Earthquake: low level movement in a group
   Eruption: individuals erupt with qualities of assigned materials (ash, lava)
   Ending: conical group shape
   Show in two groups
5. Closure
   Memory integration
6. Follow-up
   Watercolor of erupting volcanoes
   Papier-mache volcanoes

❧ *Adapting for Different Ages, Abilities, and Experience*

Because of its free nature and conceptual material, creative dance is adaptable to any age group, level of experience, or physical ability. With skillful direction it is even possible for all ages and levels to dance together with great freedom and satisfaction. Yet in most cases, especially at school, your class will share certain characteristics that influence the manner of teaching.

Major changes do not have to be made to adapt the basic content of creative dance lessons for different populations. Lesson notes and general outlines may look very much the same for different kinds of groups because the same conceptual material is covered. The language and tone, structures, and pacing in the delivery of the lesson, however, are adapted to the audience. From experience, discussions with colleagues, and written sources (Gilbert, 1992; Mirus, White, Bucek, and Paulson, 1993), considerations to guide planning and presentation for different age groups and settings are reviewed here. Ultimately, each group is unique, and the approach depends mainly on the needs of your students.

Language and Tone

The language used to present material sets the tone of the lesson and should match the intellectual development of your students. Verbalize the lesson in a way that your students feel respected and understand what to do. The language described in Part II for labeling movement concepts is appropriate for most age groups. In some cases several terms are identified that can be used for different levels. Young children need abstract concepts explained or defined simply and in context with their limited experience. They may be just beginning to understand abstract concepts (like opposites, for example). Dance experience will help them learn the words that go with their innate movement knowledge. It is crucial that these terms be clearly and simply worded and reinforced throughout the lesson. Such reinforcement, of course, is not necessary when teaching older students. For them, clarity of movement expression should be emphasized. Even advanced dancers can hone the expressiveness of movement qualities using these same lesson concepts.

The tone of the lesson should also reflect the maturity level of the student audience. Young children like playful enthusiasm and challenges. Intermediate grade level students appreciate frank and rational instruction. Adolescents begin to question the meaning of dance and want reasons for everything. So be clear in your artistic objectives, and provide explanations as you introduce material. Humor and zippy or trendy language is often well received by teens, but be careful that you use it correctly and without sarcasm lest they take offense or think you are silly in trying to be like them. Adolescents may become self-conscious when you talk about body parts (for example, the pelvis). Try to find other words (lower torso) to make them more comfortable, and don't dwell on movement of these parts.

All students need a safe harbor and genuine acceptance of their imperfections and fears before they will trust you not to judge them or make them feel inadequate. This is especially true for middle and high school students and beginning level adults. Real-life stories of personal challenges with self-consciousness or hesitancy often help students relax and relate to you as a nonintimidating human being.

Through experience you will learn how to verbally coach your students while they are moving. Constant and specific prompting can provide ideas and variations that draw movement out of inhibited dancers. Conversely, when dancers are discovering movements on their own, it's best not to interrupt their creative process.

Structures

The amount and kind of structure given to studies really depends on the group. Some groups need a lot of structure; others want little. Beginners, especially young children, need to be taught how to use space appropriately to ensure safety without collisions. Older elementary and middle school students may still need reminders about maintaining personal space. We hope adults will do this instinctually, but this is not always the case. In general, young children need space management structures that are simple and delivered in small portions. The lesson studies in this book model the breakdown of material into distinct bits. By middle school this may not be necessary, and more information or variables can be given in a shorter amount of time.

The complexity of exploration problems and culminating forms also needs to be considered. For very young children repetition is good and lessons should culminate simply. Group work for early elementary students should have a single objective and be guided by the teacher. By third grade, students are more able to work independently in groups. Intermediate and middle school students like to create their own dances but still need clear structures. This is an extremely creative age if freedom is handled appropriately. Teens may prefer complex structures that let them think up their own choreographed sequences. College students can invent their own creative problems to solve once they have learned the basic concepts and elements of movement.

Adult needs for structure vary greatly. Some groups want step-by-step instructions, but more experienced dancers may enjoy the challenge of very little structure and the freedom to create variations of their own. With more maturity, students are able to focus intently on simple structures, delve deeply into the material, and consciously combine the elements of dance. In general, as students become more experienced, more problem solving can be left up to them.

Pacing

The pace at which you move through material and the amount of physical exertion that can be expected varies from group to group. The length of a dance lesson can vary greatly depending on the daily schedule, age of students, and intent of the lesson. Classes for preschool or kindergarten may last for half an hour or less, whereas a high school or adult class may run an hour and a half or more. Lessons in schools are often forty-five to sixty minutes in length. In general, the greater the number of students, the more time it takes to move through the material. If you have less than half an hour, it may not be possible to teach a complete progression of study. In this case, you may wish to separate the material into two or more lessons. Once the material has been explored in a full creative dance lesson, many activities can be singled out and repeated in short slots of time.

Young children exert huge amounts of energy but tire easily. They need short intervals of activity—less than a minute for some studies. During early puberty, children have unpredictably changeable energy levels, so stay tuned to their needs. Many healthy active adults like a chance to really get moving and get a little workout. Others come to dance class from stressful work situations and need time to wind down and relax. Adults can spend much longer exploring each study than children and teens. Twenty minutes or more could be spent exploring a single focus. Generally classes for older adults should be taught at a slow pace. Adults, especially seniors, need freedom to move at their own pace and rest when necessary. Encourage them to pay attention to and heed their body's messages to avoid injury and exhaustion.

The best feedback on pacing comes from observing the energy in your students. Are they losing interest? Pick up the pace a bit. Are they out of breath? Slow it down. Are they impatient? Liven it up. Are they a contemplative group? Give them time. If you observe receptively, you will often be able to sense the energy level of the group. You are probably not moving as much as your students, so do not hesitate to ask if the class needs a rest or wants to go on. It takes experience to gauge the time needed for movement instructions, studies, and transitions, and it is wise to be overprepared. However, do not be tempted to jam too much material into a short time span. Save unfinished material for the next lesson.

Social Considerations

By building nonverbal communication skills, creative dance offers practice in group cooperation for all ages. In early childhood classes, dance experiences help young children understand who they are in relation to others. Expect and allow young children to mimic your movements, but also encourage them to find their own ways of moving. Primary grade children like to work in partners, gender not usually being too great an issue. In larger groups they learn how to take turns with others. Young children generally love to show off their ideas and thrive on the attention provided by demonstrating and performing. Positive reinforcement goes a long way in building confidence at this and all ages.

Intermediate grade students like to organize and invent. They are able to work in small groups, especially of the same gender. By now they are able to lead and follow cooperatively. They generally love to perform and share their ideas and emotions, although inhibitions about showing dances may come up. At any age, such inhibitions can often be overcome by having several individuals or groups show their movement at once. For very young or shy students, having the teacher dance along with them can make performing possible.

Adolescent students' needs for social interaction often outweigh their intellectual focus. Improvising group dances as well as composing dances in small groups can provide them with many opportunities to work cooperatively at a time when sharing in front of peers or large groups may be intimidating.

By later high school and college, students usually have a more solid sense of self than in middle school. They do well with both unison and independent structures for dance studies. Community service can be a great focus for creative dance at this age. In a noteworthy creative dance project for high school students in which creative dance students were matched one to one with developmentally disbled adults, high schoolers taught creative movement to their assigned students (R. Fitzgerald, personal communication, March 2004). This challenge took them out of self-absorption, demanded clarity and communication skills, and fed their needs for useful and meaningful endeavors. It provided a very immediate motivation for learning dance. Middle school students may also enjoy teaching dance skills to younger students under the direction of a teacher. These, of course, should be elective activities.

Creative dance provides a wonderful chance for senior citizens to connect with others. This may be their primary reason for taking a dance class. Circle formations and group shapes can contribute to a sense of togetherness. Singing familiar songs often offers a well-received entry into movement for such groups. Beginning a lesson with the whole group "conducting" a song with their arms enlivens the participants, begins to loosen the body and activate muscles, and brings the class together as a collective. Conversations relating the movement studies to people's lives can be a wonderful and important adjunct to the lesson. Draw specific named movements from students' own diverse experiences (past or present). These might be related to work tasks such as gardening (dig, haul, plant, harvest) or to festivals, holidays, cultural background, military service, or youth activities such as scouting or going to camp. Any important or poignant events, especially if they are commonly shared, offer good ideas for movement expression. These structures work well for any group that is seeking community.

Physical challenges excite high school and college students.

Physical Limitations or Exceptional Abilities

Age has obvious implications for a person's ability to move. Young children are learning to coordinate large and small motor skills, but they may not have developed enough bodily control to accomplish turns, balances, or complex movement combinations. Don't push them into these as that will only cause frustration and halt receptivity. If you notice a student with particularly good coordination, it is fine to acknowledge that in a way that promotes the learning of the whole class and does not put others down.

Teens and college students are at their physical prime and want complexities to be part of their experience—in fact, this may be necessary for them to feel like they are really dancing. At this time in their lives, physical challenges excite students and can be capitalized on. Be careful, however, not to get lost in purely instrumental work, and do not overemphasize skills that preclude success for less coordinated students. It is far more important to clearly express a theme than to be superathletic.

Adults vary tremendously in their physical abilities, and you may come across a wide comfort range in one class. Creative dance has an advantage with groups of differing abilities and ages because each student can solve movement problems according to his or her own capabilities. When teaching seniors, a chair can be used as "home base" for sitting movements and also to hold onto for standing movements. Many studies that are normally done standing can be adapted to sitting and lying down. All the basic qualities of movement can be done sitting, and students

Seniors can do all the basic movements and qualities while sitting in a chair.

can move their feet in locomotor patterns such as marching, galloping, jumping, and skipping while sitting in a chair.

Physical disabilities may call for special adjustments. Since creative dance is conceptually based, wheelchair bound or severely disabled dancers can experience beautiful and dynamic movement forms. Students with developmental disabilities may surprise you with the depth of their movement feeling. Movement may have remained their primary language, and they may have fewer inhibitions to overcome in expressing themselves through movement and sensing group themes.

It is very important for the teacher to be informed of students' past injuries or unnoticeable physical conditions so that the dance experience is safe. Adults will usually (but not always) take care of themselves, but be ready to offer alternatives to movements they cannot do. Physical competition has no place in these situations, and all dancers must learn to be responsible to themselves by moving in healthy ways.

Experience, Preconceptions, and Inhibitions

Beginners of any age must be approached differently from those with experience. Some groups, ages, and cultures tend to have more inhibitions about beginning to dance, and particular care must be taken when introducing creative dance to these audiences. It is fairly common for intermediate and middle school age students (especially boys) to think that dance is not cool. It is paradoxical that students who are initially the most resistant to creative dance are often the ones who need it the most. For this age group in particular, physical challenges, creative ways to work with sports movements, and using music they are familiar with can win their trust. Group unison movement, especially when led by an individual dancer, can reduce anxiety for new groups. Also, giving students a chance to lead can boost their self-confidence. Once inhibitions have been addressed, students who were initially self-conscious may thrive with dance. That said, it is counterproductive to force resistant students to dance. Their hesitancy could rub off on others and thwart the progress of the class as a whole.

Many middle school kids crave movement; others are scared to death of it. This is the time when students are most nervous about moving their bodies and portraying their image. Taking the focus off the body and putting it on the material or subjects that interest them is helpful in easing self-consciousness. Initially you may want to deemphasize introspective kinesthetic tune-ups and go right into small group activities. Good entry points are dramatic, emotional, or interpersonal themes such as those in Chapter 14 foundation lessons Interactive Forces and Lines and Shapes in Space, and in Chapter 8 in Creative Toolbox 8.2, Machines. Time element studies working with the beat, dancing with hand and foot sounds, or group orchestras with drums or found instruments all work well. Props (scarves, hoops, stretchy bands, or balls) are useful because they provide an external focus to movement explorations and interactions. All of these structures offer clear "containers" for freedom of expression and can be useful for groups of any age with inherent inhibitions.

By high school, students are usually in dance classes by choice, so resistance to dance may not be an issue. When movement is used to integrate subject areas in the classroom, short movement activities may be more appropriate than developing a full lesson in a single session. If only a short amount of time is available, but you would like to develop material as it would be done in a longer lesson, consider breaking the material into bite-sized pieces and working on the progressions in five- to fifteen-minute blocks over the course of several class periods. A curricular idea could be introduced with a group movement activity one day, explored individually another day, tried in small groups the next day, and pulled together in a culminating form at the end of the series. Alternatively, several different aspects of a problem could be covered, one per day, and pulled together on the last day. These do not have to be done by the whole class. Asking for volunteers to demonstrate an academic concept through movement provides a safe way of bringing movement into classrooms without coercing hesitant students. This structure can become contagious and open the door for students to work together collectively on more developed curricular dance projects.

In any group, the term *dance* may be misinterpreted for a variety of reasons. For some groups, it may be appropriate to address the issue of dance head-on and educate them about the many forms of dance, including dance as a creative art activity. For others, more judicious sensitivity is called for. If this is the case, you may achieve more success by approaching material as "movement" instead of dance. It is unwise to select activities that might invade religious or cultural mores, as this may alienate your audience. Instead, provide a consistent atmosphere of trust and appreciation of diversity.

When teaching in a setting or group that you are not familiar with, it is beneficial to get support from others who have experience with that population or age group. This was demonstrated in a session with a group of sixty men in drug treatment, many of whom had recently been released from prison. The workshop was preceded by a rousing introduction from one of their counselors who pointed out the value of movement expression and stepping outside one's envelope of comfort. Without this priming, the heartfelt, uninhibited, even gentle movement expression that followed would not have been possible. The encouragement of mentors and teachers whom your students trust will validate your work and make it easier for students to participate.

When entering a new venue, be alert to your own preconceptions. None of the generalizations listed here is *always* true. Even the best built lesson plan needs room for flexibility in case the audience is not receptive to your preconceived approach. Just as you expect your students to be willing to try your ideas, you need to be receptive to them. If you are experienced in working with a particular group, you can confidently follow your intuition when adapting material.

One of the great joys in teaching creative dance is crafting dance experiences that offer progressive growth for students. It is also one of dance teaching's greatest challenges. As you work more and more with movement in different class situations, the building blocks of planning will fall more easily into place. Putting together an effective creative movement lesson is not really difficult, but it does take care, practice, and an organizational understanding of your material. Your enthusiasm and commitment will go a long way toward putting your students at ease for exploring and growing through creative movement no matter what their age or experience.

CHAPTER SUMMARY

- Creative dance teaching requires clear goals, careful organization of material, and considerate methods of presentation.
- Natural principles of progression logically develop material and connections to curricular themes.
- The guiding steps for constructing creative dance lessons are:
  - Gather information about your topic.
  - Find a conceptual link to movement.
  - Narrow material down to a manageable focus.
  - Build a progression to meet objectives.
  - Consider the use of sound or silence.
- The important parts of a creative dance lesson are:
  - Introduction to concepts.
  - Kinesthetic tune-up.
  - Exploration.
  - Culminating form.
  - Closure.
  - Follow-up activities.
- Creative dance is adaptable to students' needs as determined by their age, ability, and level of experience.

REVIEW QUESTIONS

1. What variables need to be addressed when planning a creative dance lesson?
2. What is an example of a teaching progression that moves from simple to complex? Describe how this would translate to actual material.
3. What is an example of a thematic progression that moves from pure movement material to a curricular application?
4. How does the sequence of working from freedom, to awareness, to control create a spiraling progression?
5. Pick a lesson from Part V and briefly describe how each of the five guiding steps for planning have been manifested in that lesson.
6. What are the parts of a creative dance lesson? What function does each serve?
7. Pick a particular student population and explain the adaptations you might use to teach this group. Refer to the variables presented for different needs.

CHAPTER 12

CREATING A LEARNING ENVIRONMENT FOR DANCE

Learning Objectives

1. Recognize the importance of and be able to use presentation structures that ensure a positive, safe learning environment.

2. Employ management tactics to establish and maintain student focus.

3. Acknowledge personal teaching styles.

Creativity or Chaos

As one of my (Mary Ann's) first ventures into teaching creative dance, I volunteered to teach dance at the local preschool. When, I arrived, I was greeted by twenty three-year-olds running around naked. The group was going swimming after dance class, and the teachers had decided to have them change into their suits before they went. Needless to say, with this preamble to dance class, the preschoolers found it quite impossible to focus on what they were doing during that lesson. After this experience, the teachers never expected to see me again. Undaunted, I went back the next week, having learned the hard way that the more attention given to supporting factors around the class, the more successful the lesson will be.

During creative dance lessons, some of the typical physical structures that order the environment (such as desks to sit in) may be taken away. Instead, the physical space, focus of movement activities, and teacher's manner of presentation must provide those structures. Mary Ann's true story from her early teaching days is an example of what can happen when ordering structures are not in place.

To give maximum opportunity for exploration and growth, creative dance teaching strives to provide as much freedom as possible. However, there is a fine line between creativity and chaos, and knowing how to use freedom is a skill that needs cultivation. Saying "Dance any way you want to" is free, but it could result in chaotic confusion. Directing the focus and establishing boundaries enhances creativity. A teacher must learn how to structure the teaching space and lessons to help students use freedom responsibly. To help students feel comfortable with the freedom offered in creative movement exploration, provide a stable learning environment where students can focus on movement studies and their bodies' responses to movement. Without that stability a dance class can easily become disorderly. This does not mean that you need to teach choreographed steps for students to copy. Nor does it mean that the environment must be perfect. It does mean that you need to provide safe boundaries to create an inviting atmosphere where healthy, free movement expression can comfortably grow.

Presentation Structures

The Physical Space

Developed in 1995, the *Consortium of National Arts Education Associations Opportunity-to-Learn Standards for Dance Instruction* describe the environment needed to establish a safe, comprehensive dance program in schools. Sadly, few schools meet those standards,

---

CONCEPT SPOTLIGHT 12.1

Rules for Creative Dance

Posting the rules can help establish order in dance classes.

1. *Be Safe:* do not hurt yourself, others, or the space.
2. *Pay Attention* and use your senses.
3. *Speak with Movement* not your mouth.
4. *Think for Yourself,* but *Cooperate* with the group.

---

and solutions to the lack of adequate dance space often have to be creatively devised. As dance becomes more common in education, administrations will need to provide improved areas in which to hold dance classes.

Creative dance can be adapted to many kinds of physical spaces. Ideally, students should have enough room to have personal space the size of their furthest reach and ample room to move without bumping each other. Too large a space—a huge echoing gymnasium or an open playground—can cause problems. Students may not be able to focus or hear the teacher's directions. This can be ameliorated by blocking off part of the area with tables, chairs, or room dividers. It may be enough to request that students stay within visual boundaries such as lines on the floor.

A medium-sized cafeteria or multipurpose room can serve adequately. A cafeteria may have a fair amount of traffic through the room or commotion from the kitchen in preparation for meals. If this is the case, efforts to communicate with others using the space may help. Also, it is very important that the floor be kept clean. This means mopping, sweeping, or vacuuming the room before dance class and making sure that students' shoes are clean before they enter the space. Custodians and cafeteria workers are very important support personnel for providing a proper environment for creative dance. Eliciting their help in a thoughtful way, and pitching in when possible, will go a long way to ensure that a clean, open, quiet space is ready in time for class. Hard tile or carpet over concrete floors, common in many school settings, is also an issue when teaching dance. In such conditions, dance material must be chosen that does not include high-impact foot and leg work or falling.

With adaptation, creative dance lessons can be taught in classroom-sized spaces if the number of students is not too large. The room can be arranged so that desks and tables are moved to the side to create space in the center for movement. Students can learn to do this in a systematic way. If desks are pushed flat against the wall, with no gaps left between, and chairs pushed fully underneath them, a lot more space is made available than if desks are simply pushed aside. Moving small items such as wastepaper baskets, charts, and teacher's chairs can open up valuable bits of space.

In some instances, rearranging the room may not be necessary or desirable. Students in intermediate grades who are new to creative dance may feel more comfortable moving expressively in a space that is protected by desks because it provides a sense of boundaries. For classes that have trouble controlling their movements, pushing the desks back may provide too much freedom at first. Some individuals also may have social or perceptual challenges, which make the openness of the space and the freedom of a creative dance class daunting. Sometimes simply placing children in a protected area of the room (behind a desk, near the side by a wall, or near the teacher) is enough to give them the stability they need to participate without reordering the whole class structure significantly. The placement of students will vary according to their needs. Once students have become comfortable moving in a more confined space, they will be ready for freer movement in larger spaces.

When using a room where students' desks have not been rearranged, students should push their chairs in completely and scatter in any available space. Moving aside light or small charts and displays will make more room for dance. The formation of desks can be worked into structures for movement. For example, circle dances can be done around several tables or groups of desks pushed close together, leaving space at their periphery. If desks are arranged in rows, dancers can form group lines and move through the linear spaces between the rows. Lessons can also be adapted to limited space by dividing the class in half and alternating half the class sitting in their chairs and half the class exploring through space.

Management and Safety Strategies

Once a physical environment has been prepared, other structures need to be established to provide safety and order in the classroom. These "containers" establish boundaries that control students' focus. They make the class easier to manage and the presentation more effective.

My Spot

One crucial container is the sense of place or "home base" from which each student works. For most students, simply noticing where they are standing and marking it with movement can establish their place. Having the whole class jump in place while saying "It's my spot!" is a ritual that is amazingly fun for students of all ages. It works for preschoolers as well as teenagers.[1] For young children, the sense of place may require some kind of marker at first. Two props useful for marking spots are plastic hoops, which are available in a variety of sizes, or cloth loops about thirty-six inches in diameter. Small pieces of masking tape or labels also can be used as place markers. (These should be taken up soon after class to avoid damaging the floor's surface.) After a few lessons, spatial awareness will be developed enough that students no longer need these place markers. Before proceeding to further material, the class as a whole needs to reliably dance safely in place. Once students begin to move through general space, returning to place and reestablishing it by jumping and saying "It's my spot!" can be repeated many times during a lesson. It is a good way to regain control if there is danger of it being lost.

Space Bubble

The imaginary space bubble, especially when combined with "my spot," is a valuable tool for helping students establish boundaries of personal space and maintain control within a group. The boundary of personal space is defined by how far a person can reach in space. It can expand or contract depending on the dancers' positions and how much space there is between people and objects. Use the image of the space bubble at the beginning of every children's lesson and return to it when students are having difficulty organizing themselves in space. It is a very effective safety tool, and it allows students to relax enough to work creatively.

These students are moving within fabric loops that mark spots.

There are many ways of establishing self-space. The easiest is to simply "touch" the outer edges of the kinesphere (or bubble). Another useful exploration is for students to make movements of "painting" or otherwise decorating their space bubbles. In doing this it is important to make contact with all three dimensions of self-space: high, low, in front, behind, and on either side. The foundation lesson The Moving Body (Chapter 14) explains basic procedures for claiming place and establishing personal space.

The importance of personal space cannot be overemphasized. Respecting each other's space is the most frequent reminder used to control a classroom. Evoking the space bubble is much more positive than simply saying "Don't bump." Also, the space bubble image is a tool many classroom teachers have adopted for use in other school and life situations; it represents an awareness of others that is useful in relationships in many settings.

12.1 CREATIVE TOOLBOX—TRY THIS!

Adapting My Spot and Space Bubbles

Because a space bubble and my spot are used on an ongoing basis, it is stimulating for students when these structures are adapted to different lesson themes. For example, in the lesson adaption Southwest Native American Pottery Design (Chapter 14), rather than building a space bubble at the beginning of the lesson, students move as if building a life-sized "pot" around themselves, then jump inside it and say "It's my pot!" In The Three Little Pigs lesson (Chapter 19), dancers build their individual houses around themselves to represent their space bubbles.

Safe Stops

At some point during the first dance lesson, children need to be taught to stop safely. Generally this means stopping on cue with weight on both feet, knees slightly bent, and feet slightly apart. If students are doing something on one foot, they can try to stop on one foot and maintain balanced control—not by waving the arms wildly but by engaging the abdominal muscles. Children enjoy practicing this skill. If they are working at low level, they can simply stop in their low positions. It is necessary to specifically teach a stopping technique because children like to fall and slide when signaled to stop. Unless the class is working on those particular movements, they make the dance environment unsafe and should be addressed immediately. Using the directive of "Make a safe stop" and teaching students how to do that gives them an alternative to out-of-control stops.

Prevent Injuries

Sometimes dancers do unsafe movements without realizing their danger. Enthusiastic students may overstretch or place their feet so far apart that they have difficulty moving from this position. This could injure their inner leg muscles. Splits, cartwheels, and other gymnastics aren't safe in a creative dance format. Similarly, young children may bounce on their knees, seemingly with no adverse effects. However, this abuses ligaments or joints and can cause permanent damage. Specific rules about what is not acceptable should be established to prevent injuries to a body that must last a lifetime.

A safe stop: weight on both feet, knees slightly bent, feet slightly apart.

Student Attire

Encourage students to wear comfortable clothing appropriate for moving freely. For girls this may mean wearing pants. Be creative with students not wanting to dance because of inappropriate attire. Placement in the room can often solve the problem. If a girl is wearing a skirt or dress, putting her feet toward a wall when lying down or standing where no one is behind her may solve that problem.

Decide whether or not to have students wear shoes. When creative dance is taught in studio settings, it is most often taught in bare feet. To dance without shoes is a wonderful thing. Without shoes the feet can truly be used as expressive instruments. There is also a different atmosphere in a class when students work without shoes. It makes the dance time somewhat special and different from the rest of the day. There can, however, be problems with wearing no shoes in school settings. Extra time is needed for putting on and taking off shoes. In some situations floors are too hard or uneven for dance activities to be done in bare feet. There may also be concern for students stepping on pins, staples, and so forth on the floor. Some students (or their parents) object strongly to taking off shoes at school. Some may feel embarrassed or, worse yet, start holding their noses indicating real or imaginary smelly feet. Teachers need to decide whether the benefits of taking off shoes are worth these extra hassles. If shoes are removed, it is important that they be stored in an orderly fashion. This sets a tone for all the work in the dance class. If shoes are worn, we recommend that students wear gym shoes with a good tread. If individuals have inappropriate shoes such as sandals, heavy boots, or high heels, consider having them work in their bare feet. Unless the room is carpeted, students should not dance in stocking feet because of the danger of slipping.

Minimize Distractions

In creative dance, participants are asked to apply themselves intently. The atmosphere in a room changes when students begin to concentrate fully, without undue tension. The more students focus in this way, the more they generate collective "mind power," which provides a supportive environment for movement exploration. Unfortunately, it is difficult to have undistracted instruction periods in a school setting. Crises for students can arise at any time, school staff may need to speak to the teacher or a student, there may be fire drills, "pull-outs" of students, and intercom announcements. Some interruptions cannot be avoided, but planning ahead and establishing behavior guidelines for those situations can eliminate many distractions. For example, allowing time before class for using the restroom and providing ample opportunity for drinking water before and after (but generally not during) class will address issues of students needing to leave and return to class.

Students need role models when concentrating on movement problems. Adults in the room need to respect the environment required for dance by minimizing conversations while students are working. Tutoring small groups in the same room or adults conferring with each other on the side are practices that should be discouraged. (A designated dance room would minimize distractions caused by simultaneous uses of a space.) The optimal environment for dance exploration is one in which everyone in the room is focused on the dance work. It is very powerful for students to feel that they are being witnessed as they explore creative problems. Observers may not think they are doing much just watching a class, but they are helping to provide the safe container and crucible for the development of dance, which is a performing art.

Student conversations can also be problematic. Students tend to talk when they feel nervous or inhibited while moving. They fall into talking as a distraction. This can happen with any age group. Creative dance teaches nonverbal expression and communication. Therefore, students should not have verbal conversations while dancing. Although talking may seem to increase the friendliness of the class, it gets in the way of discovering the depth of movement exploration. One way to discourage conversation is by directing students to "speak" with their movements, not with their mouths. This idea may have to be reinforced many times before students get used to it. Students can vocalize in a nonconversational way by making sounds to match the quality of their movement or saying the name of a movement as they do it (for example, having students say "Strrretch" in a stretchy way as they make stretching movements). The vocalizing then becomes a kind of musical accompaniment to the movement and enhances the experience rather than being a distraction.

When students get together in groups to work, a little talking to make sure everyone understands the structure is permissible. However, simply beginning to move (rather than verbally planning out a sequence) will generally create more exciting and expedient results. Without words, language barriers are diminished, and equal opportunities are provided for everyone to be leaders through nonverbal communication. This will be challenging to students accustomed to taking charge, but even in multilingual populations, students will gain tremendously from this cooperative relationship. After an improvisation is complete, partners or groups can benefit from discussing their experience.

Arrangement of Students

Group formations used as a basis for instruction affect the tone of the class, so arrangement of students deserves careful consideration. Different groups function better in different formations, and different lessons call for different groupings. Does the material lend itself to a circle formation or line? Does it feel right to work in smaller or larger groups? There is no absolute right or wrong here; going with one's natural tendency is usually the best approach.

Clump

A loose clump is a good formation for students to sit in when they are getting detailed instructions at the beginning of class and for discussion in the middle or at the end of class. It is not as formal as a circle and everyone can't always see each other, but it is a quick arrangement for gathering students together. Returning to a clump is also a way to center the focus of the class if attention is becoming too diffuse with students spread out through the space.

Circle

Having students sit in a circle is another good arrangement for giving instructions at the beginning of a class. Some lessons can be continued in this format. This form has a nice sense of community and sharing because everyone is focused toward each other. Groups naturally travel in a circle when working on locomotor movements such as galloping and skipping. The circle is also a good basis for many culminating forms because it unites the group. The disadvantages of the circle are that sometimes the space is inadequate for everyone in the circle to move freely, students may feel inhibited in seeing each other, and in large circles the teacher may not be prominent enough for all to see and hear.

Scatter

Movement explorations usually begin with individuals equally spaced in a loose scatter formation. Each student establishes his or her personal space and identifies a place (or spot) within the scatter. The scatter formation communicates a certain amount of freedom in its looseness and demands that students be aware of each other to keep spaces even.

Lines/Rows

If students are not able to maintain an orderly arrangement in a scatter formation, they can be arranged standing side by side in several rows. This gives a more controlled, regimented feel to the environment, which can be helpful for students who lack a sense of internal order.

Working in rows is also useful for locomotor movements. Depending on the shape of the space, have students stand one behind the other in parallel lines at one end of the room (Figure 12.1). The first person in each line can do the locomotor movement across

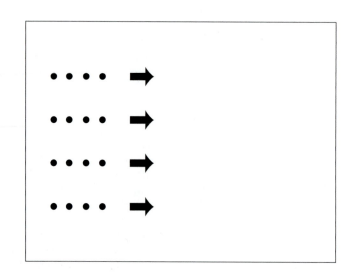

FIGURE 12.1 *Moving in lines from one side of the room to the other is a common structure in dance classes, often referred to as "moving across the floor."*

the floor as the next person in line waits his or her turn. As the students reach the other side of the room, they turn around and form their lines again one behind the other. These spatial arrangements are very common structures in many forms of dance instruction.

Establishing Group Collaboration

Establishing partnerships and small groups for dance work is an interesting activity in itself, and this can be done in several ways. Partners can be assigned by numbering off, grouping by proximity, or by using knowledge of individual needs. Many teachers already have systems that can be pulled out of the hat here such as established reading or math partners, hall buddies, and so forth. Allowing partners to choose each other gives more freedom and responsibility to students but may result in undesirable combinations. It is prudent to maintain the option to rearrange groupings if needed. A student without a partner can be honored by working with the teacher or an aide, making him or her feel special instead of rejected. This is a good opportunity to orient students to the community spirit of creative dance—to be willing to dance with anyone and to accept all partners politely. Once that standard is firmly established, students find that they can work with people they previously did not consider friends.

In many lessons partners are asked to decide who will go first as leader. Even though both will get turns to be the leader, this is a revealing process. It becomes clear who is a more active personality and who is passive. Similar personalities may have difficulty working together. Either they both want the control, or neither wants control. Work with this challenge or bypass the hurdle and assign roles.

Sharing Dance

Performance is not the primary goal of creative dance. At any point in the lesson, however, sharing a creation is an excellent way to solidify an individual's art experience and build community among dancers. Having students show their dancing to each other provides a sense of accomplishment for the performers. It is a way to validate their movement discoveries and expand ways of thinking. Fellow students find it fascinating to see the range of solutions to movement problems posed during class. In addition to highlighting the diversity of movement expression, showings can be a rich source of ideas to develop into further studies, group dances, or dance compositions for performance.

Informal showings can be done in a variety of ways. Small groups can perform individually, or if space permits, a few groups can perform at a time. This is a good format for noticing contrasting ideas. Large group dances can be demonstrated fairly well by half the class. This is especially good after the whole class has done the dance together. Observation layers a visual idea of the dance onto the kinesthetic experience, offering an integrated learning activity and practice in audience skills. During the dance, others can play simple accompaniment to the dance. After watching, those in the audience can draw what they saw or felt, write descriptive words and images, or scribe an account of the movements. Giving onlookers an assignment keeps them engaged in the dance.

If students have the confidence, they should be given the opportunity to share solos, but never push this too hard. Having three or so individuals share their dances simultaneously gives each dancer company and is a good way to build confidence gradually. Another way individuals can share is by teaching their movements to the rest of the class. During the exploration section of the lesson, having a few individuals show or teach their movements can motivate a variety of movement solutions. This is surprisingly successful even for beginners, especially when everyone takes a quick turn.

Sharing dances can be either an embarrassing situation or an empowering one. For students to reap the benefits of dance showings, they must be done in an emotionally safe and supportive environment. The goal of performance can be a great focus for a group and often pulls out the best in students, but no one should be forced to perform.

CONCEPT SPOTLIGHT 12.2

Showing Formations

When students are asked to watch others dance, choose from these formations:

Scatter: audience is seated but scattered; performers move from their scattered positions.

Circle: audience is seated in a circle; performers move inside the circle.

Proscenium: audience is seated on one side of the space to view performers moving on the other side.

Gallery: audience observes by walking around performers who are moving in place in scatter formation.

Sometimes it is necessary to teach a class how to be a receptive and respectful audience. Students should learn that the people performing need the audience's help to focus on their dances. For this they need to watch quietly with an attitude of openness. Sometimes the setting will be appropriate for applause. At other times a pause of silent appreciation, "silent clapping," or another nonverbal gesture will seem right. If there is applause, no hint of competition or silliness should be allowed. Properly presented, showings can boost students' confidence in their artistry, commitment to their work, and acceptance of diversity among peers.

Discussions about the dances should be worded in positive, helpful terms and should focus on the material of the dance rather than on the dancers themselves. Pose

---

 # Box 12.1

Structures for Sharing Dance

Individual Dances
Assign or let students choose a theme from the lesson to show.
(Used in Rhythmic Opposites and Finding Unison lessons in Chapter 14.)

Partner Dances
One or several sets of partners show their improvised dances.
(Used in Lines and Shapes in Space, Rhythmic Opposites, and Finding Unison lessons in Chapter 14.)

Small Group Dances
Have students show an improvisation or sequence they've created together while the rest of the class observes.
(Used in Lines and Shapes in Space, Rhythmic Opposites, Interactive Forces, and Finding Unison lessons in Chapter 14.)

Half and Half
Half the class dances; the other half watches.
(Used in The Moving Body and Lines and Shapes in Space lessons in Chapter 14.)

Invited Audience
The whole group of dancers performs for invited peers, parents, teachers and principals.

questions that provoke description, feeling, and correct use of dance terminology. This teaches students how to talk (or write) about dance. It is also an excellent opportunity to have students identify and analyze movements they observe. In this process, outcomes of learning objectives can be summarized or assessed.

✿ Focus Tools

To help students develop kinesthetic awareness, choose from a large repertoire of techniques for maintaining and reestablishing focused concentration. The following tools range from simple attention-getters to thinking about the flow of the entire lesson.

Kinesthetic Centering

Creative Pause

A creative pause at the beginning of an improvisational exploration helps students gather their focus and awareness. Return often to a place of awareness as a basis for movement feeling in dance material. Directives such as "Come to a neutral position" or "Begin in stillness" can prepare students before starting to work on a movement study.

Relaxation

There are times when students become too stimulated to focus. Having the class take a moment to relax can work wonders. This is best done by creating an environment conducive to relaxation instead of demanding it. Sometimes it is hard for students to relax completely; physically tiring them out before asking them to let go may help.

12.2 CREATIVE TOOLBOX—TRY THIS!

Relaxation Tips

- If possible, have students lie comfortably on the floor.
- Using a patient gentle voice, encourage them to be loose and heavy.
- Ask students to turn their attention inward toward their heartbeat or breath. Instruct them not to change their breath but to just pay attention to it. (This minimizes exaggerated breathing and fake snoring.)
- Guide students into tightening and then releasing muscles in the arms and legs.
- Go to each student and gently jiggle both arms to facilitate looseness.
- Have students take the hook-up position.

BrainGym

Developed by Paul and Gail Dennison (1994), BrainGym activities are specific movement patterns used as tools for integrating different areas of the brain, thereby bringing the mind into focus. Although not specifically developed as a management tool, these activities are effective in that realm because they bring the mind into focus. Here are four BrainGym activities useful for centering students' attention. We've adapted them for use in group dance classes. For more information on BrainGym movements, see the books and videotapes by the Dennisons and Carla Hannaford listed in the Bibliography.

- **Lazy Eights.** Draw a figure eight lying on its side. Lazy eights can be "drawn" on a desk, a chalkboard, or in the air. Do this with each hand separately and then

slowly actually requires more control than moving fast. This is a positive way for students to practice skills they may find challenging.

Sound

Start and Stop Signals

It is important for students to know when they are expected to be dancing and when they are to be listening to instructions or discussing the material of the lesson. There are many ways to signal the start and end of movement explorations. The teacher's own voice is the easiest and most adaptable instrument for signaling students. Phrases such as "You may begin," "Ready—go," and "Move" initiate action. "Bring it to an ending," "Freeze," "Stop," or "Pause" set the limits of the movement problem. Students also easily understand nonverbal signals. Clapping, beating once or twice on a drum or claves, or ringing a bell, triangle, or finger cymbal are excellent signals. The quality of the instrument's sound will influence the students' entry into and completion of movement studies. A drumbeat will elicit a sudden change; a bell indicates more gradual starting and stopping. With recorded music, starting and stopping music tells students when to begin and end their dancing. Fading volume in and out can frame the length of a movement study.

Voice and Rhythm Instrument Accompaniment

The voice is an important tool for coaching students as they move. It keeps students' attention on the concept they are exploring and can be done using words or pure sound quality that matches the movement task. The tone and rhythm of the voice are instantly adaptable to changing needs.

Kinesthetically created sound helps students focus during exploration. The voice, body sounds, handheld instruments, and drums are all good movement-based modes of accompaniment. They can be played while dancing or to accompany other dancers. You do not have to be a trained musician to accompany the class with simple rhythm instruments. Spending time playing and dancing with drums, bells, gongs, claves, and found instruments will establish a creative relationship with them. The movement feeling applied to accompaniment with an instrument is conveyed through sound to your students.

Recorded Music

Recorded music can aid kinesthetic response by providing a mood or beat. For beginners, music can help them make the shift from everyday awareness to a heightened dance focus. Recorded music can also control the activity level of the class; it can either relax dancers or liven them up.

Before using recorded music, consider to what extent it will benefit the dance and dancers. It may not be worth your time to fuss with music for a very short study. One way to keep the musical accompaniment clean is to prerecord the music you wish to use onto a single tape, compact disc, or play list in the order in which you will use it. Any electronic sound can fail at inopportune moments. If this happens, remember that dance as an art form stands on its own without the use of musical accompaniment.

Clapping or Finger-Snapping Patterns

When used effectively, patterns of clapping or finger-snapping reestablish concentration or get students' attention. These patterns also supply vitality to a class lagging in energy. Here are two simple sound structures to try:

- **Echo clapping.** The teacher claps a short time pattern for students to echo. This is effective only if the pattern is short and clear enough for students to repeat easily (about two to six claps). If needed, repeat a pattern a few times before changing to a different pattern for students to echo.

- **Steady beat.** Here the teacher begins snapping fingers or clapping hands to a steady beat and asks students to join in. After everyone is together on the beat say, "Four more snaps (or claps)." Finish those beats (possibly counting backwards), and stop with a hand signal. Then continue with instructions.

Bench Time

Especially in beginning experiences with dance, some children may not have the skills to work with others in a movement context. They may, on purpose or quite inadvertently, bump into others, endangering the rest of the class. They may interrupt the class and make it difficult for others to concentrate. In such cases, have these students sit out for a while with a nonpunitive "watching" assignment. Truly disruptive students could sit with an aide, if available, or be removed from the room so that the rest of the class more fully benefits from the dance work. Fortunately, kids will do almost anything to be able to move around, so they have a vested interest in learning the responsibility of safety early in their dance education.

Asking students to watch for a while is effective only in small doses. It's not good to get into a situation where many students are sitting out or those disrupting the class are coming in and out of participation. If there is this level of resistance, it's best to stop the class and change gears. Relaxing or centering activities, addressing the issues in discussion, or switching to a nonmovement topic entirely are possible alternatives.

12.3 CREATIVE TOOLBOX—TRY THIS!

Bench Time Assignment

If students bump into others while the class is moving through shared space, ask them to sit down while the class repeats the activity. Have them watch how the rest "look for empty space without popping bubbles." Then ask the students if they understand how to do that skill. If they say "Yes," they can be allowed to reenter.

The Lesson's Rhythm

Focusing tools address specific ways to maintain control in the classroom. These techniques should be used in context with the rhythm of the lesson as a whole. Creative dance can be very stimulating, if not exhausting. The dancer is asked for total involvement—physical, intellectual, and emotional. Working in the force and time elements can be particularly tiring. Teachers should be aware of needs that may arise for resting within the lesson. Breaks are very helpful in regrouping a class that has gotten a little wild or off track. Here are some ways to control the rhythm of the lesson and allow recuperation time:

- Balance vigorous expansive expressions in the lesson with more inwardly focused expressions. Large movements open students up; smaller movements gather energy that is getting out of hand.
- Let students rest lying on the floor as a break or while you give new directions (Figure 12.6).
- Have small groups (or half the class) show movement while the others watch.

The teacher must be both active and receptive in guiding students' activities, using the kinesthetic sense to "read" students. To sense the rhythm of the lesson, the teacher needs to bodily sense what the students are experiencing and respond to the circumstances. The foundation lesson Interactive Forces (Chapter 14) introduces skills for kinesthetically assessing what is going on in the environment and gaining sensitivity to the

FIGURE 12.6   *Be aware of needs that may arise for resting within the lesson.*

"pulse" of a group. Try to sense the endurance of your students, and stop them before their physical stamina and creative focus wear out.

∽ *Personal Teaching Styles*

Every teacher has his or her own way of presenting dance lessons. One of the beauties of creative dance is that it can be presented in many different styles. You may wish to move with your students to motivate and inspire them as you present a movement lesson. Conversely, you may simply assign movement problems and monitor students' dancing. Different parts of the lesson may call for different amounts of movement from a teacher. Many group assignments may need to be demonstrated, especially for children. Two students or the teacher and a student volunteer can often do this.

Sometimes it is hard to remember progressions planned with detailed care. Keep the lesson plan handy when you teach. Teaching dance with a notebook in hand is difficult, so jot an outline on the board prior to class, especially if teaching a new lesson.

What actually takes place in every lesson and every improvised group dance is new and unknown every time. After presenting a lesson, take time to evaluate your success. While the experience is fresh in your mind, make notes for future reference. What worked well? What didn't? Was there the right amount of material, and was it level appropriate? Did key words or group configurations help? Should the order of the lesson be changed, or does the theme need a whole new approach? Did new ideas come to mind that you

---

CONCEPT SPOTLIGHT 12.4

Teaching Tips

- Prepare the space.
- Outline lesson progressions and organizational reminders on the board if necessary.
- Minimize distracting activities and conversations.
- Establish "my spot" and the "space bubble."
- Teach students how to use freedom, and be aware of how much freedom the class can handle responsibly.
- Pose problems to reestablish control: smaller, lower, less vigorous, in place movements.
- Pace the class according to needs and stamina.

would like to develop? Maybe you found the perfect musical accompaniment. Even if it's a long time before you look at the lesson again, a few brief notes will be of great help in future planning.

One key to successful teaching and learning is the extent to which the instructor communicates excitement and enthusiasm. Be open to exploration yourself, to unexpected solutions to problems, and to modeling an attitude of discovery. Integrating movement into your teaching is largely a matter of becoming comfortable with the movement experience and understanding movement vocabulary. The more experience you have with movement, the better you will understand kinesthetic concepts. The more you teach creative dance, the clearer it will become how to present a problem and how to adapt lessons to different groups. The lesson plans in Part V provide plenty of material for getting acquainted with vocabulary, concepts, progressions, and movement experience at a basic level. As these become familiar, it will become easier to address movement as a tool for learning, and you will find the best ways of presenting creative dance problems to enhance your teaching and your students' learning potential.

Chapter Summary

- Structures that ensure a positive learning environment for creative dance include the following:
  - Well-prepared physical space
  - Claiming "place" and identifying personal space
  - Safety guidelines
  - Suitable attire
  - Minimal distractions and conversation
  - Consciousness of the spatial arrangement of students
  - Procedures for establishing student groupings
- Tools that bring the class into focus include the following:
  - Kinesthetic centering
  - Use of sound
  - Bench time
  - Attending to the rhythm of the lesson
- Creative dance can be taught with a wide range of teaching styles.

Review Questions

1. Why is it important to provide ordering structures when teaching creative dance?
2. What structures help ensure a safe and positive environment for teaching creative dance? What difficulties does each address and how?
3. What tools can be used to focus the attention of students during creative dance lessons? How do each of these use kinesthetic awareness to solve a problem?
4. Describe some personal stylistic traits that might emerge in your own teaching.

Notes

1. The ritual of claiming place with "It's my spot!" was originated by our late colleague Grace Levin. Grace was a master at opening the door of creative dance to diverse populations, including troubled boys in residential treatment settings.

The standards developed by the NDEO in the United States are organized within the categories of performing, creating, responding, and interconnecting. They are derived from categories used by the National Assessment of Educational Progress (NAEP) for assessment in all performing arts. The standards are necessarily broad so that they can be applied to a variety of dance styles and approaches. For dance, performing includes knowledge and skills that are involved in the execution of dance movement and accuracy of intention based on the dancer's understanding of the elements of dance. Creating refers to the process of problem solving by inventing original movements and effectively organizing movements into meaningful forms, again guided by the framework of the elements of dance. Responding focuses on the critical thought processes of perceiving, analyzing, and synthesizing the art experience in a way that offers constructive feedback. Interconnecting refers to the ability to connect dance to other areas of life and learning. As individual states implement standards of learning in the arts and related methods of assessment, these general categories for assessment serve as a guide. In situations where national, state, or local standards have not been adopted, achievement categories may have different names, but the same skills are addressed overall. The specific creative dance objectives presented in Appendix D can be organized in the following way to match the NAEP/NDEO categories:

- The dancer's skill in using the body as an instrument of expression (performing)
- A demonstration of understanding of the elements of force, time, and space and the ability to discriminate between different aspects of these (performing and creating)
- The ability to use accurate dance vocabulary to define, analyze, and describe the dance experience to others (responding)
- The capacity to relate dance to other areas (interconnecting)
- The ability of the student to collaborate and contribute in group work (all categories)
- Level of motivation and artistic commitment (all categories)

❧ Methods of Assessment

There are a number of ways to assess student learning, and this discussion is by no means exhaustive. We present different models that you can choose from or combine to suit the needs of the situation. Some aspects of dance knowledge can be tested with traditional multiple-choice and short answer questions or through student writing. However, because dance is an activity that participants *do,* it makes sense to evaluate students' performance. Performance-based assessment has been called "authentic assessment" because it evaluates meaningful, real-world tasks that demonstrate a student's integration of knowledge in relation to established criteria (Tombari and Borich, 1999). The authentic assessment techniques discussed here are geared toward viewing live creative dance classes and showings. That is, they are imbedded within instruction. These methods can be used as well for evaluating journals, videotaped recordings of dance, or compilations of student work in the form of a portfolio. Balanced assessments can include both dancing and writing or talking about dance.

While presenting a lesson, an effective educator continually assesses the group's reception of the material. This is a complex and demanding task and a perfect example of activity and receptivity being needed simultaneously. To sense the group as a whole, the teacher's awareness is often diffuse rather than pinpointed on individual students. It is not easy to remember individual performances unless you specifically train yourself to notice individual dancers. Familiarity with performance objectives and a selection of specific skills to look for will help focus your observations.

Ongoing assessment can begin early in a study program. After teaching each class, make notes to informally assess the effectiveness of the lesson's movement studies and progressions for the group being taught. Making anecdotal notes on individual students who performed especially well or who need assistance in specific areas of the lesson will influence planning, ongoing student assessments, and reports on student progress to parents and school staff.

Although performance objectives can reduce subjectivity, there is no way to eliminate aesthetic preferences from dance evaluations. A very expressive dance will move its audience even if skill and proficiency are less than perfect. Artistic preferences vary person to person. Explain what it was about the dance that made it particularly expressive or pleasing, and assess how clearly the dancer was able to express in movement the thematic idea or quality underlying the dance. Evaluation should focus on the purpose of the dance and not on a like or dislike of the material or subject matter.

Rubrics as Scoring Tools for Observational Assessments

Assessment notes can be organized more fully with the help of rubrics, or scoring tools. The word *rubric* was not always an educational term; it referred to the red coloring of headings in early manuscripts, which made the headings clearly visible. In the same way, assessment rubrics are systematic signposts for observation that take the mystery out of qualitative evaluation. Tombari and Borich (1999) identify three kinds of rubrics that can be used as part of authentic (or performance) assessment: rating scales, checklists, and holistic scoring. **Rating scales** focus on different aspects of the skill such as the quality of performance (excellent, satisfactory, needs improvement) and the consistency or frequency of the behavior (always, often, sometimes, rarely, never). When skills are rated on a graded scale, it is necessary to have clear criteria for each rating level. This level of specificity provides detailed feedback to students on how to improve. Performance assessment sheets should also have space for written comments or feedback for the student in addition to the score. A **checklist** is useful for dance behaviors that can be observed as being present or not present. Checklists are also useful for creating grading scales and holistic scoring tools.

Checklist and rating scale rubrics break dance performance into components, enabling teachers to offer specific feedback to students and to guide further instruction. However, when evaluating an activity such as dance—which is truly more than the sum of its parts—holistic evaluations are also called for. **Holistic scoring** looks at the activity as a whole and can assess products such as composed dances or the culminating form of a lesson. Holistic scoring allows for intuition on the part of the evaluator. Familiar examples of holistic scoring are the numerical scores given for gymnastic, figure skating, and diving performance. Holistic scoring looks at the total picture but does not, on its own, provide diagnostic information (Tombari and Borich, 1999). Combining a holistic approach with assessment of specific performance objectives produces balanced, well-rounded, useful evaluations. Graded holistic assessments should provide models of products that meet proficiency level criteria. These models should not be so rigid as to discount compelling unexpected delight in a dance or performance even if it meets few of the specified performance objectives and expectations for mastery. Checklists, graded scales, and holistic scoring should be combined in a way that fits the teacher's organizational style and the needs of each educational setting.

Rating Scale Rubrics

NDEO's Standards-based Rubric

The National Dance Education Organization's Standards for Dance in Early Childhood (2005a) and Standards for Learning and Teaching Dance in the Arts (2005b) provide a wealth of practical resources for assessing students using the voluntary national standards. These rubrics can be adapted to state and local standards or to customized creative dance performance objectives. The publication provides rubrics for all the achievement standards at benchmarks of fourth, eighth, and twelfth grades. The categories of achievement are

Box 13.1

Sample Rubric Format for Standards or Customized Objectives

Name

Content Area	Needs Improvement	Meets Standard	Outstanding
Specific dance standard I or Customized performance objective I			
Specific dance standard II or Customized performance objective II			
Specific dance standard III or Customized performance objective III			

"needs improvement," "meets standard," and "outstanding," and the chart includes a space for comments. These forms can be downloaded from www.ndeo.org and photocopied for use in student evaluations. The standards are written not only in professional language but also in language that is age appropriate for various grade levels. Students can read the standards to know what is expected of them in dance and to participate in self-evaluation. Box 13.1 provides an example of this rubric.

Graded Scale Rubrics

To assess skills of a lesson with a number or letter graded scale, a rubric can be created with performance objectives selected according to a lesson's goals. Box 13.2 presents a graded scale for evaluation.

Creative Dance Proficiency Rated by Freedom, Awareness, and Control

A system of analyzing skills related specifically to creative dance is based on Mettler's pedagogical progression of beginning with freedom and building to awareness and control (Chapter 11). This progression often (but not always) also reflects the continuum of student achievement. Because creative dance instruction generally begins on the level of freedom, proficiency in objectives in the freedom category mark the first steps toward mastery. To gain mastery in a category of skills, students must show proficiency in performance objectives from all three areas: freedom, awareness, and control.

The progression from freedom, to awareness, to control is not always sequentially developed for individual dancers and thus should not be strictly adhered to when assessing students. The rubric shown in Box 13.3 is useful, however, in pinpointing student needs in each area of dance instruction. This organization of objectives serves as a good diagnostic tool and a guide for future lesson planning.

BOX 13.2

Graded Scale Rubric

The objectives for this graded scale rubric are drawn from the Creative Dance Performance Objectives in Appendix D and relate to the Sensing Time Patterns lesson in Chapter 14.

Rating Criteria
3 = Excellent: Consistently exhibits the objective.
2 = Adequate: Exhibits the objective often and appropriately.
1 = Emerging: Occasionally exhibits the objective or does so with undue effort.
0 = Unsatisfactory: Rarely or never exhibits the objective.

Name _____   **Grade**

(Use the above rating scale to score this student's achievement.)

Body—Distinguishes between movement of the whole
body and parts of the body.   _____

Time—Enjoys moving in a wide range of tempos: Slow   _____

Fast   _____

Time—Matches steady beat patterns with the group.   _____

Time—Creates mixed beat patterns.   _____

Space—Maintains self-space; does not bump others.   _____

Group—Works cooperatively with others.   _____

Comments: _____

_____

_____

_____

All students here are exhibiting freedom in their use of the body, especially Molly (in denim skirt). The movement of Jefferson (boy on the right) stands out as showing body awareness right through the fingertips of the left hand. All show awareness and control in using the body safely, moving on the same beat, and maintaining appropriate spacing as a group.

Box 13.3

Assessing Creative Dance Proficiency

(See Appendix D for a full set of Creative Dance Performance Objectives.)

Name _____

Body/Instrumental Skills

    Circle those that apply: Freedom   Awareness   Control

Comments: _____

_____

_____

Force Element

    Circle those that apply: Freedom   Awareness   Control

Comments: _____

_____

_____

Time Element

    Circle those that apply: Freedom   Awareness   Control

Comments: _____

_____

_____

Space Element

    Circle those that apply: Freedom   Awareness   Control

Comments: _____

_____

_____

Group Work

    Circle those that apply: Freedom   Awareness   Control

Comments: _____

_____

_____

Overall

Problem solving/creativity _____

Motivation/perseverance _____

Performance _____

Assessment Tally Sheet: A Checklist with a Holistic Element

If a formal evaluation is called for to coincide with a grading schedule or as an ongoing assessment, a checklist can be organized into tally sheets that direct observations according to specific objectives guided by the emphasis of the lesson. Tally sheets provide a quick way to evaluate a whole class on a single sheet of paper.[1] The checklist can be used by the instructor after a lesson or by teachers' aides or other observers during the lesson. Some training is required to know what to look for and how to use the tally sheets. Having evaluators who are observing but not instructing can be a great help because they offer additional evaluation perspectives and because it is so easy to miss something important when actively engaged in teaching a class.

The tally sheet presented in Box 13.4 has blocks labeled with each student's name. The blocks also contain abbreviations for specific dance objectives and a little room for notes. The abbreviations representing objectives can be tailored to criteria from any single lesson or to overall goals in a program. A key accompanies the tally sheet so that everyone using the sheets understands what the abbreviations stand for and how to code them. Evaluators (including the instructor) mark a + on the tally sheet for every instance they see the performance objective being met. No negative marks are made. This methodology keeps the observation somewhat objective and postpones interpretation of scoring data until after the lesson. Some teachers may prefer to use the sheets in a leveled manner, with a + indicating superior proficiency, a / indicating adequate performance, and a − indicating a need for help in that skill. In addition to the tally procedures, observers make an intuitive rating—excellent (E), satisfactory (S), needs improvement (N)—regarding each student's general proficiency and artistry. This methodology combines checklist scoring of specific behavior indicators with holistic assessment.

Self-Assessment and Peer Assessment

Self-assessments and peer assessments are valuable in ongoing evaluation. Discussion and journal entries can include self-assessments of what students have learned, how they felt as they danced, and what they need to work on. Student reports on their movement preferences also provide valuable information and insight into skill level, enjoyment, and conceptual understanding of material from the different elements of dance. Journals are a good source of information on student understanding and should be evaluated regularly. Many thought-provoking journal questions can be used with any lesson.

General Questions for the Dance Journal

- What was the idea or concept you danced about? Did you solve the movement problems successfully? How?
- Were you able to keep your self-space bubble today? How? How did that affect the lesson?
- Did you try a new movement that you've never done before? What was it?
- Did you learn some new words? What are they? How did you show them in movement?
- What worked well for you today? Which movements felt best? What was your favorite part of the lesson?
- Were there parts of the lesson that didn't go well for you? What needed to happen differently for you to have been more successful?
- How did the class make you feel? Did different parts make you feel differently?
- What do you feel you could improve upon?
- Did you work by yourself, with a partner, in a small group, or in one large group? How was the group dance different from your own dance?
- If you or the class performed a dance, describe your dance or one you observed.
- Do you have some new ideas you would like to try?
- How does the material of the lesson relate to your daily life?

Journals are a good source of information on student understanding.

At the end of each lesson in Part V you will find questions specific to that lesson.

Self-assessment rubrics can be created for any specific lesson. The one in Box 13.5 was created for the Interactive Forces lesson in Chapter 14. These rubrics provide a handy structure for reflection about one's dance work. Peers can answer similar questions to assess a partner with whom they have been working.

Sometimes a series of creative dance lessons will culminate in more formal performances where dances are shown to peers, parents, and other members of the school community. After these events it is useful for the teacher and students alike to assess what has been learned in the lesson series and how that was reflected in the performance. This can be done with discussion, journal writing, essays, or questionnaires. These summary evaluation procedures help all involved to digest the material and pave the way for the next steps in the creative dance program.

 # Box 13.4

Performance Objectives Assessment Tally Sheet

This model assesses each student on the material of one lesson (The Moving Body, Chapter 14). Words indicate skills being assessed. A key to the abbreviations and their meaning is provided. Use one box for each student, writing the name in by hand. Generally, twenty students' blocks will fit on one page.

Lesson: The Moving Body

Body:		Body:		Body:		Body:	
whole	Beat	whole	Beat	whole	Beat	whole	Beat
relax	Bubble	relax	Bubble	relax	Bubble	relax	Bubble
swing	Free	swing	Free	swing	Free	swing	Free
balance	Create	balance	Create	balance	Create	balance	Create
k sense	Focus	k sense	Focus	k sense	Focus	k sense	Focus
loco	Safe	loco	Safe	loco	Safe	loco	Safe
Scott		*Jesse*		*Kim*		*Max*	
Body:		Body:		Body:		Body:	
whole	Beat	whole	Beat	whole	Beat	whole	Beat
relax	Bubble	relax	Bubble	relax	Bubble	relax	Bubble
swing	Free	swing	Free	swing	Free	swing	Free
balance	Create	balance	Create	balance	Create	balance	Create
k sense	Focus	k sense	Focus	k sense	Focus	k sense	Focus
loco	Safe	loco	Safe	loco	Safe	loco	Safe
Lu		*Manuel*		*MaryBeth*		*Anne*	
Body:		Body:		Body:		Body:	
whole	Beat	whole	Beat	whole	Beat	whole	Beat
relax	Bubble	relax	Bubble	relax	Bubble	relax	Bubble
swing	Free	swing	Free	swing	Free	swing	Free
balance	Create	balance	Create	balance	Create	balance	Create
k sense	Focus	k sense	Focus	k sense	Focus	k sense	Focus
loco	Safe	loco	Safe	loco	Safe	loco	Safe
Linda		*Martin*		*Walter*		*Meg*	

Key for "The Moving Body" Tally Sheet

The tally sheet objectives used in this example are chosen from Appendix D, Creative Dance Performance Objectives. Mark a + on the tally sheet by the objectives that are demonstrated.

Body

whole = uses the whole body, including bending and twisting the torso, in movement; stretches fully

relax = is able to express relaxation while resting and in movement

swing = performs swinging movements easily, drops weight, releases knees

balance = balances on one foot

k sense = expresses awareness of movement feeling

loco = performs age-appropriate locomotor movements

Beat = maintains a steady beat in movement

Bubble = maintains personal space; does not bump into others

Free = moves without inhibition

Create = solves movement problems in unique and nonstereotypic ways; inspires new ideas through movement exploration

Focus = maintains concentration/focus both while moving and observing movement; moves without talking to other students

Safe = moves and stops easily and safely

 # Box 13.5

Self-Assessment Rubric

Name _____

Lesson: Interactive Forces

Directions: Circle the statement that describes your dance work today.

Did you move safely?	Yes, easily	Sometimes	No
Did you feel and show the difference between tight and loose?	Yes, easily	Sometimes	No
Did you lead your partner responsibly?	Yes, easily	Sometimes	No
Could your partner follow your directions?	Yes, easily	Sometimes	No
Did you let your partner move you?	Yes, easily	Sometimes	No
Did you rest very loosely at the end of class?	Yes, easily	A little	No

Comments/Likes and dislikes:

_____

_____

_____

adults. The lessons are carefully constructed in an effective format, but teachers should take the liberty of redesigning the lessons in ways that work for them. Lessons are written as complete progressions of study but can be broken up into smaller units done in sequence. We hope the variety of formats for creative problem solving presented in the lessons provides you with many avenues for developing your own lessons and lesson series—pouring your own specific content into the structures described.

CHAPTER 14

FOUNDATION LESSONS

THE MOVING BODY

The material in this lesson provides a foundation for the study of creative dance. Focusing on body parts and basic body movements, it awakens the kinesthetic sense through movement exploration. It offers the experience of using the body freely as an instrument of expression. The foundations for working safely in a movement class are established by addressing the concepts of personal space and shared space.

CONCEPT SPOTLIGHT 14.1

Lesson Concepts

Personal or self-space
Shared or general space
Body as an instrument of expression
Body parts
Basic body movements
   In place
   Place to place

Lesson Plan

Introducing the Kinesthetic Sense

In this class you are going to make up your own movements and pay attention to the feeling of those movements. Let's try a few movements to learn how to do that. Move your arms and hands with your eyes closed or lowered. Without looking, raise your hand, tighten it into a fist, shake it, bring it down slowly, and notice when it rests in your lap or to your side. Now open your eyes. How did you know what movements you just did? You *felt* them. The ability to feel these and all movements is the kinesthetic, or movement, sense at work. It involves making a connection from the brain to the muscles by way of the nerves. Attending to the feeling of a movement is one thing that separates creative dance from everyday movement. [*To cultivate this ability, periodically ask students to stop and feel what their bodies are doing. Lowered or closed eyes may help.*]

This dancer is paying attention to the feeling of the movement within self-space.

Introducing the Concept

When you stay in one place, your body takes up a certain amount of space. On that spot, you can touch the space all around you: down low, up high, in front, beside, behind. It forms a sort of "bubble" of space around you. This is self-space. Sometimes self-space is as big as your outermost reaches, and other times it shrinks and becomes small. [*Using all levels and directions, demonstrate the "bubble" by moving the arms to their farthest reach and filling the self-space with body movements using different body parts.*]

You can leave your spot and move through space to another place. In doing so you move through space that is shared by others, called the shared space. [*Demonstrate moving the self-space bubble through the shared space, looking for empty spaces to move into.*] When there is a lot of space, a person's bubble can be big; other times it will need to shrink to fit into more crowded areas. The idea is to not "pop" your bubble by running into something or someone. This way you do not bump, and together you can all move safely in the space you have.

Kinesthetic Tune-Up

Stand and scatter. Find an empty space where you are not touching anyone or anything. Spread out so that everyone has an equal amount of space.

Claiming Your Place   [*When the class is scattered equally through the space, direct them to do a movement, such as jumping up and down or tapping their foot on their spots, claiming their spaces with a unison statement such as "It's my spot!" or "This is a great spot!"*]

Feeling Movement in Different Body Parts   Sit on the floor with year eyes closed or lowered. Briefly but clearly move and then relax each body part: head, shoulders, arms, hands, spine, hips, legs, feet. Combine all. Relax.

Individual Exploration

Exploring the Self-Space Bubble   Use your hands to draw a space bubble around you in all directions. Push on its edges and come to standing to establish its largest size. Touch the outer edges of your own space bubble using all levels and directions. Move as if you are "painting" the space bubble. Paint the space above, below, in front, beside, behind, and all around you. Try this with other body parts such as your foot, head, elbow, or back.

[*Stop students occasionally in still shapes. Ask them to hold that shape and feel the sensations in the muscles that arise from that position of the body. Ask students to notice what parts of their body feel stretched, what parts are bending, and what the position is of their arms, legs, or torso.*]

Basic Body Movements in Place (Axial Movements)   [*Direct students to explore the following movements, emphasizing the feeling of each movement. Introduce each basic body movement separately, providing a clear starting and stopping signal. If time is limited, choose the movements marked with an asterisk.*]

Fill your bubble with movement as you explore many different ways to move:

Stretch*
Stretch and bend
Stretch and flop
Flop and drop
Twist*
Shake*
Shake and stop [*repeat several times on a signal*]
Toss arms and hands

Toss one leg at a time
Undulate or make waves
Bounce
Swing* (say "swing" as you drop into the movement)

Moving through Shared Space (Locomotor Movements)   [*Repeat demonstration of moving the self-space bubble through space. Encourage students to look for and move into the empty spaces. Introduce props such as carpet squares or plastic hoops, if you wish, to mark students' places.*]

Notice where your place is so you can come back to it.
Slowly leave your place and walk through the general space that you all share, keeping
     your self-space bubble around you. Do not let it pop by bumping into something
     or someone.
Return to your spot and hold a shape.
Now try walking at a faster pace.

[*Have students try different kinds of locomotor movements while traveling through general space. Choose from the following.*]

Walk (forward and backward, slow and fast)
Jog
Leap
Hop (up and down on one foot)
Jump (landing on two feet)
Gallop
Skip
Roll
Crawl

[*At first introduce these movements one at a time, returning to the same spot and holding a shape. Walking in different ways may be enough for a first lesson. With more experience, students can do locomotors in freely mixed combinations.*]

Culminating Forms
Choose any one of the following culminating forms.

Staying and Going   [*Divide the class into two groups scattered throughout the room. These groups can be designated with any names such as As and Bs.*]

One group moves through space with a selected loco-motor movement (such as walk, hop, or skip) while the other group holds a shape in place. The first group returns to their spots. Repeat, reversing roles.

Next the whole class alternates moving and staying. The pattern can be:

As go, Bs stay
Bs go, As stay
All go, All stay, All go, Freeze.

The dance may be repeated without coming back to an established spot.

Moving within a Time Pattern   Establish an amount of time in which to do a phrase of movements.

The walking students are looking for and moving into empty spaces.

[This can be marked by students chanting or counting, or the teacher can use a drum or clap to mark the beat. Introduce a beat pattern and repeat it several times without movement to ensure that everyone is familiar with the basic pattern. An eight-count phrase is easy because it is neither too long nor too short, and because music is often set in eight-beat phrases. However, any number of beats can be used.]

Build a progression from the basic phrase. For example, you may begin with a pattern such as this:

8 beats walking, 8 beats holding in place

Then add some of these variations:

8 beats walking, 8 beats shaking in place

8 beats walking forward, 8 beats holding
8 beats walking backward, 8 beats holding

8 beats walking, 8 beats holding in place
8 beats jumping through space, 8 beats holding in place

8 beats walking, 8 beats shaking in place
8 beats walking, 8 beats stretching in place

8 beats of any locomotor movement, 8 beats of any axial movement. *[This can be free choice or decided on by the class.]*

These structures may be repeated using different movements from this or subsequent lessons.

Building Vocabulary   Create a movement pattern using a time frame, such as the one in the previous study. Small groups of students perform this using movements of their choice while others watch. Then ask observers to name the movements they saw.

Skip Dance   Skip freely among each other in shared space. Once a beat has been established, briefly skip with each other as partners, connecting one or two hands, linking elbows, or just skipping next to or around each other without touching. Try to skip with many people, forming and leaving partnerships freely. Go back to your original spot to let the skipping come to a stop. (Adapted from Mettler's "Skip Social," in *Group Dance Improvisations,* 1975)

[Let students start skipping at their own pace. Have the dancers say "skip" as they skip. Observe the students to discover the pace that feels appropriate for the group. From that, establish a common skipping pace for the group by clapping or beating it on a drum.]

Sharing   Half the class at a time watches the others as they perform any of the dances previously described.

Closure
Choose one of the following movements to close the lesson.

Bit-by-bit relaxation and rounding the spine
Hook-up
Shake, fling, flop and drop
Standing calf stretches

Lesson Notes

- Organizing the basic movement material of this lesson depends on the needs of your students and the time available for the lesson. A very young group or a short time frame might warrant dividing the material into two lessons. On the other hand, adults or experienced groups might be able to explore all of these studies. We suggest you try our sequences and then vary them as you wish.
- To begin the study of dance, we use movement and body words rather than imagery. By not imposing images onto the movement, we allow students to have their own rich, broad dance experience. Following the lesson, imagery can be drawn from students by giving them an opportunity to speak and write about the images and associations that these movements evoke.
- The focus of this lesson is to have students freely explore and express the feeling of basic body movements rather than doing learned exercises or copying others. Therefore, move if you wish as you name the actions or body parts, but encourage students to find their own way of doing the movements.

Kinesthetic Tune-Up

- The structure of claiming a spot by saying "It's my spot!" (or a similar strategy for identifying each student's place) is an important management tool. It is a popular activity with teenagers and three-year-olds alike! It can become a familiar pattern in each lesson as a way to reestablish students in space. A physical place marker is especially helpful with very young children. Use a carpet square, a fabric loop, a small plastic hoop, or mark spots with a piece of masking tape or a removable sticker before the lesson begins.
- The study on tracing or "painting" the edges of the space bubble can be fruitfully repeated in many lessons.
- This lesson provides good material for enlivening the body, or "tuning it up" as an instrument. Variations can be done on a daily basis for 5 or 10 minutes at the beginning of the school day or to awaken the kinesthetic sense in subsequent dance lessons.

Exploration

- Barbara Mettler (1960/2006, chap. 1) developed this lesson's sequence of axial body movements as a good way to introduce movement exploration. Stretching, twisting, and undulating activate muscles. Flopping, dropping, shaking, and tossing are done for loosening. Flopping and dropping are sudden releases of body weight into gravity. The amount of release can be guided by the teacher, ranging from a single body part dropping, to releasing into a slump, to flopping all the way to the floor from standing. Bouncing is both exuberant and loosening and helps release the knees in preparation for swinging. Swinging requires both control and letting go. Students should be encouraged to exhale as they drop into the swinging and allow their knees to bounce. Working with these movements engages a full range of kinesthetic sensations.
- Students may need more structure than simply to stretch. You can add precision by combining body movements and body parts such as "Stretch your arms. Stretch your legs." You may even add the direction of the movement as in "Stretch your arms upward. Now stretch them to the side."
- Exhaling and making vocal sounds is a natural outgrowth of these movements. Flopping, shaking, and bouncing are especially evocative of vocal sound. By encouraging sounds with movement, you encourage freedom; however, the sound should not be allowed to dominate the movement. Another way to bring in sound is by having students say the word as they do the movement, capturing the feeling of the movement in the word. This is good for vocabulary development as

Lesson Plan

Introducing the Concept

Opposites naturally occur in the world, and also in movement. What are some examples of opposites? By exploring opposite qualities of movement, your bodies learn different ways to move. This expands your vocabulary for movement expression.

Kinesthetic Tune-Up

Sit in a clump or circle.

[*Have students use arms and hands to briefly express the following qualities. Do each a few times, perhaps with eyes closed or lowered to heighten awareness of the kinesthetic feeling of the movement.*]

Stop and Go

Begin with arms and hand in a still shape.
When I say "Go," move your hands and arms any way you want without touching
    each other.
When I say "Stop," be still.
The opposite of Stop is Go.

Slow and Fast

Move your hands and arms slowly.
Now move them fast.
The opposite of Slow is Fast.

Tight and Loose

Let the muscles in your hands and arms get tight and tighter.
Now let them go loose.
Tight and loose are opposites.

[*You may wish to continue this verbal reinforcement of sets of opposites throughout the lesson.*]

Individual Exploration

[*Ask students to slowly stand, scatter, and find empty spots. Alternate commands of "Go" and "Stop" several times as they do this. When the students are evenly scattered, conclude with "Stop." This will be their home base for the lesson.*]

Small and Large

Start in a small closed shape and create a small space bubble around you.
Gradually open to a large shape. Notice how the size of your space bubble changes as
    your shape grows.
Gradually close again to a small shape.
While in a small shape, make small movements.
While in a large shape, make large movements.
Changing from small to large can also be expressed as open and close, another
    set of opposites.

Open and Close

Close into a small shape.
Open into a large shape.
Open and close on a high level.
Open and close on a low level.
Repeat a few times at any level saying "open" and "close" as you move.

Staying with open and close, add the following opposites:

Slow and Fast

Open and close, slow
Open and close, fast

Staying with open and close, slow and fast, add:

Strong and Gentle

Open and close, strong and slow
Open and close, strong and fast
Open and close, gentle and slow
Open and close, gentle and fast [*This combination may require making the movement
        smaller.*]

Now mix qualities, for example:

Open, gentle and fast/Close, strong and slow
Open, gentle and slow/Close, strong and fast
Open, strong and fast/Close, gentle and slow

Staying and Going

[*Review how to move safely through general space by moving the self- space bubble into
        empty spaces without bumping.*]
Walk in place. Let's call this "staying."
Now walk through the room, looking for empty space to move into. Let's call
        this "going."
Repeat this a few times trying both forward and backward walks.

Continue with staying and going, and vary the walk with the following opposites:

Small steps staying/Small steps going
Large steps staying/Large steps going
Fast steps staying/Fast steps going
Slow steps staying/Slow steps going
Strong steps staying/Strong steps going
Gentle steps staying/Gentle steps going

Combining Qualities   Explore walking with combinations of qualities.

Slow and large
Fast and small
Fast and small and backward
Slow and strong
Fast and gentle
Slow and small and gentle

Other Opposites   If time permits, walk with other polarities.

High/low
Tight/loose
Smooth/jerky

Culminating Forms
Choose any one of the following culminating forms.

Share Your Quality   Students each choose a quality from the lesson to express with a
walk both in place and place to place. One or a few at a time, students take turns nam-
ing their qualities and showing their walks:

Dancers express opposite qualities of high and low in the Boys and Girls Opposites Dance.

Start in a shape.
Using the chosen quality, walk in place.
Walk through space.
Walk in place again.
Hold a shape to finish.

Boys and Girls Opposites Dance   Boys and girls move with opposite qualities from each other as directed.

Boys move slowly, girls move fast.
Girls do strong movements, boys do gentle movements.
Boys do another quality from list as directed, girls do the opposite.
Girls do another quality as directed, boys do the opposite.

Continue with four to five sets of opposites. This dance can be structured so that the two groups move either simultaneously or in alternation.

Partner Opposites   With a partner, pick a set of opposites to show in movement. One person moves with one quality while the other simultaneously moves in the opposite way. This study can also be done with both partners showing the same quality and then showing its opposite. Observe several of these studies and discuss the opposites you see.

Sequence of Qualities   Choose two sets of opposites (such as fast/slow, strong/gentle). Arrange these into a rhythmic sequence to dance. Example: slow, then strong, then fast, then gentle. Freely express the qualities, repeating the pattern several times. Begin and end the dance in stillness.

[*With less experienced students, this dance can be done by the whole group all at once. In more experienced groups, it can be practiced for showing by individuals or in small groups of two to four students.*]

Closure
Choose one of the following movements to close the lesson.

Bit-by-bit relaxation and rounding the spine
Hook-up
Tight and loose
Floppy test
Standing calf stretch

Lesson Notes

- Students and dancers at all levels benefit from and enjoy working with polarities. This lesson presents a very structured way for beginning dancers to explore opposites. Movements such as opening, closing, and walking provide a container that supports and frees movement expression for beginners. You can loosen these structures if your students are able to explore movement qualities without the focus of associating them with specific movements.
- This lesson gives an overview of material from all the elements of dance. Other foundation lessons delve more deeply into each element. Working with opposites is demanding emotionally as well as physically. Be sensitive to the age, experience, and endurance of the group in deciding how many polarities and variations on opening/closing and walking to present.
- How you introduce the concepts of this lesson depends on the age and sophistication of your students. Picture books about opposites are excellent starters for very young children who may have no idea what an opposite is. Tossing a coin and labeling the sides as "heads" and "tails" illustrates that opposites are different from each other but also related.

Kinesthetic Tune-Up

Scattering, claiming a place, and establishing a space bubble were introduced in The Moving Body. This spatial orientation needs to be reinforced throughout the course of study according to the class's needs.

Exploration

- Saying "open" and "close" while doing these movements gives students unifying sound cues and coordinates the breath with their actions. You may wish to have the class continue to say opposite words or vocalize movement qualities as they move.
- Some combinations of qualities with open and close are more natural to express than others. Unusual combinations can be a fun challenge for older students, but combining three variables may be too difficult for younger students. If this is the case, do not combine both force and time qualities with these actions; rather, work with the qualities one at a time.
- When working with slow movement, ask students to show the feeling of slowness in their movements rather than having them move as slowly as possible. In the same vein, tight movements do not have to be uncomfortably tight to express the feeling of tightness. Too tight or too slow movement is extremely limited and cramps the experience.

Walking variations

- There is a different feeling with each quality of walking. Dancers should be encouraged to express fully the differences in emotional tone between the different kinds of walking. Generally, the more qualities that are combined, the richer will be the emotional content. Sometimes images or characters will emerge from these objective movement directions. In fact, these movement skills will enable students to express a wide range of thematic material. The characters, images, and associations that emerge from students are fruitful material for writing and drawing follow-ups to this lesson.
- Walking fast means that the steps occur quickly, not that one travels a great distance. The structure we suggest helps make that point by having the students make fast steps while staying on one spot before they move fast through general space. Make sure students do not confuse moving fast with traveling a long way.
- Combining fast and backward walking is a good challenge for spatial awareness. Insist that students look over their shoulders to avoid collisions.

Culminating Forms

- As children mature they are more able and interested in practicing a study before showing it. Rehearsing, even briefly, requires a bit of independence. At the same time, it also builds independence. Use your knowledge of the class to decide whether to have students work on these culminating forms before showing the rest of the class. When sharing their walks, partner studies, or sequence of qualities, several students can show at once if some are too shy to show alone.
- In structuring the Boys and Girls Opposite Dance, the fact that the groups are divided into boys and girls can be looked upon as another set of polarities. This dance can also be done with the class divided into two groups by other criteria.
- Although it seems simple to move in an opposite way from others, it is actually very challenging. Students must maintain their own quality while being aware of the contrasting quality expressed by others they can see.

Follow-Up Activities

Language Arts

Use the following questions in group discussion, or ask students to write their comments in their journals.

- Name three sets of opposites you did today. Of these sets, which is your favorite quality or pair of opposites? What do you like about it (them)?
- Which quality or pair of opposites did you like least? Why?
- Was there a quality that was hard for you to express? Did you like it or not like it?
- Use some quality words from the lesson to describe something other than movement.
- Choose words that describe the feelings you had while doing the different qualities. Contrast opposite qualities.
- Write stories based on characters or images created by combining several qualities.

Visual Arts

Create abstract gesture drawings representing the opposites by moving crayon or chalk with different qualities on paper. Create a picture while moving the crayon slowly, and then create another picture while moving it fast. Make pictures with large drawing movements and small drawing movements. Choose colors that feel like those qualities.

Music

Listen to contrasting kinds of music and discuss the opposites you hear. Possibly arrange a sequence of short bits of music that could accompany an Opposites Dance.

Lesson Adaptations

Adjectives and Adverbs

This lesson is an excellent way to teach adverbs and adjectives. Identify the movement qualities as adjectives or adverbs, depending on whether you use the actions as nouns or verbs (a *slow* walk versus to walk *slowly*). To be used as adverbs, some of these opposites will need the suffix -ly added, others are both adjectives and adverbs. With some you may want to use a synonym (such as *forcefully* for *strong*) to aid with sentence fluency. Many basic body movements such as those in The Moving Body lesson can be used with the descriptors of this lesson. This can result in interesting, even paradoxical directives: flop slowly, wave quickly; make large shaking movements or small swings. After exploring the descriptors of this lesson, students can list other adverbs or adjectives evoked by their movement experiences:

Languidly, slothfully
Hurriedly, frantically
Vigorously, viciously
Delicately, lightly, lovingly
Reluctant, hesitant
Eager, willing
Haphazard, erratic
Gigantic
Microscopic

Texture descriptors such as prickly, silky, muddy, rough, fluffy, and hard or emotional descriptors such as loving, angry, frustrated, sorrowful, and peaceful are especially evocative for movement.

Use the exploration and culminating form structures of this lesson with these or similar words. As a way to culminate this study, you may want to have some students show a favorite quality and have the class analyze their movement in terms of how the word's quality combines force, time, and space attributes. Once they are familiar with strong/gentle, slow/fast, large/small, and so forth, students can readily identify those qualities in movements they observe.

Synonyms and Antonyms

Rhythmic Opposites focuses on antonyms. After working with the material of this lesson, have students generate other opposites and explore them using the formats of this lesson. To work with synonyms, have students brainstorm words similar in meaning to the movement concepts of this lesson. By exploring these words in movement, students may be able to identify subtly different shades of meaning between the synonyms.

For young children, Tana Hoban's *Exactly the Opposite* is a good companion book to extend this lesson (Appendix F). Show pictures and elicit sets of opposite descriptors, then show these in movement. The opposites in the book can be used as options for the Partner's Opposites Dance.

Varying Curricular Material

The basic structure of taking a verb and modifying it with different movement qualities can be used to have fun with stories and action-oriented topics. Here are three examples:

The Little Red Hen   The story of *The Little Red Hen* is one of an industrious hen who does all the work involved in making a loaf of bread, from planting, through cooking, and on to eating. Along the way, she asks for help but does not receive it from her lazy barnyard companions. A version of this story, *The Little Red Hen and the Ear of Wheat* by Mary Finch, extends the story, and the barnyard animals eventually learn to cooperate and work together to plant wheat and make bread (Appendix F).

For a lesson on this story, first list its major actions: plant, scratch, water, harvest, carry, grind, mix, knead, bake, eat. Explore each action with several movement descriptors: plant slowly, plant quickly; scratch gently, scratch forcefully; mix with small movements, mix with large movements; knead high, knead low. For additional variation, have students explore doing the movements with different body parts: plant with your head, grind with your elbows, knead with your feet. These can also be combined with movement qualities.

To conclude the lesson, work with any of the culminating forms from Rhythmic Opposites, using variations on the actions from the story. A satisfying yet simple way to pull together the lesson is to have students show their own unique variation on their favorite action from the story or create a series of variations based on a movement that the students especially enjoy.

Occupational Movements   The same strategy used for *The Little Red Hen* can be used to investigate and vary any occupational movements. If age appropriate, have students brainstorm actions for each occupation. There may be one characteristic action for an occupation or several. Here are some work movements that lend themselves well to different movement qualities. Some can also be done with different parts of the body:

- Construction: pound, saw, paint, scrape, twist (as with a screwdriver), lift, carry, push, pull
- Cowboys: ride (on a galloping horse), lasso, shovel (in the barn), milk (a cow), wrestle (calves to the ground)
- Gardening: hoe, dig, plant, weed, prune, harvest, water
- Work in a factory: single repetitive motion
- Craft making: pound, mold, paint, sew, weave, knit
- Office work: type, file, write, read, talk

In some occupations, such as office work, the actions may be small and subtle. These provide an interesting challenge for students to exaggerate and modify.

Sports Variations   Creating dances from sports movement is a good way to motivate reluctant students as they begin creative dance study. First, list movements from a specific sport and have the students explore them individually with movement quality variations.

Do the movement quickly and slowly, on straight and curved pathways, in its normal sequence and in reverse. Because many sports are done with a ball, the size and weight of imaginary balls can also vary. A pass or shot done with a heavy ball will require stronger movement, a light ball calls for gentle movement.

Once movement qualities have been established with these sports actions, explorations and culminations adapted from several other foundation lessons can be employed. See lesson adaptations for The Moving Body, Interactive Forces, Sensing Time Patterns, and Finding Unison for additional sports dance ideas.

INTERACTIVE FORCES

The goal of this lesson is to introduce the force element and build the foundation for improvisational group work. When moving within a group, one can take the position of active leader or assume a role as receptive follower. Both are valuable, even necessary, skills for life and cooperative work with others. One cannot always be the leader, nor is it wise to always be the follower. When there is no leader in a group, all members must take on both active and receptive roles. This lesson will help students learn how to be sensitive to the needs of a situation and to adapt their roles accordingly. If you teach young children and think this lesson may be too complex for them, consider teaching Strong and Gentle (Chapter 16) as a first force lesson.

CONCEPT SPOTLIGHT 14.3

Lesson Concepts

Tight and loose
Centers of gravity and levity
Strong and gentle
Activity and receptivity

Lesson Plan

Introducing the Concept

Today you are going to be working with movements that teach cooperation with others and responsibility in a group. [*Either now or at the end of the lesson, discuss situations where cooperation and responsibility are necessary.*] You will do some movements that are strong and some that are gentle, and you will practice skills of both leading and following. When working with each other, you'll use movement, not words, to communicate. Let's start by feeling the difference between tension and relaxation in our muscles. Being a leader with movement requires some tension, and being a follower requires relaxation.

Kinesthetic Tune-Up

Scatter, claim a spot, and establish a space bubble.

Stretching and Shaking   Briefly stretch in different directions, stretching all the parts of the body, then shake loosely.

A small group responds to the leader's active direction.

Alternating Tight and Loose   Begin to move and get tight all over so that you hold a tight shape with your whole body. Keep breathing and do not get so tight that it hurts. Feel it in your whole body. Let go, breathe out, and let gravity pull you downward as your muscles get loose. Stop in a loose position.

[*Direct students to alternate tight and loose positions several times. Vary how they change from tight to loose, choosing from gradually tight, suddenly tight, gradually loose, and suddenly loose. Encourage students to release down onto the floor, becoming as loose as possible to finish.*]

Moving with Sustained Looseness and Sustained Tightness   From a relaxed position lying down, gradually begin to move loosely with as little tension as possible. Roll to the side and loosely come up to sitting. Let everything be droopy and heavy. Loosely come to standing and begin walking. Your arms hang, your torso and head droop.

Now become tight. Move with a tight feeling. You can't go very fast because you are tight. Keep breathing. Feel the resistance in your muscles.

Now move loosely again. Find your spot and sink down onto it, resting completely loose.

Assisted Relaxation or Floppy Test   [*With a student, demonstrate the following way to help another feel looseness in the muscles. Then have the whole class try this activity in partners.*]

One person lies down on his or her back and relaxes as fully as possible. The relaxing person lets the helper support and move the arm without resistance. The assisting partner gently lifts the relaxed partner's arm, supporting it under the elbow and at the wrist. Move the arm slowly in circles, and bend and unbend the elbow. Sometimes jiggle the arm gently to help it feel loose. Carefully put the arm back down on the floor. Do not drop it. Repeat with the other arm. The helper may also loosen both arms at once by standing astride the resting person and picking up both arms at the wrist to gently jiggle them. Replace them carefully on the floor.

When finished, lie down near your partner but in your own space. Relax completely. Repeat the Floppy Test, switching roles.

Exploration

Cultivating Receptivity: Individually Moving with Looseness and Lightness   Come to a sitting position. Gently place your hands on the upper chest in the area of the sternum bone, upper ribs, and heart. Feel how your ribs rise and sink with your breath. This is the center of levity or lightness. Gently and lightly lift this area and let your hands fall loosely downward. Place your hands over the heart area again and repeat this rising up, but this time move as if you are being drawn up to standing. Move through the room lightly, yet loosely, with your arms relaxed downward. Move smoothly as if you were willingly being drawn along by something moving you. Return to your places.

Moving and Being Moved Guided Walk: Contact with Partners   [*To prepare for the guided walk, demonstrate with a volunteer how a leader can help a partner cultivate the feeling of receptivity by gently guiding him or her with touch. Show examples of both responsible and irresponsible ways of leading and following.*]

Leaders and followers both begin lying loosely. Leaders get up and help their partners, who remain loose and light, stand. Briefly the leaders gently move the followers' arms to check for looseness, and then they guide their partners on a walk through the room. Use two points of contact to guide the follower (for example, with hands at shoulder and elbow, or holding on to both hands or wrists). The points of contact can change during the walk. The leaders then help their partners back down to the floor, and join them, lying loosely.

- The element of trust is very important in group work. Before relaxing into a receptive role and letting themselves be moved by another, students must feel safe with their partners. The Floppy Test and Guided Walking help establish trust between partners. The leader must accept responsibility for the partner's safety by not moving too quickly, running into things or other people, and by stopping gently. In fact, the leader's focus needs to be "How can I help my partner have a pleasant time as I lead them?" rather than "What can I make my partner do?" If you detect an inability to demonstrate responsibility in a leader, it may be necessary to remove that student from the activity and ask him or her to watch how others show responsible leadership.
- When doing the Guided Walk with Contact, you may wish to have followers experiment with closing their eyes when being led versus having their eyes open enough to be able to see. It is easier for some people to give up control with their eyes closed; for others it's easier if they have the security of being able to see. When doing the Guided walk without Contact, the follower's eyes need to stay open to see the leader's directions. Here the eyes should be slightly lowered and relaxed to aid the follower in expressing receptivity.
- The leaders' and followers' movements are different and express very different feelings. The follower is loose and light, whereas the leader needs some tension and forcefulness to actively affect the follower. Encourage students to feel and express these two different roles. This is not the same as mirroring a movement in which both partners try to do the same thing.
- If nonverbal leadership is unclear, the person being moved will not know how to move. This is a problem for the leader to solve by finding another way to express the message. If a follower is uncertain, he or she should move in the most responsive way possible, or not at all. Words are unnecessary.

Culminating Forms

- When Moving and Being Moved is done in larger groups, spatial formations can be developed more fully than is possible with just two people. The leader can spread the group out, bring it close together, have it move in a circle, or make part of the group rise and part sink.
- Although moving and being moved is a very basic skill, very young children—kindergarten and younger—will probably have more success with unison movement as their first group experience because mimicking others is a prime learning modality at this age. See the Finding Unison lesson (Chapter 14).

Follow-Up Activities

Language Arts

Use the following questions in group discussions, or ask students to write their comments in their journals.

- In the dance work today you danced in two different roles, active leader (moving) and receptive follower (being moved by someone else). What was challenging and satisfying, or what did you like and not like, about being in the leader and follower roles? Write some words that describe how each of these felt to you.
- Which did you prefer—active leadership or receptively being moved? Why?
- What are some situations in life when the skills of leading and following are needed?
- Write an observation from daily life that illustrates an active/receptive relationship.

- Using literature or other classroom materials, list verbs that imply active leadership or receptive follower roles. Teach/learn, request/comply, and toss/catch are some examples. List adjectives or adverbs that describe how these roles feel.

Drama

Create or select from literature a dramatic situation that represents an active/receptive relationship. Act it out.

Visual Arts

Draw pictures of partner or group studies showing Moving and Being Moved.

Express in color and abstract design the two contrasting qualities of active moving force versus receptive willingness to be moved.

Lesson Adaptations

Wind: Weather, Seasons, and Sailing

After working with moving and being moved in pure movement, apply these studies to demonstrations of cause and effect. This is easily applicable to lessons involving the wind. Wind is an active moving force that moves clouds, autumn leaves, and sailing ships—all of which move loosely and lightly. The active force of wind can move leaves as part of a lesson on autumn. Some dancers can represent the wind while others portray the objects being moved.

Political Forces

The studies in this lesson are about cooperative relationships between active and receptive forces. They can be used to demonstrate political situations where people willingly follow a leader. Conversely, the lesson studies can be adapted to less copasetic political interactions. These can include situations where two or more forces vie for influence over an electorate, where there is lack of leadership and the group is passive and without direction, where there is resistance to the leader's influence, or where the leadership is irresponsible such as in a malevolent dictatorship. In the latter scenario, students will need to keep their movements safe while expressing this potentially dangerous relationship. These studies can clarify political dynamics and lead to insightful discussions with older students.

Sports Interactions

Exploring movement themes based on interactive sports such as basketball draw on the skills learned in this lesson. To construct a lesson that will emphasize the responsive part of sport movements, prepare students with pure movement studies of tight/loose, forceful/forceless, and especially moving and being moved. Then vary the size, speed, and force of throwing, catching, shooting, and dribbling actions (as detailed in Rhythmic Opposites lesson adaptations).

Next, have students work in partners, passing an imaginary ball that changes size and weight. Partners must watch each other to see what size and shape of ball is being passed to know how to respond appropriately as they "catch" it. Actions need to be clear and qualities exaggerated to make this work. Another good partner study is for one to be the offensive player and the other to defend. The defender must modify his or her movements in accordance with the player with the imaginary ball. If the offensive player moves gently and in slow motion, so will the defender. In essence the offensive player is expressing activity while the defensive player is receptive.

LINES AND SHAPES IN SPACE

This lesson builds on the spatial awareness introduced in The Moving Body lesson. It acquaints students with the opposite qualities of curviness and straightness and asks them to use those qualities in personal and general space while moving along pathways and holding shapes. Awareness of visual design is heightened by focusing on the empty space created while the body holds a shape. Group designs are then made as students build Human Sculptures together.

CONCEPT SPOTLIGHT 14.4

Lesson Concepts

Moving on lines or pathways
Holding shapes
Straight and curved
Positive (filled) and negative (empty) space
Group body

Lesson Plan

Introducing the Concept

Lines and shapes in movement can be straight, curved, or a combination of the two. The skeleton gives the body its basic spatial design, so awareness of the shape and placement of the bones is a good way to prepare for space element studies.

[*To orient students to visual design, show pictures of straight and curved lines or have them point out straight and curved lines and shapes in the classroom. Show a skeleton. Have students point out curved and straight lines in the skeleton.*]

Kinesthetic Tune-Up

Stand, scatter, and claim a place.

Sensing the Bones   Take one hand and lightly run the fingers along the long straight bones of your arm. Close your eyes and sense the straightness as you trace the bones of one arm and then the other. Move the arm bones. Picture these bones as they fold and unfold at the joints. Close your eyes if you like when moving any of the bones to sense them more fully.

- Run the fingers along the long straight leg bones, tracing the line from hip to ankle. Move the bones of the legs. Picture the leg bones as they move.
- Curve the spine forward. Using the hands, feel the bumpy vertebrae and the curviness of the spine. Curve the spine in several different directions, sensing the bones.
- Lightly feel the rounded, curvy "container" bones: the skull, rib cage, and pelvis. Move those three bony structures in relation to each other. Let the spine curve when these parts are moved.

Individual Exploration
Straight Lines in Personal Space   [*Have students switch hands at any point.*]

With one hand and arm draw a straight line in the air downward to the floor (vertical).
Draw a straight line upward.
Make a straight line sideways, and to the other side (horizontal).
Trace a diagonal line from as high as you can reach to as low as you can reach and
    back up again. Repeat several times, and to the other side.
Draw a zig-zag line with the arm and hand.

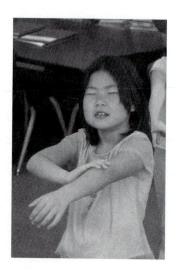

Feeling the bones helps create a kinesthetic base for the expression of shapes.

Use different body parts to draw zig-zag lines: feet, head, navel, back, elbows, nose, or
   chest. [*Elicit suggestions of body parts from students.*]

Straight Shapes
Make the shape of a single straight line with the body.
Try another way to make one straight line with the whole body.
Make a shape with one angle. This is a bent line.
Make shapes with the whole body that have many straight lines and angles. Try this at
   different levels.

Curved Lines in Personal Space
Draw curvy lines with the hand and arm, switching hands as needed.
Draw curved lines with different body parts. [*Elicit suggestions of body parts from students.*]

Curved Shapes
Make a curved shape with the whole body. Make sure the spine curves.
Make different curved shapes.
Explore shapes at different levels.

Shapes with Empty Space   [*Demonstrate with the help of a student volunteer how held
body shapes create empty spaces. There can be enclosed spaces ("holes") or open spaces within
and around the body's design. If desired, show sculptures or pictures of sculptures that have
both filled and empty spaces.*]

Make shapes with the whole body being aware of the empty spaces within them.
Make shapes with empty spaces that are closed.
Now open up those closed spaces.
Again, make shapes that have open and closed empty spaces.

Lines through Shared Space
Make straight pathways through general space holding the body in a straight shape as
   you move.
Travel along your own straight pathway, being aware of empty space.
Make one line at a time, stopping at the end and turning, then make another line. An
   angle is formed at the stopping point.

Make curved pathways through the room.
Curve the body's shape as you curve your
   pathway into empty spaces.

Partner Exploration
Human Sculptures   [*Demonstrate the following partner
studies with a student before the class tries them. As one
person makes and holds a shape, show how a partner can
fill some of the resultant empty space with his or her shape.*]

Alternate Shapes   [*Use a signal to indicate when students should change movement roles.*]
One person makes a shape and holds it. The second
   person makes a shape which relates to that
   shape. In this way the two people create one
   group shape.
While the second person holds a shape, the first

person carefully moves out of position and takes a new position, relating to the
partner's shape in a new way.

These dancers are relating to the empty
(negative) space in and around the
spatial design of their bodies.

Now the second person again moves and finds a shape in relation to the first partner. Partners continue alternating, holding a shape and finding a shape in relation to their partners.

Simultaneous Shapes

With a partner, find a shape together in which the shapes of the two bodies relate in some way to each other.
Pause in this form.
On a signal from the teacher, change shapes simultaneously.

Culminating Forms
Choose one or more of the following culminating forms.

Sculpture Garden

Partners make a shape in relation to each other.
One partner holds the shape while the other partner leaves and moves around the empty space of other human sculptures in the room.
Movers return to their own partner on a signal and make a shape with them.
Partners reverse roles. The partners who had stayed in a shape move around the room as their partners now hold shapes.
Finish with everyone back with their partners holding a shape together.

Human Sculpture Variations

- Show the human sculpture partner work to the rest of the class.
- Groups of three to five: First, have one person at a time change position. Do this several times. Then have all change together on a signal. Each group can show their study to the whole class.
- Large group: One person comes into the center of the room and makes a shape. One at a time, others add to that shape. Then all change shape at the same time on a signal. Repeat changing shape as a group several times. The whole class can do this at once, or half the class at a time can show their dance.

Closure
Choose one of the following movements to close the lesson.

Bit-by-bit relaxation and rounding the spine
Hook-up
Memory integration
Sitting stretches

Lesson Notes
Kinesthetic Tune-Up
Sensing the Bones   This space element lesson begins with the shape of bones because awareness of the skeleton provides a concrete experience of spatial form. Students enjoy locating different shaped bones on a model skeleton. Inexpensive skeletons that are accurate enough for this lesson are often sold as Halloween decorations.

Bones of the legs, toes, arms, and fingers are straight.
The skull, pelvis, and rib cage all form curved boney containers.
The small bones of the spine fit into each other in a curved stack, even though an upright spine can give the torso a straight feeling.
Arching or curling the spine in any direction will naturally form curved shapes.

Individual body shapes interrelate to create a group shape in Human Sculptures.

Exploration
Making Shapes

- Encourage students to close or lower their eyes when holding their shapes. This helps them to experience their design internally. Stopping and holding a shape is a good way to tune in to the kinesthetic sense during any lesson.
- Holding shapes with a straight feeling requires some tension in the muscles. Coach the students to feel that straightness in the whole body. Encourage students to make shapes at different levels and to find many ways of making shapes. At first they may find it difficult to find variations on a single straight line shape. With encouragement, however, some will soon discover that they can lie down in a straight line on their back, belly, or side.
- Curvy shapes have a different more fluid feeling than straight shapes. Emphasize the curve of the spine, and direct the students to change from shape to shape slowly.
- In the individual body, enclosed empty space is created by bringing two body parts together or by creating an empty space between parts of the body and the floor. Open empty space surrounds the body in any position. Some interesting open empty space designs are made by separating the parts of the body that created enclosed spaces.

Moving on Pathways through Space

- Young students enjoy the image of having paint on the bottom of their feet, which would leave a line on the floor.
- The limitations of maintaining a straight shape and walking on a straight pathway are fun and create a robotic image. Discuss with the class how to maintain a straight path and avoid bumping into others. This can be done by slowing down to let others pass, stopping, or possibly turning with a sharp angle and changing direction. Because they are making straight paths on the floor, curving around each other is not an option. Children and beginners tend to blur the sharp angles when doing zig-zag pathways. Make sure they stop fully before turning. Making a sound or saying "stop" and "turn" can clarify the angularity of their lines. You may want to direct students to each travel on a straight pathway, then stop and turn at the same time before freely moving in zig-zag lines on the floor.

Culminating Forms
Human Sculptures in Groups

- Great care must be taken in the group work to respect others' self-spaces. The space bubble needs to shrink in close to the body to allow getting very close to each other. The image of a "spacesuit" might be helpful here. The stationary person in the pair should make shapes that allow his or her partner to be safely successful. For example, a low shape is easy to move over; a wide high shape can be moved under; a small shape can be moved around; and a "holey" shape can be moved through, if only by an arm or leg.
- To maintain the spatial clarity of human sculptures, students should avoid leaning heavily on each other. Cue students to maintain empty spaces between themselves. Depending on your class's level of awareness, you may allow them to lightly connect with each other, or you may direct them to relate without touching.
- When creating individual shapes, dancers are aware of the design of their individual bodies. When making shapes in relation to each other, partners create a single design formed by both their bodies. They are then functioning as a group body rather than as separate individual bodies. This shift of focus is very important for group dancing.

- For a more complex culminating dance, the large group Human Sculptures Dance can be done with students numbered into grouping by counting off 1, 2, and 3. The whole group initially makes a shape together. Then direct each subgroup to change shapes in turn. You can regulate the amount of time it takes this way and gradually shorten the amount of time given to finding new shapes. Conclude by everyone changing shape on the same signal several times.
- After changing shapes as a group on your signal, the class may be ready for heightened concentration. If so, allow each group to sense their pauses together and to change positions with their own timing. This becomes more difficult as the size of the group increases.

Use of Sound

- Spatial studies have a clarity that is often very beautiful when done in complete silence. However, especially for beginners, some use of sound may be helpful. Saying the word "straight," "vertical," "horizontal," "zig-zag," or making a "straight" sounding vocal sound while making straight lines helps focus attention on that one movement and provides a simple musical accompaniment. Saying "curve," "round," or making a continuous "curvy" vowel sound enhances the curvy feeling of the movement.
- You can clap or use a drumbeat to signal the change from one straight shape to another. Changing from one curvy shape to another can be signaled by a triangle or bell. The quality of sound of these rhythm instruments supports the feeling of straight and curved.
- Ambient or flowing music without a prominent beat can enhance the performance of any of the culminating forms, especially the Sculpture Garden dance.

Follow-Up Activities

Language Arts

Use the following questions in group discussion, or ask students to write their comments in their journals.

- What kinds of lines and shapes did the class make today?
- How do curved movements feel different from straight movements? Find as many words or images as you can that describe the two different qualities. Which quality do you like better?
- Who was your partner for Human Sculptures? What did you have to do to make the Human Sculpture dances work well?
- If you made Human Sculptures in a group larger than two, how was that different from working just with a partner?

Visual Arts

- Create torn paper collages of shapes that relate to each other. Use black or other single solid color paper for abstract shapes and fill empty spaces with designs drawn with oil pastel, crayon, or colored chalk. This creates a bold representation of the Sculpture Garden Dance.
- Create paper, aluminum foil, or clay sculptures based on straight and curved lines. These may be abstract or representational.

Lesson Adaptations

Letter and Number Shapes

After working with straight and curved shapes, make shapes of letters and words with the body individually, in partners, or in small groups. Pay close attention to the correct differentiation of straight lines from curved. These spatial studies are great to use when students are first learning letters and number symbols, with phonics concepts, and with words from a spelling list.

Prepositions

Prepositional phrases in language represent spatial relationships that can be expressed in movement. This lesson's material can be steered toward language by developing the explorations with defined spatial relationships in mind. After tuning up by sensing the bones, individually use lines and shapes to explore the relationships of over, under, beside, around, and inside between parts of the body ("Make a shape with your hands over your head, then under"; "Draw lines around your torso, then beside your leg."). Saying the words while demonstrat-

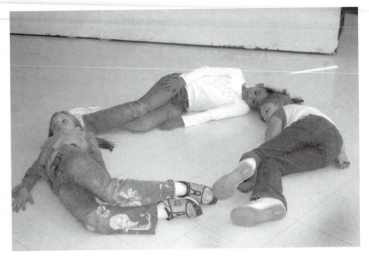

A small group cooperates in making a single letter *O*.

ing their meaning is super reinforcement for new language learners. Using the partner Human Sculptures skills, demonstrate these words: over, under, around, and through empty spaces in their shapes. These can be done with held shapes or with one person holding a shape and the other moving in relation to that person ("Move over your partner, then under." Reverse roles.). Use the same format as Human Sculptures with groups of three to five, keeping the focus on the stipulated spatial relationships. As the group holds their group shape, one person moves in relation to the whole group: beside, around, above, below, and so on. When movers finish their brief turn, they return to their place, and everyone changes to a new shape to hold while the next person moves. Continue until all have had a turn. This makes a nice culmination to share.

Cursive Writing

This lesson can emphasize curved line studies as a connection to cursive writing. Emphasize the smooth, continuous feeling of moving in curved pathways. When making Curved Lines in Personal Space, use the toes to draw curved lines on the floor. Try writing all the vowels using a different level or body part for each one. Say the vowel as you write it. As students move on Lines through Shared Space, encourage them to feel their bodies carving the space and banking inward. Suggest many variations on curved pathways, such as walking in small circles, moving backward, or putting two small circles together to form a figure 8. Finally, put lots of circles together, big ones and small ones, making continuous loops and curved pathways through the space. Finish the individual exploration by having students move along the pathway of a short word written in cursive. The word "it" makes a good study. Let individuals find their own unique ways of crossing "t"s and dotting "i"s.

Several culminating forms for a cursive lesson make lovely dances for sharing. Individuals can compose a Cursive Name Dance in which they write the letters of their name very big, as if the whole room were the paper. As a variation of Human Sculptures, with one person moving at a time, have groups choose a word that has as many letters as there are people. Each person will dance one letter. After working individually with their letters for a bit, arrange the group in order so that the word is danced sequentially. Each person takes his or her turn, then connects to the next person with a gentle touch, signaling the beginning of the next letter. A similar word study can be done by the whole class making up movements for one letter at a time and moving it together. Then combine all the letters to dance the whole word.

Curvy pathways with the arms are one part of the Cursive Name Dance.

Geometry

Lines and Angles   The beginning exploration on straight lines can easily teach geometry vocabulary such as vertical, horizontal, and diagonal lines by simply having students say those words while drawing them in the air. To make this a lesson on acute, obtuse, and right angles, have students draw and name those angles when making zig-zag lines and create those specific linear designs when making angular shapes with their bodies.

Perpendicular and Parallel Lines   After moving on straight line pathways through shared space, go a little further with the idea and create a Grid Dance. Embodying the concepts of perpendicular and parallel lines, everyone moves simultaneously on straight line pathways that form an imaginary grid on the floor, like graph paper or the tile lines in linoleum flooring. The dancers go as far as they can on one line. When they would bump into something, they stop and turn (90, 180, or 270 degrees) to go on another straight pathway. This can go on with interest for quite some time. Often all dancers end up walking the periphery of their squarish space, which makes a good ending for the dance. Many variations on this theme can be developed. Offer different locomotor movements for traveling, varied levels of movement, interesting movements to mark the turns, and so on. A fairly "square" metered (4/4 time) energetic piece of music works well if it is at a reasonable walking tempo. Do not, however, emphasize the need to mark time with steps. Keep the focus spatial.

Predator/Prey

The aggression inherent in expressing the relationship between predators such as meat eating dinosaurs, big cats, and praying mantises is most naturally aligned with the force element. However, some classes find it very hard to control their energy when working with predator/prey studies. Luckily the forcefulness of this theme can be tamed by using the space element. After basic work on making human sculptures, have students create shapes in partners with one taking the role of the predator, the other its prey. The predator takes an aggressive shape; the prey responds with a cowering one. Continue alternating shapes in this fashion several times, and then reverse roles. It is especially important to remind students to maintain empty space between them for this study.

Human Sculptures "Diorama"

Students can re-create scenes from historical events, ecosystems, literature, and so forth by becoming representational human sculptures as if they were in a diorama. The scene can evolve by having dancers simultaneously change shapes on a signal. The studies in this Lines and Shapes lesson prepare students for using their whole body to create shapes and hold them with full awareness of their position in space. Encourage use of different levels. Human dioramas are useful for classes that may be either too shy or too rambunctious to successfully enact scenes in free movement. This can also be a good step in increasing spatial interest when students are dramatizing stories.

Southwest Native American Pottery Design

Students gain a greater appreciation for prehistoric Southwest Native American pottery by dancing those designs in a lesson based on this study of lines and shapes in space. Byrd Baylor's *When Clay Sings* offers many abstract curvy and angular designs as well as pictures of stylized bugs, mountain lions, bears, fish, antelope, monsters, rabbits, and Kokopelli (the bent flute player) to show students (Appendix F). After reading and showing the book, the lesson begins with students "building a pot" (rather than a space bubble) on their spot. Following the model of the Lines and Shapes lesson, students "draw" straight and curved designs on their pot and make shapes as if on the surface of the pot. Some of these shapes are abstract designs; others represent the kinds of figures typically found on this pottery.

A wonderful dance is for dancers to make a shape as if on the pot and then let the designs come to life. The shape will leave the pot, dance through the room, and return to the pot. Challenge the students to maintain the character of the design as they travel and to return to the same shape at the end of the dance. This dance can also be done in partners, with the two dancers starting in related shapes on a pot, dancing away from the pot, and returning to the same relationship on the pot.

Southwest Native American music such as that composed and performed by R. Carlos Nakai is recommended. This lesson has been taught and favorably received in schools in the Navajo Nation.

SENSING TIME PATTERNS

Every action begins with a movement impulse. The use of time in creative dance refers most simply to awareness of when a movement impulse occurs. This is felt as the beat of a movement. The pace of movement is determined by the frequency of impulses, fast meaning that the impulses come close together, and slow meaning they come further apart. The arrangement of impulses determines the time pattern of movement. When fast and slow impulses are mixed together, they create an uneven time pattern. When the pace remains constant, the result is an even time pattern or steady beat. In this lesson vocal sound and clapping are used to mark the beat pattern of movement.

CONCEPT SPOTLIGHT 14.5

Lesson Concepts

Pace: fast and slow
Feeling the impulse as a beat
Beat patterns
     Mixed or uneven beat
     Steady or even beat

Lesson Plan

Introducing the Concept

When you dance, your movements create patterns of beats. Every beat marks the beginning of a new movement. It is fun to dance with music that has a beat; however, today we are going to feel the movement beats without the help of recorded music. Instead, you will move your bodies and mark the beat with your voice or clapping.

Clapping is a movement where you can hear the beats. Let's try some clapping movements. Now make those claps closer together. That is a fast beat pattern. Now try the opposite. Clap slowly. There is a long time between each clapping movement in a slow beat pattern.

Kinesthetic Tune-Up

Stand, scatter, and claim a spot. Before starting to work with beats, let's feel the difference between slow and fast.

Moving Slowly

Move your head slowly. Take lots of time, enjoy the slowness.
Move your shoulders slowly.
Move your arms slowly, very slowly.
Move your back slowly.
Now move your whole body slowly.

FINDING UNISON

Unison movement is group movement in which all the dancers simultaneously make the same movements, matching each other in their use of force, time, and space. Rather than strained togetherness, the goal is a feeling of unity, so that the whole group feels like its parts are moving "as one." This lesson builds skills for finding unison, beginning with individual exploration of organic forms in which one movement leads naturally to another. Organic form studies provide practice in letting movement evolve; this in turn helps students follow the natural flow of group unison movement. If you have limited time and wish to simplify the lesson, eliminate the Repeatable Pattern study in the individual exploration and end the group exploration after Exchanging and Letting Go of Leadership.

CONCEPT SPOTLIGHT 14.6

Lesson Concepts

Organic form
 One movement
 Creative pause
Repeatable pattern
Gradual/sudden
Unison
 Mirror relationship
 Circle form
Echo format

Lesson Plan

Introducing the Concept

Today we are going to work in groups and match each other's movements. Doing the same movement at the same time is called unison movement. [*Demonstrate unison movement by having students explore making the same movement with both arms. Both arms simultaneously rise, both sink. Both move apart and together, and so on.*] Here both arms are moving in unison. We can also match movements as an echo. To echo a movement means to watch and repeat the same movement after it has been completed. [*Demonstrate, and have students make a movement with one arm and then repeat (echo) that movement with the other arm.*] To build your feeling for matching movements, we'll start with some individual movements that will help you in your group work.

Kinesthetic Tune-Up

Stand, scatter, claim a place, define a space bubble.

Basic Body Movements

- Use your whole body to stretch. Then stretch and bend, twist, shake, undulate. [*Emphasize that each person makes these movements in their own way and tries different ways of doing them.*]
- Make swinging movements and say "swing" as you drop. [*At first direct students to swing in their own way, then ask them all to swing on the same beat.*] Swing from side to side with the whole class going in the same direction, saying "swing," and all dropping at the same time. This is matching each other in a unison swing.

Partners mirror each other's movements as exactly as they can, which requires clear leadership and attentive following skills.

Individual Exploration

One Movement at a Time

- Make one single movement and pause. Then make another movement. And another.
- Make a series of movements (four to ten) one movement at a time, with a pause between each movement. Let the feeling in your body tell you how to move next.

Gradual Movements   Make single gradual movements. Move continuously, and make sure there are no sudden changes in your movement. This will have a feeling of slow motion. [*If students need further coaching, direct them to gradually move their arms, bend in different directions, twist and untwist, rise and sink, walk in place.*]

Sudden Movements   Now move suddenly. You can move parts of your body or the whole body. Make a few sudden movements and pause. Then make some more.

Repeatable Patterns   Explore and create patterns of about one to four movements that can easily be repeated over and over. These movements can be gradual or sudden. Or make a pattern that combines both qualities.

Group Exploration

[*Before having the class try each of these studies, demonstrate them with a student volunteer. Discuss effective leading strategies, such as avoiding quick changes and turning away from the follower.*]

Partner Unison: Mirroring with a Leader   Partners begin standing, facing each other. The leader makes clear gradual movements. The follower moves simultaneously and matches the leader's movement as exactly as possible in a mirror relationship. That is, if the leader moves the right side, the followers move their left side; if the leader leans forward, followers lean forward; if the leader goes backward, the followers go backward. Both partners concentrate on making the same movement at the same time. Come to a stop. Switch roles.

Exchanging and Letting Go of Leadership   With the same partner, continue unison movement. Students reverse roles on a signal without stopping the dance. With each exchange of leadership, they are given a shorter and shorter time for leading. After a few minutes of exchanging leadership, both students let go of leadership and continue moving simultaneously in unison without a leader. They follow each other and the flow of the movement. [*Signal the change of roles with a predetermined sound, such as ringing a bell or triangle, or saying "change."*]

Partner Echoes   The leader makes a short movement pattern (approximately one to four movements). The follower watches and, after a brief pause (less than a second), repeats that movement, matching it as exactly as possible. The leader continues creating movements for the follower to echo until signaled to stop. Switch roles.

Finding Unison

- With the same partner, both students begin moving individually, making simple repeated movements. Soon they begin to watch each other and to modify what they are doing to be more like their partner. [*This can be thought of as putting their antennae out to receive information about the other's movement.*] Partners should not impose movements on one another. The unison pattern evolves by partners adapting their movements to each other.
- Once a repeating unison pattern has been established, the partners may gradually change the amount of force, the pace, size, or direction of the movement. Any changes must be done in unison, silently, without one person taking a leadership role.

Students pass leadership around the circle in this small group unison study.

[If desired, this lesson can focus on partner work. In that case, finish exploration here and culminate with Partner Showings.]

Small Group Unison Circles   In groups of four to six dancers, form a standing circle. Each person leads the circle in unison movement. The teacher signals when the leader is to stop and pass the leadership around the circle to the next person. There is a moment of pause between leaders, but the continuity of the dance is maintained throughout. *[Different leaders may be assigned specific structures. Leader 1: holding hands in a circle. Leader 2: Holding hands and making the circle turn. Leader 3: Choice of contact or no contact, circle expands and contracts. Leader 4: Choice of contact or no contact, circle rises and sinks. Leaders 5 and 6: Any gradual unison circle movement.]*

Culminating Forms

Choose one or more of the following culminating forms.

Partner Showings   Show unison movement in partners, half the class at a time. This can be done with leaders changing on the teacher's signal or as leaderless movement.

Small Group Showings   Allow small group circles to practice their unison movements and show them to the rest of the class.

Repeated Unison Patterns   Whole class or small groups assume circle or close scatter positions. One person at a time leads the group in a short, repeatable movement pattern. The leader begins the pattern, and the rest of the group joins in as soon as possible, repeating the same movement pattern in unison. To end each pattern, the leader senses the rhythm of the group and gradually directs the movement to come to an ending. There is a brief pause between one leader's movement pattern and the next. *[Depending on class time and the experience of the group, there can be one leader, several volunteers, or each member of the group may have a chance to lead. With less experienced groups, the exchange of leadership can be predetermined with numbers or by being called on by the teacher. More experienced groups can exchange leadership without prearrangement.]*

Leaderless Unison Circle   As a whole or small group, form a standing circle. Without a leader, the group moves in unison, making the circle rise and sink gradually. Dancers watch each other to stay together at the same level. Each individual's movement contributes to the form of the circle going up and down. Repeat rising and sinking as many times as feels appropriate. Finish after the sinking phrase.

   If the students can successfully rise and sink in unison, have them try expanding and contracting the circle in unison.

Closure

Choose one of the following movements to close the lesson.

Bit-by-bit relaxation
Rounding the spine
Hook-up
Sitting stretches
Shake, fling, flop and drop
Open and close whole body

Lesson Notes

Kinesthetic Tune-Up

Although this lesson emphasizes matching others' movements, it begins by encouraging students to freely explore basic body movements in their own way. This enables students to bring the richness of their individual movement imagination to the group work and also primes them to feel the difference between group movement and individual expression.

Exploration

Individual Exploration

• The direction to make one movement at a time means literally that—the result of one movement impulse as felt by the dancer. It does not mean to do one kind of movement over and over. It means one jump, one turn, one stretch, or one of any unnamable movement.

• Movements naturally occur one at a time, each movement giving birth to the next. Young children quite naturally let one movement follow another, letting the dictates of their kinesthetic sense guide them. Older students and adults may have lost the sense of letting the body lead and may intellectualize their movement choices rather than feel them. Making movement choices by tuning in to movement feeling and being guided by the natural sequence of movements results in organic dance forms. By preceding unison movement with work on organic form, all participants will be able to sense more clearly the movements that feel natural for the group. Briefly pausing between movements gives the dancer a moment to kinesthetically feel what the body wants to do next and can reinforce a sense for organic form. This pause is called the "creative pause." Practice moving and pausing as individuals will help students sense the pause within the group work of the lesson as leaders change or between echo movements. (See Chapter 5 for further discussion of organic dance forms and creative pause.)

Group Exploration

• Before young or inexperienced students begin their partner work, you may want to introduce the unison and echo formats by having the whole class mirror your movements in unison and also repeat your movements as an echo.

• When working in unison, the leader's job is to move in a way that the follower can easily match. This often means moving gradually without trying to surprise or test the follower. Another way to maintain unison is to make predictable movements, such as occur in a repeated pattern. If the pattern is predictable, the movements do not have to be gradual. All participants strive to make the unison so complete that an observer would not know who is leading.

• In partners, mirror relationships work best when dancers directly face each other. In this arrangement, it is natural to move in mirror fashion by kinesthetic feel rather than thinking about the relationship. If partners turn so that they are side by side, the mirror relationship is much harder to maintain, especially for young children. Sometimes it is best to direct students to stay facing each other to avoid this problem. Depending on your students' skill level, use your judgment on how rigorously to demand adherence to the mirror relationship in partners who move away from the facing position.

• The echo format has been used formally and informally for centuries as a versatile teaching method in movement, drama, singing, and speaking. To effectively work with an echo, the leader's pattern must be clear, simple, and short enough to be easily copied. In this lesson the echo format helps students discover short patterns that will be appropriate for repeated unison movement.

- Beginning individually and then adapting to a partner is a basic procedure used in dance improvisation for groups of any size. This process honors the individual's contribution as well as the need of dancers to receive information and respond to others.

Culminating Forms

- The basic movements of a circle are to rise and sink, expand and contract, and rotate. When moving in a group formation such as a circle, the movement of the circle itself is much more important than the movement of the individual bodies that comprise it. Encourage the leaders of the circle to explore these "circle movements" rather than emphasizing individual body movements of students who just happen to be standing in a circle.
- Progressing from partner mirroring to unison movement in a circle requires a shift in orientation. Dancers need to orient themselves to the movement of the circle rather than mirroring the leader. That is, if the leader is moving the circle to the right, all followers should move to the right. Students across from the leader may naturally want to mirror the leader, but if they did so, they would move left—causing a collision in the circle. Also, a follower standing near the leader may not be able to see the leader's movement. These dancers should look across the circle and match the movement of the group rather than turn their head to see the leader.
- When dancers are arranged in less formal relationships (such as scattered), the issue of which sides of the body are matching each other is no longer important. Dancers can simply copy each other without concern for "what foot" they are on.
- Moving in a clump or in scattered positions in unison provides an experience of flocking, schooling, or swarming. Dancers engage group skills shared with other social animals such as matching direction, speed, and spacing while traveling from place to place. A variation for exchanging leadership while in a "flock" is to follow the dancer who is the most easily visible. When the group changes the direction it faces, the dancer in the most prominent position takes over as leader without a break in the movement. This variation works best with experienced groups.
- Expanding and contracting a circle may present difficulties because moving toward the center is so compelling. Some students may rush to the middle, causing a congested and often unsafe clump. The circle form and the group feeling may be lost. If you choose to do circle expansion and contraction, coach your students to move gradually inward with awareness of each other. Slow motion is a good idea here. Holding hands (gently, without pulling) can help establish spacing, and combining contracting with rising sometimes helps to avoid breaking the form.
- In a study on leaderless movement, it is tempting for dancers to become impatient and just begin moving. Encourage students to truly be receptive and allow the movement to emerge from the group.
- Moving in unison requires that dancers blend individuality with the needs of the group. In return, they receive the communal benefits of being a part of a larger creation. The merits of and relationship between these two modes of operating will provide fruitful class discussion.

Follow-Up Activities

Language Arts
Use the following questions in group discussion, or ask students to write their comments in their journals.

- Is it easy or difficult for you to clearly feel one movement at a time? Explain.
- Who were your partners for unison movement?

- What did you have to do to lead effectively?
- What did you have to do to follow effectively?
- Were you and your partners able to move in unison without a leader?
- If so, how were you able to do that? What movements did you do?
- If not, what were the problems?
- How did circle unison movement feel the same as or different from partner unison?

Visual Arts

- Draw pictures of partners or circles moving in unison.
- Make bilateral symmetrical designs that represent the mirror relationship of partner unison movements.
- Make radially symmetrical circular designs to represent the circular unison forms. These visual art works will likely resemble mandala or kaleidoscope patterns.

"Ice-breaker" Unison at Tables is a great way to engage hesitant students in group movement.

Lesson Adaptations

"Ice-breaker" Unison at Tables

Unison movement can be adapted to a classroom setting with students sitting around tables. Begin with a brief tune-up of moving their heads, shoulders, torso, and arms while sitting. Then at each table have one person at a time lead their table's group in gradual unison movements. Most of these will be done sitting, but adventuresome leaders can experiment with the group standing and sitting in unison. Allow time for each person at a table to be the leader.

Next, choose one person to lead the whole class. The leader leads the movement, the class follows in unison, watching each other. Some students will have their backs to the leader; they will follow by watching whomever they can see. A fun variation on this idea is to choose a leader without the rest of the class knowing who was chosen. When finished, students guess who the leader was. This activity pulls a class together and makes a great "ice-breaker" and introduction for upper elementary and middle school students who may be hesitant about trying creative dance.

This variation on unison movement was taught to us by Margo Taylor.

Symmetry and Asymmetry

Unison movement in a mirror relationship produces bilateral symmetry, and circular unison creates radial symmetry. Therefore, unison studies can be used to teach symmetry. To adapt this lesson, first have students do a body parts kinesthetic tune-up. Have each student draw the line of symmetry along the vertical axis of the body. Students can then individually explore symmetrical movements by having both arms and legs match each other in movement. To explore asymmetrical movements, have them move their arms and legs differently from each other. Distinguishing between symmetrical and asymmetrical movements with an individual body often proves more difficult than one would expect. Challenge students to be clear in showing these opposites. For work in partners, have students draw a line of symmetry between partners and do the mirroring studies from this lesson. For asymmetry, cue your students to make different movements from those of their partners. Finish the lesson with symmetrical circle dances.

Your Own Folk Dance

Most folk dances exemplify unison movement and are bonding activities for a group of people. Your class can make up its own folk dance based on common threads among students. This may take several class sessions and can be worked nicely into a performance piece if desired.

First, establish skills for finding unison by teaching this lesson. Especially important will be the Finding Unison partner exploration study where dancers adapt to each other's movements to establish unison. Precede work on Your Own Folk Dance with a class discussion about things everyone has in common. These commonalties will later be translated into movement.

To create the folk dance, begin with a basic body movement tune-up and exploration in partners or small groups that reviews how to find unison without a leader. Students will use this method to arrive at movements for their folk dance. Assign each group one of the specific themes that unite the whole class. One group could find movements that express the geography or climate of the region. Another could express a local industry. Common activities (like sports) can be used as themes. Social values, such as freedom or helping others, could be expressed in movement. (Keep themes specific. For example, choose "mountains" or "desert" instead of "landforms.") In each group, dancers begin to improvise individually around the chosen theme. Very soon they tune in to the other movements being improvised and adapt their movements until all are doing the same movement. This movement then becomes a motif for the final dance.

As a whole class, discuss how the space element could be used to lay out the dance. Do students live in a crowded community or in a rural area? Can the spacing of students in the dance express this? (One class's dance began in a serpentine line that "picked up" each student on the "way to school.") Discuss the feeling or mood for the dance. Should it be energetic or calm? Should it be fast or slow? Are instruments or vocal sounds appropriate? These general qualities apply to the whole dance.

Decide on a logical order in which to sequence the movement motifs invented by small groups. Work out transitions between the parts, a general spatial pattern, and the underlying pace. Because folk dances often repeat themselves several times, decide if you want to organize the parts so that the ending feeds into the beginning. Keep the dance simple enough that it can be learned without much difficulty; the pleasure and point of the study is a unison group dance.

Sports, Occupational Movements, Vocabulary/Verbs

Unison partner and group studies can be integrated in the many foundation lesson adaptations that use action words from sports and occupations. Partners can mirror specified verbs from vocabulary lists, occupations, or sports. These named unison movements can also be done in circles and loosely formed groups with a leader. Using sports as an example, partners can find leaderless unison by beginning with a specific repeatable sports movement, such as kicking, swimming, or throwing. The partners adapt their movements to each other and create a unison version of that movement, which repeats. For larger groups, use the Repeated Unison Patterns structure and have leaders introduce a repeating sports movement that the rest of the group joins in together. (See lesson adaptations for The Moving Body, Rhythmic Opposites, and Sensing Time Patterns for explorations that lead to unison studies on these themes.)

CHAPTER 15

EXTENSION LESSONS FROM THE BODY ELEMENT

Lessons	Page
Pure Movement Lesson: Body Parts	213
Curricular Lesson: Spiders	216

PURE MOVEMENT LESSON: BODY PARTS

Body parts are used as the theme for dances in this lesson. Exploring body parts does not mean that the dancer isolates that single body part and ignores the rest of the body. It means that that part is the focus of the dance. The dancer's whole self is involved with full awareness of the whole body. Attaching parts of the body to one another changes the body instrument, creating new possibilities for movement forms.

CONCEPT SPOTLIGHT 15.1

Lesson Concepts

Body parts
Relating body parts
Leaderless group work
Group body

Lesson Plan

Introducing the Concept

Today's lesson focuses on the movement of different parts of the body in relation to each other. You will do this on your own and in groups. Pay close attention to your movement sense and how you move differently when different body parts are the emphasis of the dance. This will help you to discover new ways of moving.

Kinesthetic Tune-Up

Sit or stand, scattered. Move each part of the body separately: head, shoulders, trunk/spine, hips, legs/feet, arms/hands.

Individual Exploration

Move two parts of the body in relation to each other. Sense the whole body even though specified parts of the body are the main focus. [*Coach the students, if needed, that parts can move the same or differently; they can approach and separate, move around, over, or under each other.*]

Two hands
Two feet
Elbows and knees
Top of the spine and bottom of the spine
Any two parts

Connect two parts of the body. Let this new relationship guide your movement. Choose from the following:

Palm to palm
Hands on knees
Hands on head
Knees or feet together
Any connection

Group Exploration

Body Parts Relationships   Improvise in small groups on themes of the relationship of the following parts of the body. Use the whole body but emphasize and initiate movement with the specified body part. In this study there is no leader; all respond to the movement and how it is evolving. [*These studies are done with no contact between dancers. They can be done as duets, trios, or quartets. Begin the series with duets. Students can change partners after each study.*]

These girls are finding interesting ways to move together with hands connected.

Hands and arms
Heads
Feet and legs
Elbow and knees
One shoulder from each dancer

Body Parts Attached   [*The theme of these small group dances is how the group body can move as one connected unit rather than focusing on the point of contact between individuals.*]

Explore the group movements that naturally evolve with these limitations:

Head to head duet. Place heads together.
Hands attached duet. This study can be done with partners holding both hands crossed or uncrossed, or single hands attached (right to right hands or right to left hands).
Hands attached duet or trio, changing contact. Begin holding hands and exploring group movement. Hands can be released and reconnected as the movement dictates.
Feet attached duets or trios. Improvise with group members' feet connected.
The connection may change as the movement evolves. [*This is a very limiting structure.*]

Culminating Forms

Choose one or more of the following culminating forms.

Showings   Students show any of the previously described small group dances to the class.

Medium-Sized Groups   Groups of five to eight students improvise on any of the previously described themes. These can be shown to the class.

Whole Group, Together and Apart   Group members move among each other, leading with different parts of the body. As dancers pass each other, they gently and momentarily connect with an elbow, hand, knee, head, or foot and then disconnect and continue moving through the group, reconnecting briefly with others. The dance ends in a moment of stillness with all members connected with some point of contact. A variation is for dancers to say their name or another word at the moment of contact.

Closure
Choose one of the following movements to close the lesson.

Sitting stretches
Hook-up and rest

Hand-to-hand connection helps create a sense of moving as a group body.

Lesson Notes

- Working with body parts attached, both individually and in groups, creates new body configurations that have creative limitations. These limitations can help dancers find new ways of moving to meet the demands of that particular configuration. The studies of two or more dancers attached by hands, head, or feet give a strong experience of being part of a group body. The experience of being a group body can be extrapolated to functioning with a sense of group body even when not physically attached.

- This lesson can easily be divided into two lessons, using the same kinesthetic tune-up. One lesson covers the material without attaching parts of the body individually and in groups. The other lesson emphasizes the studies with body parts attached.

Lesson Adaptations

The Skeletal System
Introduce the lesson with a model skeleton, having students trace the bones of the body before moving each part. Use the anatomical names of the bones when working with each part of the body. Say the names of the bones being connected in the Whole Group, Together and Apart culminating form.

Prepositions
While moving body parts in relation to each other individually and in partners, have students say the prepositions that express that relationship. Partners may be saying different words: for example, as one moves hands and arms *over,* the other is moving *under.* See the lesson adaptation for Lines and Shapes in Space (Chapter 14) for additional dance work with prepositions.

Creatures, Nouns, and Fantasy Stories
When students connect two parts of the body together, they form a different body configuration, which can be viewed as a new and unique "creature." After individual body parts connected explorations, have students create unusual names (nouns) for their creatures and have the creatures dance together. Also, have students dance creatures that are formed by two or more dancers connected to become a single creature. As a follow-up, create fantasies about the adventures that these creatures encounter. This can be done orally as a group or as an individual writing assignment. A subsequent lesson can focus on dancing these adventures, working with the sounds the creatures make or even writing songs based on their adventures.

CURRICULAR LESSON: SPIDERS

Grounded in scientific observations of spiders, this lesson investigates the way spiders move their characteristic body parts. Spider web designs are explored and then combined with the spider movements in a logical sequence for the culminating dance.

CONCEPT SPOTLIGHT 15.2

Lesson Concepts

Characteristic spider movements
  Opening and closing
  Joint actions
  Crawling
  Multi-focused movements
  Swinging (re: swinging and ballooning)
Center of gravity (re: swinging and ballooning, the nursery web)
Center of levity (re: swinging and ballooning)
Group formations (re: the nursery web, partner spiders)

Lesson Plan

Introducing the Concept

[*Show pictures of spiders, drawing attention to their number of legs (eight), the way the legs have more joints than humans' legs, and the number of eyes they have (eight).*]

Spiders have bodies that are very different from human bodies. They have four times as many legs and eyes. To move, spiders stretch their legs out from the center of their bodies. Spiders move delicately and quietly, either on the ground or on their webs. They also hold very still sometimes. Try to capture these qualities in your own movement.

Kinesthetic Tune-Up

- Lie on your back. Stretch and twist in any way.
- Still on your back, curl up with arms and legs pulled in close to the body. One limb at a time, extend the extremity away from the navel, or center of the body. Then curl it back in toward the body's center. Now move all of your arms and legs at the same time, feeling how they connect to the control coming from the center of the body around the navel.

Exploration
Delicate Wandering Spider Steps

- Now come to all fours. Lift the knees off the ground so that you use your hands and feet to bear weight. Use the same idea of moving the limbs out away from the center of the body as you slowly crawl through the space. Take your time and feel the joints of the limbs flexing and extending. Spread the limbs out before taking a step in any direction. Move from the center of the body and reach outward, staying low to the ground.
- Still on all fours, move your head to look around you in all directions as if you had many eyes. Use your spider crawl to move as if you were stepping on the tiny threads of a spider web. Place your hands and feet very carefully. Look all

around as you move. Keep your head moving, and do not stop to focus on a single point as you wander through space.

Swinging and Ballooning   [*These movements take a lot of space and may need to be done by only part of the class at a time.*]

- Spiders sometimes move through the air by hanging from a thread they have spun and letting the wind blow them to a new location. Stand up, giving yourself plenty of personal space. Let your knees bend slightly and begin to swing the arms and then the whole torso side to side or forward and back. Feel the control and balance coming from the center of gravity (abdominal area) while you let your arms and head swing freely. Stop.
- Keeping the knees loose, spin in place slowly, as if suspended by a thread attached to the upper chest (the center of levity or lightness). Now begin to move from that center of lightness. Gently, weightlessly, move as if you were sailing, floating, swinging, lifting, and turning through the air. Come to a stop (landing) on all fours. Curl up and rest.

The Nursery Web

- Scatter evenly through the space, but stay within reach of others. Start individually lying on the floor, curled up in a little ball, as if you were a spider egg. As you slowly "hatch" from your egg, spread your limbs out until you can touch the hands or feet of another person. Stop there, and wait until everyone has found a connection and you are all connected as one group. Spiders do this when they are very tiny because it stabilizes them until they are strong enough to move on their own.
- Stand up, again within reach of others. Can you find a way to connect two limbs (one arm and one leg, or two arms) to someone else? Stabilize your center of gravity to help you balance. Rest.

Building a Spider Web   Stand with plenty of space around you. Use your fingertips to draw connecting straight lines in the shape of the periphery of a spider web. Then draw criss-cross lines through the middle, like spokes of a wheel. When you are finished drawing the web, spread your arms and legs to form the shape of an *X* with your body. Hold still as if you were waiting in the middle of the web.

Culminating Forms
Spider Dance

- Dancers start as individuals, curled up like eggs. Slowly they begin to "hatch" and delicately crawl through space to lightly touch other "baby spiders." When all are crawling, they rise to a middle level and connect into the nursery web formation, at which point they must stop and be still.
- Starting with students on the periphery of the group, several at a time do ballooning movements (swinging, floating, turning) away from the center of the group. Continue until all students have moved out of their nursery web formation in this way. Each student does three ballooning sequences and then comes to a stop, resting in a new place, curled up on the floor. Then they stand up, spreading their limbs from their centers into an *X* shape. Hold the position until all students are in this shape.
- Now students draw their webs. When finished, they wait in the *X* shape for all to be done. Then, as if a fly got caught in the web, the "spiders" delicately crawl to their prey, wrap it up, and curl themselves up around it and rest. This marks the end of the dance.

Two people combine to make one "spider" with eight legs.

Partner Spiders   Create one spider with two people. This allows the dancers to represent a spider with eight legs. Allow any safe method of representing an eight-legged creature, which usually entails connecting or moving very close to each other in some way. Partners can try crawling, curling, and ballooning as one spider. One or more groups at a time show their spider dances to the class.

Closure

Choose one of the following movements to close the lesson.

Sitting leg stretches
Rest and floppy test

Lesson Notes

- Although the story line and imagery of the final dance add dramatic interest and connect parts of the lesson into a whole, the expression in the dance will be richer if pure movement exploration is emphasized early in the lesson. Keep the focus objective when introducing the movements. It is more important for students to experience the basic movements than to look like or act like spiders.

- If space is limited or the group is large, split into two groups at the end to watch half the class do the final spider dance.

- A fitting piece of music for the final dance is Eric Chapelle's song "Skippy" from his album *Contrast and Continuum: Music for Creative Dance, Volume 1*. It has a cheerfully loose and springy sound quality.

CHAPTER 16

EXTENSION LESSONS FROM THE FORCE ELEMENT

PURE MOVEMENT LESSON: STRONG AND GENTLE

Learning to control and form the way energy is expended while moving is one of the primary skills for expressive dancing. This lesson investigates the poles of expression ranging from using a lot of force in strong movements to using less force in delicate, gentle movements. In this lesson dancers also practice instrumental skills that support these movement expressions. The studies introduced here provide the basis for curriculum-related lessons where the force element dominates, such as dramatic expression and forces in nature.

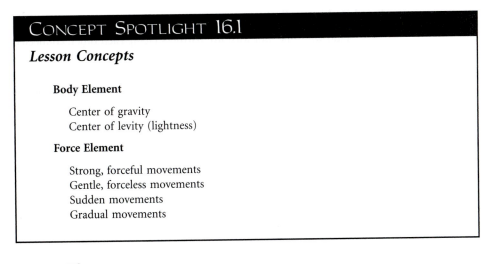

CONCEPT SPOTLIGHT 16.1

Lesson Concepts

Body Element

Center of gravity
Center of levity (lightness)

Force Element

Strong, forceful movements
Gentle, forceless movements
Sudden movements
Gradual movements

Lesson Plan

Introducing the Concept

Muscles make your body move. To make muscles work, you exert force. You can feel and control the amount of force by noticing the quality of your movements. Strong movements use a lot of force. When you use just a little energy, the movements are gentle.

Kinesthetic Tune-Up

Sit in a loose group or circle.

Gentle and Sudden Movements of the Lower Body

In place, move legs gently and suddenly.
Work to make no sound with the feet. [*This will have a prancing feeling.*]
Prance delicately from place to place.

Culminating Forms
Choose one or more of the following culminating forms.

Circle Push and Pull   In this study, the goal is to stay together as a group, matching each other's strength in pushing and pulling. It is a unison movement, meaning that all dancers do the same thing at the same time, with the same amount of force. Do not take steps forward and backward, simply shift weight as was done in the pushing and pulling explorations.

[*Direct students to use a lot of force or little force as they perform the following patterns.*]

Stand in a circle facing each other.
Working together as a group, use the arms and support of the full body to push
    toward the center of the circle.
Now reverse the motion by pulling away from the center of the circle.
Try strong pushing and pulling several times.
Do gentle pushing and pulling several times.

[*You may wish to mix strong and gentle pushing. Provide directives like these for your students.*]

Push strong; pull strong.
Push strong; pull gentle.
Push gentle; pull strong.
Push gentle; pull gentle.

Opposing Push and Pull: Partners

Stand facing your partner, a few feet apart.
Together and apart: Partners push toward each other and pull away from each other,
    saying "push" and "pull" as they perform the movements.
Back and forth: Without touching, one partner pulls as the other partner pushes.
Each person says "push" or "pull" when performing that movement.
Try these studies using a lot of force (strong) and a little force (gentle).

Opposing Push and Pull: Two Groups

Have two clumps or lines of people stand facing each other with several feet of space
    separating the two groups.
Try the together and apart, and back and forth studies as described for partners.
Work with the feeling of whole groups relating rather than working one person to
    another.
Try using a lot of force (strong) and a little force (gentle).

Line Push and Pull: Small Groups

Members of the group (three to five) stand in a line side by side, facing the same
    direction.
Together they move an imaginary wall or object across the floor, first pushing it
    forward, then pulling it back.
The amount of strength they use should be unified. For example, push forward and pull
    back strongly (as if moving a building, dump truck, or elephant) or push forward
    and pull back gently (as if moving feathers, cotton balls, or soap suds).

Line Push and Pull: One Long Line

Members of the class stand side by side, facing the same direction.

As in the partner study, the whole line works together to push and pull one imaginary
object across the floor and back.

Locomotor Sequence of Qualities Use the movement words from the lesson to make up
a sequence of locomotor movements that represent strong and gentle, sudden and sustained. After doing one movement for a short amount of time, freeze in a shape to stop.
Then proceed to the next movement in the sequence. Repeat the sequence several times.
Older students can eliminate the freeze.

Examples:

> Prance, freeze, stomp, freeze, push, freeze, float, freeze.
>
> Stomp, freeze, float, freeze, prance, freeze, push, freeze.

Group Improvisations: Strong and Gentle Qualities or Movements For students in
intermediate grades through adult, form groups of two to five people and assign themes
from this lesson with which to improvise together. Themes can include the following:

All strong
All gentle
Contrasting strong and gentle

While relating to your group, improvise with different movements:

Pushing
Stomping
Punching and stomping
Contrasting stomping and prancing
Contrasting floating and punching

[*Limit the number of themes assigned for each study according to the experience level of the
students.*]

Groups can show their improvisations to the class.

Closure

Choose one of the following movements to close the lesson.

Bit-by-bit relaxation
Floppy test

Lesson Notes

Center of Gravity

- The deep and subtle engagement of abdominal muscles is an important basic
  technique for proper body alignment, whole body connectedness, and
  instrumental support of forceful movements. To help students further tune in to this
  action, have them come onto their hands and knees, drop the navel down toward
  the floor, and arch the back. While exhaling, move the navel toward the spine,
  feeling the abdominal muscles retreat into the pelvic cavity. As the pelvis tilts, the
  back will naturally lengthen and then round. After repeating this a few times, find
  the position of the spine that is neither arched nor rounded, but long and neutrally
  aligned with the rest of the torso. In this position, with abdominals engaged, the
  body forms a solid tablelike structure with core support. The feeling in the belly can
  be described as a sense of hollowness, deep scooping, or internal lifting.

- The same awareness can be practiced while lying on the back with the knees bent up and feet planted on the floor under the sit bones. To find neutral alignment, engage the abdominals enough to press the small of the back into the floor. As the navel recedes, the belly sinks into a concave sensation and the tailbone reaches toward the heels. Once the kinesthetic image of the lower back pressing into the floor is sensed, it can be recalled in a vertical position. Frequent practice of this core awareness is recommended.
- Tilting the pelvis under while sitting, kneeling, or lying are exercises that help students experience abdominal contraction and reverse the overextended lumbar curve that is prominent in many people. In normal functioning, however, care should be taken not to grab the abdominals so much that the pelvis is locked into this "tucked" position and movement in the hip joint is restricted.

Equal Pushing   Be very clear that this is a cooperative, not a competitive, use of force. Because students get a chance to feel and express muscular resistance in equal pushing, this activity is an excellent study for expressing resistance in a healthy way.

Strong Movements

- Saying "push" and "pull" with strong movements helps dancers coordinate their breathing with the movement impulse.
- Emphasize that these are individual studies and that the strong movements are not to be directed toward others. Remind students to build space bubbles around themselves and to look for empty space when moving through general space.

Push and Pull Culminating Forms   For younger students, draw an imaginary wall between facing groups or partners to help them do the opposing push and pull studies without touching. It may be helpful in the partner study for the teacher to direct the amount of force to be used.

The one long line formation requires a large amount of space. The large group could be divided in two to create shorter lines, but the energy of the whole group working together makes a nice closure to the material of the lesson.

Lesson Adaptation

Fighting and Friendly

After exploring strong and gentle movements both gradually and suddenly, have students individually explore fighting movements such as punching, slashing, and kicking. Try these at normal speeds and then in slow motion. Students should be well scattered when doing these explorations to avoid collisions. In partners, students do a Fighting Dance expressing fighting movements without any physical contact. You may wish to call these studies Slow Motion Fighting if safety is an issue and also to turn the focus of this dance away from the personal. Previous experience with the Human Sculptures studies from Lines and Shapes in Space helps students establish interesting and safe spatial relationships in their "fighting." The Moving and Being Moved studies from Interactive Forces provide prior experience in responding to movement impulses of a partner. Some students may want to show their partner Fighting Dances. This can be done with the class sitting in a large circle and the students "fighting" in the center.

With the same partners the students then create Friendly Dances. Because most of the cooperative group work done in creative dance is inherently friendly, there are many ways to solve this problem. This open-endedness may be difficult for some students. You may cue them with suggestions such as light skipping around each other, moving while holding one or both hands, light floating together, or suggestions from the class.

To culminate the lesson, finish with a group Friendly Dance such as the Skip Dance (see The Moving Body, Chapter 14), where the whole group skips among each other with a common beat, briefly dancing with others and then going on to other group members. In this dance they may briefly join and release hands. The end of the dance can bring a return to their original partners, or the whole group may skip together in a circle with or without holding hands.

This lesson can be part of class work on learning how to get along with others, using dance to express or release negative feelings in a nonthreatening way. It is based on Mettler's Fighting and Friendly Dance studies in *Group Dance Improvisations* (1975).

In the dramatized Fighting Dance, partners use forceful movements with no physical contact. The "crowd" cheers the "fighters" on.

CURRICULAR LESSON: RAIN DANCE

The lesson develops awareness and control of changing force patterns in movement. Gradual changes in force and time, contrasted with sudden forceful movements, are used to create dynamic patterns in a group dance in which the amount of energy begins slowly and gently, builds to strong and fast, and returns to slow and gentle. These force and time qualities are related to parts of weather that contribute to a rainstorm. The lesson works with the development of a story with a beginning, middle, and end, which is demonstrated by the sequence of the culminating dance.

It is assumed that students have explored the concepts of activity and receptivity (or passivity) as introduced in Interactive Forces (Chapter 14).

CONCEPT SPOTLIGHT 16.2

Lesson Concepts

Combining elements
Dynamic qualities
    Strong/gentle
    Sudden/gradual
Pace: acceleration/deceleration
Group work
    Activity/receptivity (passivity)
    Group spatial forms
    Complementary form
Sequencing a story
Weather

Lesson Plan

Introducing the Concept

Today you will explore the changing relationship between the parts of a storm. You will finish by dancing a story of a rainstorm. Most forces of nature operate at levels of energy that do not remain constant; they change either suddenly or gradually. A rainstorm builds gradually with wind moving clouds and may climax with sudden bursts of thunder and lightning. Before getting up to move, let's investigate gradual changes with clapping.

[*It is helpful to use a drum throughout this lesson, particularly in the beginning, to demonstrate the gradual changes in the amount of force and time used in the dance.*]

Clap along with a steady beat on the drum. Use the same amount of force (moderate) for each clap.
Repeat, making your claps gentle.
Now make them all strong.

This time, gradually change the amount of energy you use in the claps.
Start gentle, gradually get strong, and then gradually return to gentle.
Stay together as a group.

Repeat this activity, gradually changing the pace of the beats as well as the amount of force in the claps.
Start slow and gentle, gradually build to strong and fast.
Then return gradually to slow and gentle.

Kinesthetic Tune-Up

Scatter and claim a place.
Stretch, shake, stretch, then flop and drop, ending loosely lying on the floor.
From this loose position, very gradually become tight and hold a tight position.
Very gradually return to lying loosely.
Suddenly become tight, and suddenly loose.
Again gradually become tight, and very gradually return to looseness.

[*Emphasizing gradual changes of tension will prepare students for gradual changes within the rainstorm.*]

Individual Exploration

Moving with Gradual Changes of Force   Staying in one place, use the whole body to begin moving with a gentle amount of force. Gradually add strength to your movements until they are strong and forceful. Now decrease the amount of force gradually until you are moving gently again.

Different Aspects of a Storm   Explore the parts of the Rain Dance individually first.

- Wind: Wind represents the active force in this dance. Remember what it felt like to be the active moving force in Interactive Forces (Chapter 14). Begin to move gently, as if you were moving something very light such as airy clouds. Gradually increase the amount of force in your movement until you are moving forcefully as if pushing large and dense clouds. Now gradually decrease your use of force to return to gentle movement. Rest.
- Clouds: Move as if you were the cloud being moved, the passive force in the dance. Express the size, shape, and density of clouds. Start with a light, gentle feeling. Build your energy to express a large, dense mass. Return gradually to being moved easily. Rest.
- Rain: Express the feeling of light rain. Now gradually increase the force and pace of your beats until you are expressing the feeling of hard, fast rain. Now gradually slow down your beats and return to light, diminishing rain.

[It is helpful to offer words that inspire images of different kinds of rain: drips, sprinkles, light rain, showers, hard rain, or cats-and-dogs rain so that movements do not all look alike.]

- Thunder and lightning: Experiment with large, strong, sudden movements to represent thunder and lightning. These movements represent the climax in the middle of the dance. Pick three movements that you like and repeat those in a sequence. Rest. [*Remind students to be safe with these movements and not bump into others. It may be helpful to split the class into two groups to allow for more personal space.*]

- Rainbows and puddles: Explore movements and shapes that express the aftermath of a rainstorm: puddles and rainbows. After moving with qualities related to both of these, decide which you would like to use for your ending to the dance.

Small Group Exploration

Clouds   Form small groups of three to five people. Each group will represent a single cloud. Find a group shape showing that your group is one cloud. Move together as if you were being pushed by the wind: first, easily, showing the light fluffiness of a white cloud; then gradually with more tension and strength, expressing the ominous churning of a dark thunderhead. Then gradually return to more gentle movement.

Culminating Forms

Choose any one of the following culminating forms.

Small Group Rain Dance   In groups of five to seven, decide how you will tell the story of a rainstorm. You may all dance all the parts, or you can decide who will dance each part (wind, clouds, rain, thunder, and lightning). Use movements you created in the explorations. Decide how you will finish the dance either as individuals or as a group, or a combination of both (some form the rainbow, others are puddles). Share your dance with the class.

Large Group Rain Dance   Divide the class into groups that will represent the different parts of the storm. One group will be wind, another clouds, another rain, and yet another will be the thunder and lightning. All choose their own way to finish as either a rainbow or a puddle. Decide on the ending before the dance begins so that the dance has a clear ending form.

   The dance begins with the wind moving the clouds. Rain begins. As the intensity of the storm builds, this energy is expressed in the dancers' movements. At the height of the storm, those dancing the parts of thunder and lightning enter with their sequence of sudden strong movements (from the exploration). As they exit, the dancers reverse the intensity of their movements, gradually returning to slow and gentle. The dance ends with all dancers expressing either rainbows or puddles.

   The dance can be repeated with students choosing different parts to dance.

Closure

Bit-by-bit relaxation, including rounding the spine and melting into a "puddle" on the floor

Lesson Notes

- Imagery is a useful tool in developing movement ideas in this lesson. Even so, be sure to have students emphasize the *feeling* of the different parts. It may be

Strong, sudden movements express lightning at the climax of the Rain Dance.

(Show that the force used at the beginning of the eruption may be different from the way the material settles.)

[*After exploring these themes some students can show their studies. The rest of the class can notice and describe the force qualities used to express the different materials. That there can be a variety of ways to express these themes can also be highlighted.*]

Culminating Forms

Small Groups   In groups of four to six, students compose a dance sequence demonstrating formation of a volcano. Show the Volcano Dances to the class.

Large Group   Create a Group Volcano Dance using the same sequence as in the Volcano Movements exploration, with the dancers sensing themselves as a group. Beginning the earthquake in a close configuration will heighten this feeling. Assign students roles of which type of material to express, erupting from the volcano on a cue. Congeal into a volcano cone shape. This improvised dance works well with half the class performing and the other half watching as the audience.

Closure

Choose one of the following movements to close the lesson.

Memory integration
Lying or sitting hook-up

Lesson Notes

Other natural disasters can be studied with the same approach. Floods, tsunamis, earthquakes, tornadoes, hurricanes, avalanches, landslides, and forest or prairie fires can be analyzed by qualities of force. Then movement explorations can be sequenced in the same order as the disaster would occur. Pay special attention to the actions, the different materials involved, how they change, and the gradual or sudden buildup and release of energy in each case.

CURRICULAR LESSON: THE WATER CYCLE

In this lesson, students emphasize qualities of movement of parts of the water cycle (condensation, precipitation, saturation, and evaporation). It is helpful to identify these qualities in reference to polar opposites from the elements of dance, especially those that relate to the force element: tight or loose, strong or gentle, sudden or gradual, direct or scattered. Movement inquiries rooted in these basic qualities help students dance images of the water cycle, which are then sequenced into a dance.

CONCEPT SPOTLIGHT 16.4

Lesson Concepts

Contrasting qualities (re: parts of the water cycle)

Tight and loose
Strong and gentle
Sudden and gradual
Direct and scattered

Box 16.2

Parts of the Water Cycle with Descriptive Word Lists

Condensation
Cloud: thick, light to heavy; rise, congeal, float, roll
Fog: low, gray, dense, opaque; linger, hover, engulf, shroud

Precipitation
Snow: gentle, delicate, unique, six-pointed, scattered; float, drift, twirl
Rain: gentle to strong; drip, shower, fall, lash, splatter, plop, drizzle
Sleet: direct, strong; pelter, pierce
Hail: cold, round, layered, hard; rise and fall, freeze, pound, bounce

Saturation
Melting ice: gentle, gradual; shrink, disappear, droop, release
Streams: lively, bubbly, bumpy, swift; trickle, flow, bounce, ripple
Raging rivers: powerful, turbulent; shoot, push, cut
Waterfalls: direct, rough, fast, steep, foamy; tumble, fall, drop, careen
Lakes: calm, flat, level, expansive; shimmer, lap
Big rivers: wide, slow, strong, muddy; swirl, meander
Estuaries: slow, gradual, spread out; split, seep, spread
Ocean: heavy, powerful, vast, deep, repetitive; wave, shove, pull, splash, sparkle, ebb
    and flow

Evaporation
Mist: gentle, gradual, light; lift, float, diminish, lighten, disappear, attenuate

Lesson Plan

Introducing the Concept

[*The use of a visual aid showing the parts of the water cycle is helpful.*] Name the main parts of the water cycle (condensation, precipitation, saturation, and evaporation). Describe the parts in detail, telling what might be included in each part. [*Particularly elicit nouns along with the actions and qualities associated with them (as illustrated in Box 16.2). List ideas on the board, grouping ideas together for each part of the cycle.*]

Kinesthetic Tune-Up

Stand and scatter.
Make your whole body tight; hold the position.
Let your muscles release as you drop heavily
    into a loose position. Repeat.
Move with a feeling of tightness. Move loosely.
Move loosely down to the floor. Move loosely but
    easily on the floor, undulating and twisting the
    spine, rolling and slithering through space.

Individual Exploration
Polarities of Force Briefly contrast the following qualities, which are polar opposites from the force element.

These dancers portray ice gradually melting in the saturation phase of the water cycle.

Make strong, forceful movements. Feel the strength coming from the center of gravity as you push, lift, press, or punch.

Now make gentle, forceless movements. Lift from the center of levity as you float and flutter.

Make sudden movements. Try gradual, sustained movements.

Move with direct and pinpointed focus. Now move in a scattering manner.

Movement Words from the Water Cycle

- Select four or more words from the list generated about parts of the water cycle and explore each in movement. [*Be sure to choose at least one word from each part of the cycle.*] Try different movements to express verbs that describe actions from the water cycle. For each word selected, pay attention to the way you use force to express the term. [*Refer to Box 16.2 for suggestions of actions and qualities.*]
- From the improvisations, choose one movement to represent each water cycle word. [*Individuals can make their own movement choices, or the whole class can adopt the same movement.*] Do the movement several times until you know it well.
- Continue exploring words describing parts of the cycle, picking a single movement for each word.

Culminating Forms

Simple Sequenced Group Dance
After exploring many different words, select those you will use in your culminating dance and devote time to each key word. Choose at least one word for each part of the water cycle. After reviewing the movement choices, connect the movements together in order of their sequence in the cycle. First, do the movements for condensation, then move through precipitation, saturation, and, finally, evaporation. Find workable transitions from one movement to the next, changing the movements slightly if necessary. Establish beginning and ending shapes.

Dance the sequence you have established all together as one group.

Small Group Sequenced Dance

- Form four groups of dancers. Each group is assigned one part of the water cycle. Allow a few minutes for groups to decide how they will dance their part of the cycle using movements from the explorations. Each group should find a way to finish their part in a still shape that leads into the next group's movements.
- If the space is large, arrange the groups throughout the room in the order of the water cycle. All groups are ready to dance their part. Begin the dance with the condensation group. They dance their part of the cycle, then hold their finishing shapes until the next group begins to move, at which time the finished group quietly sits to watch the rest of the dance. The precipitation group comes second, saturation group comes third, and the evaporation group finishes the dance.

Small Group Water Cycles

- Groups of five to seven decide how they will dance the full water cycle. They may select words and movements from the explorations or vary these slightly. They can all dance the whole cycle, or they can assign parts to the dancers and have them relay their movements in sequence. Have clear beginning and ending shapes.
- Show the dances to the rest of the class.

Closure

Bit-by-bit relaxation (melting), followed by rounding the spine and resting on the floor

Lesson Notes

- The complexity to which you develop the material of this lesson can be adapted to your age group. For a simple version of the lesson, choose only four words, one for each part of the cycle. Students in third grade and up should be able to explore several words and put them into a sequence. The more details and parts that are added to the cycle, the more challenging the study will be. The words suggested help students be specific and clear with their creative explorations and economize the lesson's time, focus, and energy.

- To teach a sense of the cyclical nature of the water cycle or other natural systems, repeat the culminating dance two or three times without stopping in between.

- Student-created sounds can be added in a subsequent lesson. Students can make vocal sounds to go with their movements, or appropriate instruments can be chosen to support the qualities of each part. Many handheld instruments can produce sounds fitting to one part of the dance or another. Extending the lesson in this manner can segue nicely into musical studies. Refer to the Rain Dance in this chapter and the Pure Movement Lesson: Sound and Movement (Chapter 19) for more direction on using sound with movement studies.

- The list of words in Box 16.2 is an excellent example of using the linguistic analogy strategy to generate lesson material in terms of nouns, verbs, and descriptors. Examples of different aspects of each part of The Water Cycle are nouns; the descriptors and verbs provide movement cues to deepen and add detail to students' movement expression.

CHAPTER 17

EXTENSION LESSONS FROM THE TIME ELEMENT

PURE MOVEMENT LESSON: MEASURED TIME PATTERNS

In this lesson beats are divided to make measured time patterns, using vocal sound and clapping to mark those patterns. It builds on the material in Sensing Time Patterns (Chapter 14). For clarity, the material is presented here in two parts that can be taught as separate lessons. Part 1 covers even, steady time patterns; and Part 2 covers uneven, mixed time patterns. These concepts can also be taught in a single lesson if appropriate for the group.

Here are several strategies for marking or notating divided beat patterns:

- Use syllables developed from the traditional music of India to vocalize beat patterns.
- Use suggested English words that mark beats and note their pace.
- Represent subdivisions visually as parts of a circle.
- Mark beat patterns with dashes of relative length.

These simple techniques are helpful in clarifying concepts, and even young children can create interesting patterns. Yet they challenge students at any level.

Comprehending time patterns from written explanations takes focused attention. We recommend that you read the lesson notes and familiarize yourself with the strategies for making beat patterns before doing these studies on your own or with your students.

Lesson Plan Part 1: Even, Steady Time Patterns

Introducing the Concept

Today you will continue the work you started in the Sensing Time Patterns lesson (Chapter 14). Pay attention to the beat or impulse of the movement and mark when it occurs

CONCEPT SPOTLIGHT 17.1

Lesson Concepts

Even or steady/uneven or mixed pulse
Marking and measuring beats with sound
Dividing beats
Slow/fast or quick
Common pulse

with sound. In this lesson you will work with a steady pulse and divide beats to produce quicker series of beats.

Kinesthetic Tune-Up

Stand scattered or in a circle.

Stretch in any way. Make one stretch at a time, marking the impulse of the movement by saying "stretch." Then do four stretches in a row, saying "stretch" on each movement.

Twist. Repeat the same sequence as in stretching, saying "twist" on each movement.

Stretch and flop; exhale audibly on each flop.

Flop four times then stop, exhaling audibly on each flop. Repeat this movement phrase a few times, saying, "flop, flop, flop, flop, stop."

Bounce in place saying "bounce" on each movement. Then try the pattern "bounce, bounce, bounce, bounce, stop". Do this first in place, then from place to place.

Bouncy walk. Say "walk" on each step. The whole class walks with the same steady pace. Alternate in place with place to place movement.

Exploration

Sit on the floor or at desks.

Making Sounds with Hands   Explore different ways to make a sound with your hands, including tapping on different parts of the body or other surfaces. Use one hand or both hands and different parts of the hand. Individual students may show different ways of making sound with their hands.

Even, Steady Beat   [*This exploration is described using the syllable system from India. English alternatives are placed in parenthesis. (See figures 17.1 and 17.2.) In all of these studies, the class as a group will keep the same beat.*]

[*Show a whole circle marked Ta (Slow.) If also teaching notation, draw a long dash on the board.*]

Clap or tap on a surface with slow, steady beat. Say "Ta" (Slow) on each clap.

```
Subdividing a Steady Pulse

Steady underlying beat


____        ____        ____        ____

Ta          Ta          Ta          Ta
(or say "Slow" on each beat)

Dividing beats in half

__    __    __    __    __    __    __    __

ta-   ki    ta-   ki    ta-   ki    ta-   ki
(or say "quick" on each beat)

Dividing beats in quarters

_ _ _ _    _ _ _ _    _ _ _ _    _ _ _ _

ta- ki- di- ma  ta- ki- di- ma  ta- ki- di- ma  ta- ki- di- ma
(or say "very-quickly" to mark the four subdivisions of the beat)
```

FIGURE 17.1   *Subdividing a Steady Pulse.*

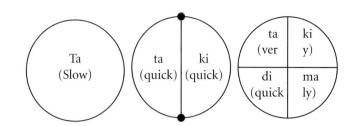

FIGURE 17.2   *Visual Aids for Subdividing Beats.*

[*Show a circle divided into halves marked with ta and ki (quick-quick). Draw two dashes below the first dash.*]
Clap at a pulse that divides the above beats in half. Say "ta-ki" (quick-quick) as you clap—one syllable per clap.
Return to clapping the slower pulse, saying "Ta" (Slow).
[*Show a circle divided into quarters with the sections marked with ta, ki, di, and ma (ve-ry quick-ly). Draw four short dashes on the board under the others. (See Figure 17.1)*]
Clap at a pulse that divides the first slow pulse into four equal parts. Say "ta-ki-di-ma" (very-quickly) one syllable per clap.

Marking the Beat with Movement   Stand scattered.
Repeat the "Ta," "ta-ki," and "ta-ki-di-ma," or "Slow," "quick-quick," and "very-quickly," sequences, making one movement on each syllable. Be sure to continue saying the syllables along with the movement. Use the whole body or parts of the body.

Stepping and clapping are movements that help students mark beat patterns.

Emphasize the bounce of the knees and stepping. Work with each pattern in place and traveling through the space.

Culminating Forms

Individual Showings   Individually show different ways to move using one of the uneven beat patterns explored.

Subdividing Circle Dance (Even Beat Pattern)   Divide the class into three groups.

Group A stands in a clump in the center.
Group B stands in a circle around Group A.
Group C forms an outer circle.

- Group A establishes a moderately slow, even pace, moving their whole bodies in place, marking the beat with "Ta" (Slow). [*Large whole body movements that alternate moving and pausing work well here.*]
- Group B moves in place, dividing the beat in half, saying "ta-ki" (quick-quick).
- Group C moves around in a circle with little steps, dividing the slow beat into fourths, saying "ta-ki-di-ma" (very-quickly). [*Smaller movements of the extremities are easier to do quickly than large position changes.*]
- Repeat this dance three times so that each group gets a chance to express each beat pattern. Groups should also change places when they change roles.

Lesson Plan Part 2: Uneven, Mixed Time Patterns

Introducing the Concept

Today we will continue to subdivide beats as in the previous lesson on Even Beat Patterns, but we will combine slow and fast beats to create uneven beat patterns that can repeat.

Kinesthetic Tune-Up

Stand scattered or in a circle.

Stretch in any way. Make one stretch at a time, marking the impulse of the movement
  saying "stretch." Then do four stretches in a row, saying "stretch" on each
  movement.

Twist. Repeat the same sequence as in stretching, saying "twist" on each movement.

Stretch and flop, exhale audibly on each flop.

Flop four times then stop, exhaling audibly on each flop. Repeat this movement phrase
  a few times, saying, "flop, flop, flop, flop, stop."

Bounce in place saying "bounce" on each movement. Then try the pattern "bounce,
  bounce, bounce, bounce, stop." Do this first in place and then from place to place.

Bouncy walk. Say "walk" on each step. The whole class walks with the same steady
  pace. Alternate in place with place to place movement.

Exploration

Briefly review the steady beat patterns and divisions in Part 1.

Uneven Patterns with a Steady Underlying Beat   Set a pattern that combines different
beat subdivisions to create uneven patterns that mix slow and fast paces within the structure of an underlying steady beat.

  A simple combination of slow and quick beats is a good pattern to start with:

"The Foxtrot"
(Slow, quick-quick)

Ta	ta-	ki
S	q	q

[*Have the whole class work on the beat patterns, progressing through the following steps:*]

Clap the pattern.

Explore the pattern in place, moving different parts of the body such as head, hips,
  elbows, or knees.

Move through space using the pattern forward, backward, on tiptoes, with big steps,
  with small steps, or combine big and small steps.

Explore your own way of moving with the uneven beat pattern.

Here are some other patterns to explore one at a time. [*These are offered as suggestions.*
Do not do too many patterns in one lesson.]

"The Tango"
(Slow, Slow, quick-quick, Slow)

Ta	Ta	ta-	ki	Ta
S	S	q	q	S

"The Magic Rhythm"
(Slow, Slow, quick-quick)

Ta	Ta	ta-	ki
S	S	q	q

"The Two-step"
(quick-quick, Slow)

ta-	ki	Ta
q	q	S

"Unnamed Pattern"
(very-quickly, Slow, Slow)

ta-	ki-	di-	ma	Ta	Ta
v	r	q	l	S	S

Partners or Trios

- In sound and movement, each group makes up an uneven beat pattern that can be repeated. If desired, name the pattern (see Lesson Notes) and make movements that reflect the pattern's name. Repeat the pattern over and over. The movements can change, but the pattern of beats should stay the same.
- Show the patterns. Possibly have the whole group echo the pattern.
- Or two groups can combine and teach each other their patterns. Combine the two patterns into a sequence that can be shown or taught to the whole class.

Whole Group: Uneven Jogging Dance   Stand in a circle. [*As an order for entering the dance, assign numbers to half of the class (or call the names of students to enter).*]

Number 1 enters first, moving on a clear uneven beat pattern such as ta-ki-di-ma Ta Ta). Students standing in the circle clap that pattern as accompaniment. Number 2 joins in, doing the same movement and time pattern. Then 3 enters, and so on until all numbered dancers are moving within the circle, weaving among each other, doing the same movement. Number 1 leaves the center when directed and joins the others in the clapping circle. Number 2 follows, then 3, and so on until all dancers are back standing in a circle. This is the end of the dance. Repeat this form with a different beat pattern so that all have a chance to move in the center.

Closure

Choose one of the following movements to close the lesson.

Standing calf stretches
Lying hook-up

Lesson Notes

- The importance of preceding this material with the foundation lesson Sensing Time Patterns (Chapter 14) cannot be overemphasized.
- Terms such as *beat*, *beat pattern*, *even*, and *uneven* have specific technical meanings within the context of this approach to time. These meanings may be different from how they are used in music instruction and everyday language. Refer to discussion in Chapter 6 for clarification of their meanings if necessary.
- Because time patterns do not require a lot of space, this lesson can easily be done in a classroom. Seated movements can be done at a desk, and the desk can be used like a drum. Because this movement material can be very stimulating, sitting provides a good container for students' attention. Also, half the students can clap or play drums or mark beats on their desks while the other half moves.

Kinesthetic Tune-Up

This series gets the whole body moving, coordinates the voice with the impulse, and establishes relaxation in the torso and legs, which is helpful for keeping a beat.

Exploration

- The lessons are written for dividing beats into halves and fourths. These patterns have a march feeling. You can use the same sequence to teach dividing beats into

Music Syllables from India	English Words	Symbol
1 beat Ta	Slow	S
2 beats ta-ki	quick-quick	qq
3 beats ta-ki-na		
4 beats ta-ki-di-ma	very-quickly	vrql
5 beats ta-ki ta-ki-na		
6 beats ta-ki-na ta-ki-na		
(or) ta-ki ta-ki-di-ma		
7 beats ta-ki-di-ma ta-ki-na		

FIGURE 17.3   *Vocalizing Beats.*

thirds and then into sixths (which have a swinging or waltz feeling). It is possible to teach patterns based on threes in the same lesson as the marchlike patterns, but tertiary patterns may be more clear if taught in a separate lesson emphasizing patterns that have a waltz feeling.

- The syllables used in this lesson are derived from Indian music and have been passed down through a long oral tradition. Therefore, you may come across variations in pronounciation and notation when using this subdividing technique. The Kodály method of teaching note values that is used in many music programs can be substituted for the words listed here. The point of the spoken syllables is to mark beat divisions. Any syllabic sound could be used—choose what works best for you.

- Marking the beat with vocal sound anchors students to the beat both audibly and with the breath. This can be done with counting or any spoken syllable. Different ways to divide an underlying beat and mark all the beats vocally are shown in Figure 17.3. Use any or all according to your needs. These words and notations can be used as outlined simply or in complicated patterns according to the age and experience level of the group.

- The image of the space bubble can reinforce the circle visual aid. When dividing the beats in half, students can draw a line through the center of their space bubbles, making the ta movement in one half of the circle and the ki movement in the other half. Similarly, the space bubble can be divided into quarters, and the students can make a movement in each quadrant when chanting "ta-ki-di-ma." (For example: arm, arm, leg, leg.)

- There are several ways to organize explorations of this material. You can have students learn subdividing first by having the whole group clap and then have the students move, as described in the lesson. Another method is to have half the students seated clapping to the Slow or Ta beat while the other half moves. Then reverse roles before dividing that beat in half (quick-quick or "ta-ki"). These choices of organization and pacing depend on your class's activity level and response to the material.

- As noted in the lesson, many of the uneven beat patterns are named rhythms from social dancing. Students enjoy knowing these names, and they also like to create their own names for these patterns and ones they invent.

- See the Curricular Lesson: Word Rhythms with African Animals (next lesson) for additional studies using syllables as a basis for time patterns.

Culminating Forms

For Subdividing Circle Dances, if there is not enough space to form three circles, groups can stand near each other and perform their respective roles. A clear spatial pattern helps distinguish each group's role and keep the groups organized.

Condensing the Pattern   Keeping the words in their one-, two-, three-, and four-syllable order, clap and say each word only *one* time. Repeat the sequence four times through, then stop. Stay together with voice and claps.

With Voice and Claps:

ape	zebra	elephant	rhinoceros
ape	zebra	elephant	rhinoceros
ape	zebra	elephant	rhinoceros
ape	zebra	elephant	rhinoceros

Review the movements that were just created for each word. Now put the movements into sequence, moving each *one* time. Repeat the sequence four times consecutively, saying the words while performing the movements.

With Voice and Movements:

ape	zebra	elephant	rhinoceros
ape	zebra	elephant	rhinoceros
ape	zebra	elephant	rhinoceros
ape	zebra	elephant	rhinoceros

Culminating Forms

Large Group Rhythmic Sequence   Mix up the words into a new pattern that does not follow the one-, two-, three-, four-syllable progression. Say and clap the new pattern several times to get familiar with it. Then say and clap the pattern four times through in unison.

With Voice and Claps (example only):

zebra	elephant	rhinoceros	ape
zebra	elephant	rhinoceros	ape
zebra	elephant	rhinoceros	ape
zebra	elephant	rhinoceros	ape

Add the movements. Say and move the pattern four times consecutively.

With Voice and Movements (example only):

zebra	elephant	rhinoceros	ape
zebra	elephant	rhinoceros	ape
zebra	elephant	rhinoceros	ape
zebra	elephant	rhinoceros	ape

[*The pattern can be changed and danced many times in the lesson period by rearranging the words. Follow the same procedure (voice and claps, then voice and movement) with each new pattern.*]

Small Group Rhythmic Sequence   Divide into small groups of three to five students.
Each group comes up with its own arrangement of the word pattern. Groups should be able to say and clap their pattern four times consecutively in unison. Then, using the same movements that were created by the whole class, add movements to the words and practice the sequence in unison several times.
Perform the small group dances for the rest of the class.

Closure

Choose one of the following movements to close the lesson.

Open and close, ending lying on the floor. Rest.
Standing calf stretches

Lesson Notes

- The Word Rhythms format can be used with any topic as long as you can find four words with the appropriate number of syllables. Here are some examples of words from other thematic topics:

  Seashore: whale, starfish, sea otter, anemone
  Insects: fly, inchworm, centipede, cecropia
  Fruits: pear, apple, raspberry, watermelon
  Birds: dove, peacock, whip-poor-will, golden eagle
  Farm sounds: moo, oink-oink, quack-quack-quack, pawk-pawk-pawk-pawk

- Traditional syllables used in drum music from India can be put into the sequencing structures of this lesson. These syllables (Ta, ta-ki, ta-ki-na, ta-ki-di-ma) were introduced in the lesson on Measured Time Patterns. They are spoken with a steady cadence and divide beats into equal parts.

- In the exploration, it is less challenging to say and move the sequence when the words are repeated four times because this establishes a strong memory of each pattern. For early learners, you may need to stay with this structure for the whole lesson. Older students will be able to make the shift to saying each word one time in the sequence.

- The repetitive nature of this patterning study is intentional. Repeating the beat patterns over and over (whether with claps, words, or movements) seats the pattern in the kinesthetic memory. With ample repetition, a movement pattern becomes easier to perform and to recall later. Soon it will feel like those movements were meant to go together! Give students plenty of time to repeat the patterns, especially their final arrangements, and particularly if they will be performed for an audience.

- Saying the words while creating or performing the movements is essential. The vocal sound regulates the time pattern of the movements. Because sound is heard, not seen, sound serves as a tool for maintaining unison among dancers even when they cannot see each other.

- For more experienced students, the structure could be changed to include the use of locomotor movements. In this case, assume a scatter formation rather than a circle. Be sure that the visual aids can be seen by all students. Hang them up if possible.

- To use in the small group culminating form, you may want to make a small set of cards for each group with the words written on them (use pictures for nonreaders). This visually reinforces manipulation of the pattern, making it easier to learn, change, and remember.

- To further develop this lesson, groups can teach their patterns to others. Then all small group patterns can be added together into a long sequence. It is amazing how quickly this can be mastered. It makes a good performance piece.

- Older students may prefer to make up new movements in their small group studies. This offers a great deal more freedom with the form. However, if the small group sequences are to be combined into one long composition, learning all the new movements can be very demanding and complex. Assess the capabilities of your class before offering this much freedom and challenge.

- Making music on hand drums adds excellent accompaniment to this lesson. If enough drums are available, let a small group of students play the beat patterns and accompany other dancers' movements. Hang the pictures so drummers can see the patterns they are to play. This addition may be worth a subsequent lesson.

CURRICULAR LESSON: MULTIPLICATION

Multiplication—based on recognizing equal sets of numbers—is taught by working with sets of an equal number of movements. The sets are measured by counting the beats of the movements and grouping them with accents. The number of beats (or counts) included in one set represents a factor in a multiplication problem. For example, if five beats are grouped into a set, this represents a factor of five. In five sets of five beats, twenty-five beats will be counted, representing the product of the multiplication problem. A variety of ways to demonstrate accents are explored. After individual and group explorations, small groups present a multiplication problem demonstrated in movement and share it with the rest of the class. When first teaching the lesson, we recommend following the progressions and procedures closely. The lesson progression carefully builds the concepts and the organizational details suggested help ensure a successful lesson.

CONCEPT SPOTLIGHT 17.3

Lesson Concepts

Tension/relaxation
Breath
Steady beat
Strong and gentle
Accent
Measured beat patterns (re: sets)
Unison

Lesson Plan

Introducing the Concept

Today you are going to study multiplication by marking the beat of movements, counting the beats, and grouping them into sets. You can define sets of beats by accenting the last beat in a series. After tuning up, you will explore ways to create accents in beat patterns.

Kinesthetic Tune-Up

Stand and scatter.
Stretch and then flop loosely.
Now start in a loose position and begin to move loosely and gently, with little tension in the muscles.
Rest.

Make a tight position suddenly, then suddenly release into a loose position.
Repeat several times beginning to coordinate your exhalation with the suddenly tight position.
Contract the abdominals as you suddenly exhale with a sound.
Continue until there is an audible sound on the tightening.
Rest.

Individual Exploration
Feeling Accents

Start by moving gently, with looseness. [*Accompany gentle movements with a gentle drum beat.*]
Every time you hear a strong drum beat, make a strong sudden movement (kick, stomp, pound, slash, or jump). Otherwise move loosely and gently. [*Accompany the strong movements with a strong beat on a drum.*]
Rest.

The strong movements stand out from the others. They are more noticeable than the gentle movements. They create accents in your movement patterns.

[*Throughout the rest of the lesson, play a drum to support students' marking of the beat.*]

Marking a Steady Beat

- Sit down, still scattered.
- Clap along with a steady beat. Stay together as a group, and make all the claps sound the same.
- Clap the beats strongly now by putting more force into the movement of the clap.
- Now clap the beats gently, using less force. Notice the difference between the feeling of gentle and strong claps.
- Stand up. As you clap the steady beat, let your feet mark the beat as well. You can stay in one place or move through the room. Step precisely on each beat. Stop clapping, but continue the steady beat with your feet. Stop.
- Repeat stepping on the beat, with no claps, but this time count your beats out loud in unison as a class. Count up to twenty beats, and stop precisely on count twenty. Pay attention so you stay together as a group. [*If necessary, repeat this until all students are stepping on the beat, counting out loud, and stopping on count twenty.*]

Creating Accents in Beat Patterns to Indicate Sets

[*Continue working with twenty beats, exploring different ways to group the beats into sets. You may want to assign one student the job of counting the number of sets created by the claps or accents.*]

Multiples of Two

- Repeat the stepping on the beat, but this time add a clap on every second beat. Continue to count out loud consecutively until you reach twenty, then stop. [*Claps will occur on counts 2, 4, 6, 8, 10, 12, 14, 16, 18, and 20.*] The accented beats mark multiples of two. How many times did you clap? [*10*] $2 \times 10 = 20$.
- Still working with multiples of two, instead of clapping on the accent, change your shape suddenly on every second count. Continue, counting to twenty, then stop.

Accented beats are expressed by strong movements that stand out from others.

Multiples of Four

- Create sets of four by clapping on every fourth beat until you reach twenty. [*Claps occur on counts 4, 8, 12, 16, and 20.*] How many times did you clap? [*5*] $4 \times 5 = 20$.
- Now instead of clapping, raise your arms overhead on multiples of four. Keep the accented movement sudden and strong so it is clear. (Lower arms on unaccented beats.)
- Try turning a sharp corner (changing your facing) on multiples of four. [*This may be clearer if students actually stop to change their facing on every fourth count and then continue to walk.*]
- Next change your level on multiples of four.

Multiples of Five

- Demonstrate multiples of five by touching the floor on every fifth beat. How many times did you touch the floor? [*4*] $5 \times 4 = 20$.
- Staying with multiples of five, show the accent in this different way. Hold still on unaccented beats, and move suddenly on the accented beat. Or move gently on the unaccented beats, and make a strong movement on the accented beat.

Multiples of Three

- Demonstrate multiples of three by jumping on every third count.
- Keep counting out loud and stop on twenty.
- Go.

[*Three does not go evenly into twenty, so there will be leftover beats in this problem. It is very common for students to add a beat on twenty-one because this feels right rhythmically. See if they can identify the "incomplete" set or point this out as an interesting variation of the problem: 3 × 6 = 18, which leaves two extra beats.*]

Large Group Exploration

- Stand in a large circle.
- Choose one number as a factor to work with. [*This factor should be small for less challenge. Factors over six are much more challenging in this study.*]
- Begin counting around the circle, saying only your own count. When a number is reached that is a multiple of the factor that has been chosen, sit down and hold your shape. As you count around the circle a second time, skip those who are seated. Continue counting until all students are seated. Notice the finishing number. This number represents the product of the factor multiplied by the number of students.

   Example: Choose a factor of five. Every fifth student will sit down. If there are twenty students in the class (this number represents the multiplier), the ending number (product) will be one hundred: 5 × 20 = 100.

- Try a different number as the factor and repeat the study. (The multiplier is again the number of students.)

[*This study can also be done with the class beginning seated and standing up on the factor.*]

Culminating Forms
Small Group Multiplication Problems

- Divide into groups of three to five. Provide each group with a complete multiplication problem.

   Example: 3 × 5 = 15. For simplicity and time saving, keep factors under ten.

- Each group creates unaccented and accented movements to define sets and express the completed problem. They may use movements suggested early in the lesson or find others. Unaccented movements should be expressed more gently than the accented beats, which are expressed more strongly. The group repeats their sequence of movements until the product is reached, at which point the movement stops.
   In the equation 3 × 5 = 15,   3 is the multiple that will be acccented
                                  × 5 is the number of sets they will do
                                  15 is the ending count
- Groups should practice their movements and counts until they can perform the whole problem in unison. Counting aloud (either by the dancers or the audience) will keep the problem clear. [*It is helpful to also have a "counter," a person who counts the number of sets as they are performed.*]
- Share the dances with the class. The problem can be identified either before or after it is performed. Clearly expressing the problem in movement is the goal, whether the class is "guessing" the problem or not.

[*For groups less experienced with multiplication, ask for three to five volunteers to improvise a multiplication fact for the rest of the class to observe. Assign the number of sets and repetitions and agree on the movement that will indicate the accent. Accompany their dance with the drum. Repeat until all who wish to show have had a turn.]*

Closure
Choose one of the following movements to close the lesson.

Rounding the spine
Bit-by-bit relaxation

Lesson Notes

- The lesson Strong and Gentle (Chapter 16) is a precurser to this lesson. Students should have a sense of the difference in the qualities of looseness and tightness in the muscles to support the clarity of accents in movement.
- For methods to learn and practice marking steady beat patterns, see Sensing Time Patterns (Chapter 14).
- Accompanying students with the beat of a drum (rather than just clapping with them) is very useful because it separates sound from the clapping movements that are used to show accents.
- Audible counting in the exploration is essential. It unifies dancers so that they are all counting at the same pace, enabling them to mark beats in synchrony with each other. This is very important for students to clearly express specific multiplication problems.
- In music, the accented beat marking a measure usually occurs at the beginning of the measure. For this lesson, however, the accent occurs at the end of the measure so that its emphasized "count" will mark a multiple of the factor being multiplied.
- If a student is assigned a job of counting sets, either for the whole group or in small groups, have the student count the number of accents visibly on his or her fingers. In this way the number of sets (or the multiplier) is very obvious.
- If necessary, you can insert a pause after the accented beat to provide more emphasis and allow students to complete the accented movement.
- The accented number can be shown in a variety of ways. It is important that the accented beat be demonstrated by a more noticeable movement—one that stands out from the other beats. This often requires an extra amount of force. In the small group problems, students can use accent movements from earlier in the class, or they can make up movements of their own. Opposites make good choices because they are clearly different such as small accented with large or low accented with high. See the Rhythmic Opposites lesson (Chapter 14) for sets of opposites that would work. Students will need to identify the more prominent quality of the two opposites.
- In the Small Group Multiplication Problems in culminating forms students may arrive at solutions using different movements than those explored earlier in the lesson. Sometimes a brief pause after the accented number helps students organize their forms. Also, students may move successively (one at a time) so that each student represents a set. As long as their dances express the problem clearly, accept their solutions.
- The large group study in a circle is easily convertible to a study in division. To make this change, count around the circle using a base number as the divisor until all students are down. When finished, the total number of students down would be the quotient, and the dividend would be the ending count. If the divisor is five and there are twenty students (quotient), the ending count (dividend) is one hundred: $100 \div 5 = 20$. When the last person goes down, ask students how many times the divisor went into the final number. See if they can figure out on their own that the quotient is the same as the number of students.

They will catch on to this "trick" quickly, so you can change the dividend (final count) to any number. Even though the answer will seem obvious (number of students down), it is a fun way to approach and reinforce division skills.

Lesson Adaptations

Rhythmic Accents

This lesson can be adapted to teach the concept of accents in a pure movement context instead of relating the idea to multiplication. To do this, tune up in the same way, but instead of relating to multiples of a number, use the number to define measures of beats (two-beat measure, four-beat measure, and so on). Once the measure has been established, you can change the placement of the accent to any beat in that measure, not just the last beat or those that are typically accented. These unusual accent placements create interesting syncopation. Be clear and consistent in marking the accented beat, repeating the pattern several times so students gain a sense of the pattern kinesthetically. For example, working with a four-beat measure, accent count one in clapping and in movement several times before moving the accent to a different beat. Perhaps even establish a form of repeating the pattern four times as a phrase.

It is helpful for students to have a visual sense of the pattern as well. You can write the pattern on the board, underlining the accented beat (1, 2, 3, **4**), (1, **2**, 3, 4), or use contrasting colored (e.g., light and dark) cards, one color representing unaccented beats, the other representing the accents (see Figure 17.4). Once the class has the idea, they can separate into small groups and create their own patterns, find movements to express the pattern, and share these with the rest of the class.

To keep the creative problems simple, stick with accents on the same beat of each measure in the pattern. For more complexity, add variations such as having two accents in the last measure of the four-measure phrase, which provides a feeling of completing a phrase, or sequence the movements of two or more patterns from small group studies.

Another way to vary the study is to divide the class in half and have one group move on unaccented beats, the other group move on accents.

Skip Counting

This lesson is adaptable to work with skip counting (by 2s, 3s, 4s, and 5s), which is a readiness skill for multiplication. Work with the same studies but eliminate counting the number of sets and working with multiplication facts. For young students, choose one kind of skip counting per lesson for students to explore.

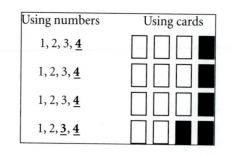

FIGURE 17.4   *Rhythmic Accents Forming a Four-Measure Phrase.*

CHAPTER 18

EXTENSION LESSONS FROM THE SPACE ELEMENT

PURE MOVEMENT LESSON: GROUP LINES

Working in a group as part of a line enables students to experience the unifying nature of a spatial form. Group lines demand very different kinds of participation from dancers depending on their placement in the line. Whether they are placed at the beginning, middle, or end, all line members are integral, needed parts of a whole. In preparation for group lines, students individually explore making many different kinds of pathways through space. The lesson explores many different kinds of group lines and culminates with showings or groups moving in relation to each other.

Lesson Plan

Introducing the Concept
Today you will draw lines through space as an individual (as done in Lines and Shapes in Space) and also as part of a group line. Many different kinds of lines will be explored.

[For young children use a chart with examples of different kinds of lines as listed in Concept Spotlight 18.1. You may also have pictures or a model of a skeleton in preparation for the kinesthetic tune-up.]

CONCEPT SPOTLIGHT 18.1

Lesson Concepts

Qualities of Line

Straight/curved
Long/short
High/low
Wavy/zig-zagged (angular)
Rough/smooth
Wide/narrow

Group Body

Line

In group lines, students experience the unifying nature of spatial forms.

Kinesthetic Tune-Up

Lie, sit, or stand scattered.

Move different parts of the body, noticing the bones that are being moved: skull, shoulder blades, arm bones, rib cage, pelvis, spine, leg bones.

Individual Exploration

Start lying, sitting, or standing.

Staying in place, draw lines through personal space with different parts of the body. Choose from these types of lines:

Long lines
Short lines
Straight lines
Zig-zagged lines
Curved lines
Wide lines
Narrow lines
Rough lines
Wavy or undulating lines
Low lines
High lines
Lines that change level

Moving through space, draw pathways with the whole body cutting through general space. [*Choose from the listed qualities of line.*]

Group Exploration

Forward Moving Unison Lines   Divide the class into groups of four to seven dancers lined up one behind the other. Each person in the group will have a chance to lead the line, which is assigned one of the following structures. After the first dancer in the line has had a chance to lead, he or she goes to the end of the line. [*Cue the leaders to move their lines slowly so the group can maintain uniformity of movement and its integrity as a line.*]

1. Connected, hands on shoulders of person in front of you, curved lines
2. Hands on waist of person in front of you, long lines and undulating lines
3. Holding hands, curved lines into and out of circles
4. No contact, wide and narrow lines
5. No contact, straight lines with sharp turns and angles; some short lines
6. Any contact with the line slowly changing levels
7. Any forward movement of a group line

Side-by-Side Unison Lines (optional)   In groups of three or four, line up side to side. A dancer in the middle will lead. Switch positions after each turn so that each person has a chance to be the leader from the middle of the line. The leader carefully leads the line through level changes, forward and backward, and sideward movements. Followers create unison movements with the leader by using their peripheral vision to sense the line's movement. If followers are not next to the leader, they watch the person standing next to them without turning their heads. [*Side-by-side unison line explorations are a challenging problem and best suited for experienced dancers.*]

Indiv
Defin
tions
dicula

 •

 •

 •

Plan

 •

 •

[*Use*

Doo

Tal

Culminating Forms
Choose any one of the following culminating forms.

Showing   Assign each group line a specific quality of line movement to show. The class observes and describes the lines (straight, curved, long, short, and so forth).

Group Line Relationships   Two or more lines move in relationship to each other through general space. Leaders guide their lines close to, far from, parallel or perpendicular to, higher or lower than, beside, in front of, or behind other lines.

Free Line Dance   Dancers begin moving individually, making lines through general space with awareness of their relationship to other dancers. As they wish, the dancers begin following others (to form forward moving lines) or stand near others (to form side-by-side lines). When dancers find themselves in leadership roles, they lead. When they find that they are part of a line behind others, they follow. Side-by-side lines move without a leader. At times lines may stop and hold a linear position. The lines can form and dissolve according to the evolution of the dance. [*This dance requires a measure of experience, maturity, and control.*]

Closure
Choose one of the following movements to close the lesson.

Open and close whole body, ending closed on floor
Sitting or lying stretches

Lesson Notes
The seemingly simple task of creating line dances is often difficult for dancers not familiar with group dance improvisation, in part, because it is so simple. Leaders often try to do movements that are much too complicated for a line to perform. The followers' roles in a line require willingness to give up individually complicated movements for the sake of clarity of the group form. Children often sense how to do this more easily than adults. However, once a group of dancers is committed to working with line forms, beautiful configurations such as those seen in line-based folk dancing can evolve through improvisation without any verbal discussion.

Follow-Up Activities
Visual Arts
Draw or make collages using only linear forms.

Lesson Adaptation
Geometry
Using the movement structures of this lesson, students can draw specified lines with their bodies that relate to geometry vocabulary: vertical, horizontal, diagonal, intersecting lines, specified angles, as well as specific geometric shapes such as triangle, square, rectangle, trapezoid, parallelogram, hexagon, and circle. These can be done in the air or on the floor in personal space or through general space. Group lines can also draw geometric figures. Classes new to working with space may find it difficult to draw straight pathways with the sharp corners required to show geometric forms such as squares or hexagons. An alternative to making geometric shapes with the movement of group lines is to have the whole class nonverbally form group shapes of specified geometric shapes—square, triangle, rhombus, and so forth.

This pair is expressing the sagittal or wheel plane.

Wheel Plane

- A sagittal pull combined with a vertical pull creates a plane that resembles a wheel. Make your body into a vertical line. Extend one or both arms on a sagittal (forward/back) line of direction. This creates a shape that expresses the wheel plane. Make an *X* shape on the wheel plane. To do this, step one foot forward on the sagittal line. Raise the opposite arm forward and raise the other arm back. Move your shape in a swinging motion back and forth on the surface of the plane. This will resemble the action of a rocking wheel.
- Again, move into two other shapes that express the wheel plane, pausing briefly in each, then continue back to the original *X* shape.

[*These body-oriented planes have been described and explored while standing. If students lie down and perform the same movements, they will continue to move in the door, table, and wheel planes because the plane is defined in terms of anatomical body movement, not in terms of its spatial placement.*]

Planes in Relation to the Space
Vertical Plane

- By establishing vertical and horizontal direction pulls, create a standing plane that is parallel to the front of the room. Move in this narrow area in any facing you wish (facing forward, sideward, or to the back of the room). The position of your body movements will change if you face different directions, but the plane in relation to the room will remain the same. Extend the area of the plane by traveling through general space along it.

Horizontal Plane

- Create a low-level horizontal plane by lying in a straight line parallel to the front of the room. You may be on your front, back, or side. This creates a side-to-side directional pull. Extend limbs toward the front and back of the room, creating a forward/back directional pull. Explore the feeling of moving within this low, flat plane. If you change your facing, stay as low as possible to maintain an expression of a flat, low plane.
- Now stand and find shapes that express the feeling of a horizontal plane at a higher level even if your legs (or other supports) are not within the plane.

[*The body cannot assume a shape that is truly in the horizontal plane without using some base of support. If the dancer stands or sits, the feeling of the plane is the intent, and the necessary vertical support in the body must be excused.*]

Sagittal Plane

- Create a standing plane that is perpendicular to the front of the room by standing tall (this creates the vertical pull) and then reaching toward the front and back of the room. You may face in any direction as you move in this narrow area, traveling toward and away from the front of the room.

Culminating Forms

Choose one or more of these culminating forms.

Individual Planes Dance Split into two groups, and have half the class dance while the other half observes.

Dancers start in a small shape. They extend their arms and legs to make a shape on the
    vertical (up/down) plane.
Moving each limb separately on the plane, they swing back and forth on the plane and
    then circle all the way around, "wiping" the plane.
Slowly, dancers drop to the floor and curl up into a small shape.
Then start the same sequence pattern of establishing, swinging, wiping, and curling to
    express a horizontal plane.
Repeat the same sequence on the sagittal plane.
End the dance in a small curled up shape.

[*This dance expresses planes in relation to the space. It can also be done in the door, table, and wheel planes (in relation to the body), in which case the curled shape will be at a middle level.*]

Small Group Dance of Planes   In groups of three to five, students create a dance that demonstrates each plane. The dance should include still shapes as well as movements that "wipe" or move along the plane. Dancers decide whether their planes have a body or space orientation and the order of presenting the planes. They then find ways to express the planes using different individual shapes, matching shapes, connected shapes, or a combination of all three. For example:

1. Horizontal plane: Individuals start lying on the floor in flat shapes. They slowly rise to midlevel or standing, keeping the feeling of the horizontal shapes. Then they find ways to move that show the surface of the plane.
2. Vertical plane: Individuals all make matching *X* shapes (perhaps connecting hands) to show the vertical plane.
3. Sagittal plane: One by one each member of the group does a somersault forward and comes to standing. Sequentially form a line, one person behind the other, to finish in a group shape that expresses the sagittal plane.

Students should find interesting and contiguous ways to make the transition from expressing one plane to another. Start and end the dance in still shapes.
    Show the dances to the rest of the class.

Closure
Choose one of the following movements to close the lesson.

Rest lying loosely on the floor
Hook-up

Lesson Notes
- Since these terms may be new to your students, a chart or words written on the board may help them to keep the different planes straight and learn vocabulary correctly. The names used for the planes in relation to the body are taken from Laban terminology, which uses names that evoke the image of their movement. The synonymous anatomical names for each plane are: coronal or frontal plane (door plane), transverse or horizontal plane (table plane), and sagittal plane (wheel plane). Diagrams and discussion of axes and planes in relation to the body are in Chapter 7.
- Obviously the body is three-dimensional and cannot be confined precisely to one line or plane of movement. Expressing the narrow, flat *feeling* of the plane in still shapes or movement within one's physical abilities is what is important.
- There is an interesting relationship and overlap between working with planes from a body perspective and working with planes in relation to the surrounding space. For example, lying down and extending arms and legs upward expresses the wheel plane from a body perspective. From a relationship-to-space

perspective, it could express the vertical or sagittal planes, depending on the position of the movement in relation to the front of the room. Advanced students may wish to explore and compare these relationships.
- Props can add to the visual clarity and expression of these studies. Fabric loops, pieces of cloth or paper, and hula hoops work well for expressing planes. Remind students that their own shapes and movements, not just the props, need to express the planes.
- The individual exploration can be varied to be a partner study with fabric loops. One student stretches the loop into a line on the first directional pull of the study. The partner adds the second pull by pulling out on the loop in the second direction. This will create a geometric shape on the plane being expressed. Explore this activity on different levels and using different body parts to hold or pull the shapes.
- Explorations of dimensions and planes within the kinesphere are an introduction to Laban's Space Harmony, which goes on to develop complex scales of movement. For further work in this field, see Laban's *The Language of Movement: A Guidebook to Choreutics* (1974), Irmgard Bartenieff's *Body Movement: Coping with the Environment* (1980), or Peggy Hackney's *Making Connections: Total Body Integration through Bartenieff Fundamentals* (2002).

Lesson Adaptation

Geometric Motions

Math studies about shape and area can include movement studies that demonstrate the three basic geometric motions: slides, flips, and turns. Using these motions, a geometric shape is moved to cover a new area on the surface of a plane (Figure 18.1).

To "slide" the shape, move it up, down, or sideways along the surface of the plane or "wipe" it around on the plane.

To "turn" the shape, fix an axial point and rotate the shape around on its axis to a new position.

To "flip" the shape, imagine a line of symmetry on one edge of the shape and flip the shape over the line to create a reflection of the original shape.

These geometric motions can be added to this lesson or explored in subsequent lessons. The motions are best experienced by moving shapes on the floor (horizontal plane). Have students work in groups of three. One person makes a flat shape on the floor and holds it securely. The other two physically move the first person's body shape, without changing it, to another position using a slide, turn, or flip strategy.

Some objects make an effective addition to these geometric motion studies. As individuals or groups, hold flat rigid objects such as paper or hoops or stretchy fabric loops in ways that form geometric shapes. Keep the shapes intact as they are moved to a new position on the plane by sliding, turning, or flipping. The focus of this variation is on the prop more than on the dancers' bodies.

Individuals and groups can share the results of their explorations with the rest of the class.

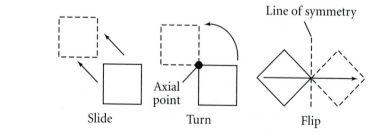

FIGURE 18.1   *Geometric Motions.*

CURRICULAR LESSON: THE SOLAR SYSTEM

Movements based on curved shapes and pathways are related to phenomena of the solar system (planets, orbits, sun) in this lesson. It extends the curved movement ideas explored in Lines and Shapes in Space (Chapter 14). By working in group shapes in relation to other groups, students further develop group spatial awareness. The lesson culminates in a dance about the solar system.

CONCEPT SPOTLIGHT 18.3

Lesson Concepts

Spherical shapes (re: planets)
Curved pathways (re: orbiting)
Rotation and revolution
Spatial relationships
Group spatial forms

Lesson Plan

Introducing the Concept

[*Use a globe to demonstrate how the earth moves, distinguishing between rotating on an axis and revolving around the sun.*]

What is the shape of the earth? (A sphere.) How does the earth move within its "self-space"? (It rotates on its axis.) When the earth moves through space, it revolves around the sun.

In this lesson you will use your awareness of self-space traveling through shared space to move like planets orbiting around a central sun.

Kinesthetic Tune-Up

Scatter, claim spots, and establish self-space kinesphere.

Open and Close   Start in a small, rounded shape. Slowly open the shape, feeling how the spine uncurls and extends. Now close the shape and feel the spine rounding. Repeat a few times.

Slow Twisting   Slowly rotate the spine into and out of twisting movements. Keep the movement flowing and sequential.

Individual Exploration
Curved Shapes and Movements

Turn attention to creating curved shapes and movements.
Again, curl and uncurl the spine, curving in many directions and freely changing
    levels.
Let the arms, head, and legs complement the curving movements of the spine.
Pause occasionally in curved, rounded shapes.
Explore place-to-place movements that express curviness, including slow turning and
    rolling. Use a curved shape in the body as well. Do these movements slowly, and
    pause if you get dizzy.
Reestablish spots and awareness of the self-space bubble.

Spherical Shapes

Make your body into the shape of the earth (sphere). Try a few different ways of making this rounded shape on different levels.

Now see if you can "rotate" your shape around a central axis. Keep the movement in one place. If it is too difficult to rotate your shape, try a different one or change to a different level.

Moving the Sphere

Pick one of your spherical shapes. While maintaining the shape, try to find a way to move the shape through space.

Can you rotate your shape at the same time that you move it through space? You may have to make slight adjustments to your shape to do this. Rotate and move slowly so you don't get dizzy. [*Try this with several students at a time moving in straight pathways across the room before going on to the "orbiting" pathway.*]

Partner Exploration

Orbiting   One person will represent the sun and find a still shape that expresses radiant light. Always face your partner, turning slowly as he or she moves around you. If desired, express the burning of the sun in movement as you turn.

The other person will represent the earth. Choose a spherical shape (yours or someone else's) that was easy to move through space. Staying in one place first, begin to slowly rotate your shape. Now carefully begin to move around your partner (the "sun") as if you were on an orbital pathway. Move slowly, stopping briefly if you get dizzy. Stay fairly close to your partner as you orbit on a curved pathway around the "sun." Go one full orbit, then stop.

Switch roles and repeat the exploration.

Small Group Exploration

Group Shapes   Form groups of three to five people, and scatter the groups evenly in the room. [*This may need to be done by half the class at a time if the dance space is not large.*]

Before forming and rotating your group shape, simply walk on the pathway that will be the orbit for your planet. All groups will orbit around the same central point. The orbital pathways are like tracks and do not intersect another planet's pathway.

Find ways to form a group shape to represent a spherical planet. Then rotate the shape in place. Now move the group shape while it rotates. Move in your curved pathway around the room without bumping into another planet. Outer planets circle the room one time, then stop. Notice that it takes longer for a larger orbit on the periphery of the space. Inner groups may go around more than once in the time it takes an outer group to orbit one time.

Culminating Form

Solar System Group Dance   In discussion, decide on a way to begin and end your group dance. This could be based on classroom science studies or be an abstraction. One idea is to start in the center of the room in a clump. A few people at a time move away from the center and take their places scattered through the room, forming the spherical shapes of their planets. The ending of the dance could reverse this movement and come to a stop.

Decide who will take which roles in the dance. You will need a sun (one or several students) and a number (eight for accurate study) of planets. The planets can be individuals or small groups of two or three dancers.

Four group "planets" revolve in circular orbits around a central "sun" represented by the back-to-back girl and boy.

When "planets" are in their places, they make their spherical shapes and begin to rotate in place. Then slowly they begin to orbit around the central sun. When all the planets have made a full orbit, the dance finds its ending.

Repeat the dance so that students change roles or sizes and placement of group planets.

Closure

Choose one of the following movements to close the lesson.

Open and close
Sitting and lying leg stretches
Lying hook-up

Lesson Notes

- It is not uncommon for students to get dizzy from the many turning movements in the lesson. Strongly emphasize safety, and keep students spaced adequately to allow for imperfect pathways. If you notice dizziness, stop students and practice skills. Here are three things you can do in case of dizziness:

  1. Slow down the turning; slow motion is great.
  2. Stop moving; a short pause will usually restore the equilibrium. This does not have to interrupt the flow of a study—simply pause for a moment, then continue. In severe cases, sit down until the dizziness is gone. The support of a wall might be welcomed.
  3. Jump up and down a few times in place. This reestablishes the vertical axis quite quickly and is useful during explorations.

  Dancers often "spot" when turning, whipping the head around to keep eyes on a certain spot while the body turns. Spotting fixes the focus and keeps the body oriented toward that point of reference. Although a technique of interest, it is probably not necessary to go into this much detail for the material presented.

- If age appropriate, students can explore rotating around a tilted axis rather than a vertical axis. This is helpful for demonstrating why the earth has seasons. However, it is a much more difficult physical feat and can usually only be maintained for a short time.

- New planetlike bodies are being discovered. If they are a part of your study, they can be included in the Solar System Group Dance. If desired, have students apply characteristics of their planet to their movement (for example, Jupiter is large, Saturn has rings, and Mercury is small). More details could be added to the dance: shooting stars, asteroids, even a spaceship. Be sure to explore the kinds of movements these objects would make (dart, float, propel, hover) and how their pathways might intersect others without bumping.

- New age music works well to accompany the dance. "Whales" by Eric Chappelle and music from Philip Glass's *Einstein on the Beach* support an ongoing, rotational quality (see Appendix F).

Lesson Adaptation

Chemistry

The spatial pattern of bodies orbiting around a central core (which characterize the solar system) is also found at the submicroscopic level of atoms and molecules. Therefore, the ideas in this lesson can be used to teach chemistry concepts such as electron sharing (covalent bonds) and electron transfer (ionic bonds). Hydrogen molecules (H_2) are comprised of two hydrogen atoms (each having one proton and one electron) that share electrons and are held together by a covalent bond. The hydrogen molecule can be danced by groups of four students. Two students will be protons of the two hydrogen atoms and two

perseverance because it will be very rewarding for them once they have broken through those barriers. On the other hand, young children generally love making sound and movement simultaneously. Free vocal sound can be used in most lessons even before addressing it specifically in a lesson. Cultivating sound in its own lessons will, however, improve children's control and imaginative use of sound.

- Sitting back to back with a partner is another way to organize students for making sounds. This position enables students to feel the resonance and movement quality of their sounds through their connection to the back of another person who is also making vocal sounds. In a sitting or lying position, encourage students to close their eyes while making sounds. This takes the attention inward to the source of the sound.

- Sound is most meaningful in relationship to silence. Be sure to observe your students closely and allow for rests of voice and body. Combining sound with movement can be emotionally demanding and physically tiring.

Lesson Adaptations

Phonetic Sounds

Letter sounds can be explored with movement as part of a phonics study for beginning readers. Working with phonetic sounds benefits all dancers as preparation for uniting dance and speech or song. Moving the sounds of vowels helps open a dancer's body to toning and singing while dancing.

In the tune-up for this lesson, include making vowel sounds while sitting back to back with a partner or moving single body parts while making specific vowel sounds. For example, say or sing "Oo" while moving the hips, "Oh" with the waist, "Aa" with the ribs, "Ah" with the upper chest, "Ee" with the head. Vowel sounds can also be made while moving shoulders, hands, and feet. This can lead adults into any of the sound quality explorations and culminating forms previously discussed. For young children, one or two vowel sounds may be emphasized in the tune-up and then further explored with movement words containing those sounds. For example, tune up with sounds of the short and long "A," then explore words such as shake, skate, snake and cat, rabbit, fast, fat. Put these words/movements into a sequence and show them to each other.

Consonant sounds such as *Mm, Nn, Rr, Ss,* and *Zz* all evoke sustained movements with different amounts of tension. Others such as *Pp, Tt,* or *Kk* are more explosive and evoke sudden movements. Letter combinations such as *Sh* and *Ch,* which may confuse youngsters, can be readily differentiated through movement because they are sounded

---

Box 19.1

Short and Long Vowel Movement Words

Long A	shake, skate, snake
Short A	cat, rabbit, fast, fat, gallop
Long E	reach, eagle, free, me, leap, freeze
Short E	stretch, bend, pet, elephant
Long I	rise, high, ride, I, kite
Short I	sink, wiggle, spin, swish, swim, fish, wind
Long O	go, open, close
Short O	drop, dog, jog, stop, hop
Long U	glue, cute, flute, music
Short U	jump, up, duck, under, bubble, lunge, punch

Box 19.2

Initial Consonant Movement Words

B	bounce, bubble
C	clap, collapse
D	dive, duck, dig
F	fall, fast
G	gallop, go
H	hop, happy
J	jump, jiggle
K	kick, kitten
L	leap, lunge, laugh, look, Look out!
M	move, march
N	no! nod
P	pound, press, push/pull
Q	quiet, queen
R	run, roll
S	swing, shake, skip, stop, stamp
T	twist, turn,
V	vibrate
W	wave, waltz
X	x-ray
Y	yes! yawn
Z	zig-zag, zebra

with such different movement feeling. When using these techniques to teach phonics for reading, focus on one or a few consonant sounds per lesson. After exploring the consonant sounds with movements, words that begin with those sounds can be moved in sequential forms.

Sounds and Movements Derived from Familiar Things or Actions

Once dancers are comfortable with combining sound and movement, vocal sound can easily be integrated with representational movement. A whole lesson can be devoted to this topic, or it can be included when addressing different subjects in the curriculum. When working with representation, take care that movement quality is not lost to dramatic expression of the topics. Direct students to sense in their muscles the qualities they want to express. Move as the thing would move or as the action implies, including sound to support the expressive qualities.

Box 19.3

Ch *and* Sh *Movement Words*

Ch	reach, punch, scratch, catch, choo-choo, chop, stretch, chicken
Sh	push, splash, shrink, shiver, shake, shine

Here are some nouns that evoke expressive sounds and movement:

Fire
Water
Wind
Thunder
Lightning
Rain
Frog
Snake
Cat
Bee
Cricket
Airplane
Bulldozer
Computer
Eggbeater
Machine

Provide, or select from classroom topics, verbs that inspire sound and movement combinations. Express ideas like these in unified movement and sound:

Explode
Melt
Ooze
Crash
Glide
Slither

To culminate the lesson, arrange words in a sequence and dance as a group.

Sound and movement collages make a nice visual aid to use with these studies. On one page, layer pictures of things that make sounds. These can all be related to one topic (animals, transportation, weather, and so on), or they can be a combination of topics. Individuals, small groups, or the whole class can improvise movements and sounds inspired by the collage. If desired, they can be put into a sequenced form.

PURE MOVEMENT LESSON: DANCING WITH OBJECTS

The dancer moves as if her body and the cloth are one.

This lesson provides a progression for exploring movement with an object, working with a piece of cloth as an example. It is primarily a lesson in visual design; the focus is on the spatial forms created by the movement of the dancer and object together. The principles and progressions of this lesson can be used similarly when dancing with rhythm instruments or any object—cloths, scarves, or streamers; objects from nature such as shells, feathers, flowers, and branches; everyday objects like chairs, hats, hoops, pots and pans, and newspaper. Each object's specific characteristics will evoke different movement responses from dancers.

Lesson Plan

Introducing the Concept

Today you will dance with a piece of cloth. Let the qualities of the cloth show you new ways to move so that you dance differently than you would without the cloth. Use your whole body, and notice the designs you and the cloth create together.

Kinesthetic Tune-Up

Stand and scatter
Move separate parts of the body, then the whole body.
Occasionally stop and close the eyes to feel the shape of the body in that position.
    [*Have students tune in to the movement of the bones if desired.*]

Individual Exploration
Exploring New Body Configurations

Place two parts of the body together; this will create a new body configuration.
Improvise, discovering the new ways that the body moves because it is in this
    configuration.

Dancing with Cloth   [*Pass out folded pieces of cloth to each student.*]

Place the folded cloth somewhere on the body where it will stay; the head, shoulder, or
    back are good choices.
Sense how having the cloth on your body affects your movement.
Be influenced by this new situation and explore moving in ways that reflect that you
    have a cloth resting on your body.
Try not to let it drop.

Unfold the cloth.
Explore moving with the cloth, holding it in different ways.
Move the whole body as if the body and the cloth are one entity.
Let your movement adapt to and be derived from holding the cloth.
Sense the movement designs you and the cloth make together.

[*If students need direction, coach them using the following suggestions.*]

Hold the cloth in two hands.
Hold in one hand.
Run with the cloth held high over head with one or two hands.
Have the cloth rise and sink; move it around the body and under parts
    of the body.
Hold the cloth by unlikely body parts; for example, with a foot or between
    knees.
Toss and catch the cloth on different parts of the body.
Wrap the body with the cloth in ways that restrict movement, and see what
    new movements arise.
Put the cloth on as a costume, allowing a dramatic character to emerge. Exaggerate the
    movement.
Place the cloth on the floor and arrange it in an interesting position.
Move in relationship to the cloth, paying attention to the sculptural designs you and
    the cloth make together.

Group Exploration
Duets

Two people sharing one piece of cloth
Two people each with a piece of cloth

[*Partners improvise freely with these structures.*]

Unison Movement

Two people, each with a piece of cloth, match each other's movements simultaneously
    in a mirror relationship.
First one dancer leads, then dancers switch roles.
The leader establishes the beginning position of the cloth in each dance.

Small Groups

In groups of three to five dancers, explore the previously described group
    structures.
Do unison movement in a circle formation.

Culminating Forms
Choose one or more of the following culminating forms.

Sharing

Show partner or small group studies

Visiting Cloths

Begin scattered through the space.
Each dancer arranges his or her cloth into a sculptural design on the floor.
First, dancers move with their own cloth sculptures, then dancers move throughout
    the room briefly dancing with different cloth sculptures. If more than one
    person is by a cloth they relate to the other dancers too.
On a signal, dancers return to their cloths and (without talking) arrange their cloths
    carefully into one large cloth sculpture. [*This can be done with one dancer at a
    time placing a cloth into the design.*]
When all the cloths have been placed, dancers take positions in relation to the
    cloth design.
Hold the ending shape briefly. [*There is a contemplative feeling to this dance.*]

Large Group Unison Circle Dance

Begin standing in a circle with all dancers holding their cloth in the same way.
Each person briefly leads the circle in unison movements with the cloths.
Or a few volunteers lead the whole group in unison movements.

Unison Line Dance

Depending on the size of the group, form two, three, or four lines with dancers one
    behind the other. Each dancer has a cloth.
The first person in line moves the line through space and leads unison movement with
    the cloths.
Leaders pay attention to the other lines and move the lines in relation to each other.

Closure
Choose one of the following movements to close the lesson.

Rounding the spine
Memory integration

Lesson Notes

- This lesson builds on material introduced in Lines and Shapes in Space and Finding Unison (Chapter 14), Body Parts (Chapter 15), and Group Lines (Chapter 18). It is helpful if students are familiar with this material before the lesson.
- If approached sensitively, dancing with an object brings about an attitude of respect for the object and an appreciation of its particular qualities and beauty. Once students have experienced dancing with objects, they can readily incorporate them into other dance lessons.
- Working with objects while dancing highlights the space element because the visual design of the object has the greatest influence on the movement. The force element enters when the object is used in a dramatic way or when the object evokes strong or gentle qualities. If moving with the object produces sound, the time element will become involved.
- Newspaper is an object whose physical characteristics evoke space, time, and force elements (sometimes simultaneously). Its use with movement promotes a great deal of freedom of expression. Include a cleanup dance in the culminating forms.
- With young children, make sure you have a strategy for the orderly distribution and exchange of objects or musical instruments. Teach students how to play the instruments respectfully. Use signals indicating when they are to play the instruments and when to keep them silent. This preplanning will make a huge difference in the success of the lesson.

Dancing with found objects develops an attitude of respect and appreciation for beauty in nature.

Lesson Adaptation

Dancing with Found and Traditional Rhythm Instruments

When dancing with instruments, strive for unity of sound and movement. After the kinesthetic tune-up, the class sits and briefly explores the sound that an instrument or object makes. Use instruments such as drums, shakers, claves, jingle bells, and triangles; found sound makers such as keys, paper bags, books, shoes, and combs; or objects from nature that create sound when they are moved such as seed pods or branches. Have students individually move with the instruments as objects of visual design, without sound. (Some instruments are difficult to move silently. Ask students to do their best in those cases, but do not require complete silence.)

Without making sound, Marco is moving with the drum as an object of visual design.

Next, students play their instrument while dancing. The movements reflect both the action of carrying the instrument and a response to the sound of the instrument. As with the cloth, coach students to be receptive to the way the instrument affects their movements. The lesson can be built around one or two instruments, such as drums and shakers, or it can provide the chance to explore several different instruments, in which case give students a chance to switch instruments.

For partner work, couples dance freely while playing instruments, relating to their partners' movements and to the sounds created by the two instruments. Partners may each have the same kind of instruments, or two instruments that complement or contrast with each other.

Additional studies that can be done with instruments include having one person dancing while the rest of the group sits in a circle and plays their instruments. Here the music follows the dance, matching the impulse and quality of the dancer's movements. This can also be done in partners with one person moving and one person playing an instrument. This study is similar to Marking Others' Time Patterns from the Sensing Time Patterns lesson (Chapter 14).

The dancers can also respond to the music. Have students play their instruments and move minimally while standing in a circle, relating their sound freely to the others' sounds. The group may or may not establish a steady beat. One or a few at a time, dancers put down their instruments, enter the circle, and dance to this music.

To create a processional with instruments, dancers move in a line through the space while playing instruments. In this line dance, the movement of dancers is not necessarily in unison although a common underlying beat is maintained by the group.

CURRICULAR LESSON: THE THREE LITTLE PIGS

The story of *The Three Little Pigs* is amazingly rich for dance. The following material is best taught in three short lessons each emphasizing a different element. Material can also be chosen from each lesson and taught in a single, condensed lesson, if desired. Before beginning the lesson series, read or have the students read the story. There are many variations of this tale, and some versions have different endings, which may require adaptation of the third *Three Little Pigs* lesson. Although this is a story for young children, the three strategies used can be applied to stories for any age level.

CONCEPT SPOTLIGHT 19.3

Lesson Concepts

Force Element (re: quality of building materials)
  Forceful/forceless
  Sudden/gradual
  Direct/scattered

Lesson Plan Part 1: The Pigs' Building Materials

Introducing the Concept
[*Show examples of straw, sticks, and bricks. Allow students to touch the objects. Elicit and list words that describe the shape, weight, texture, and movement quality of each kind of building material.*]

Kinesthetic Tune-Up
Stand, scatter, and establish space bubbles.
Stretch, twist, flop, shake, toss, swing.
Make tight movements.
Make loose movements.

Exploration
Open gradually; close suddenly.
Open with a forceless quality; close with a forceful quality.
Open while turning; close directly inward.

Explore Qualities of Each Material in Movement

Straw: light, bendable, thin, floating
Sticks: straight, stiff, rough surface, falling
Brick: solid, hard, unmovable

Culminating Forms

Small Groups   Divide class into groups of three to ten dancers. To make "houses" of each material, dancers individually assume the shape of each material and then form a group shape that represents a structure or house. The teacher takes the role as the wolf and exhales forcefully or plays a horn, gong, or drum to represent the wolf's breath. The straw and stick houses blow down. The brick houses change shape several times but remain standing. After dancing each of these houses, have groups practice the dance for one kind of house and show the class.

CONCEPT SPOTLIGHT 19.4

Lesson Concepts

Time element
    Even and uneven beat patterns (re: syllables)
Matching sound and movement
Echo format
Unison movement

Lesson Plan Part 2: Wolf and Pig Chants

Introducing the Concept

While sitting, have students chant repeated phrases from the story and clap on each syllable. Students can also move their legs to tap out the beat of the chants. [*You may want to try different pacings and beat patterns, paying attention to the evenness and unevenness of the beats.*]

Kinesthetic Tune-Up

Move one part of the body at a time: arms, shoulders, hips, legs.
Walk, kick, jump in place.

Exploration

Explore movement for the following chants, making one movement on each syllable. [*Have students work with each line separately at first, then combine the lines into a longer phrase. If students need suggestions, cue them to match the beat of the chants using the parts of the body and movement introduced in the tune-up.*]

Little pig, little pig
Let me come in.

No, no
Not by the hair
On my chinny, chin chin.

Partner Echoes

One person works with the wolf's chant, moving and varying it in any way.
The partner repeats the leader's sound and movement after a short pause.
Switch roles and explore variations and echoing of the pig's chant.

Culminating Form

Whole Group Echoes   In a circle have volunteers demonstrate movements for a section of the chant. The rest of the class echoes those movements. Conclude by choosing one part of a chant or the whole chant, and repeat over and over with unison movement.

Lesson Plan Part 3: Wolf Movements

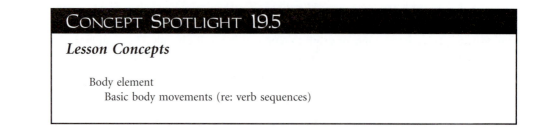

CONCEPT SPOTLIGHT 19.5

Lesson Concepts

Body element
    Basic body movements (re: verb sequences)

Introducing the Concept

From the story, have students recall the actions of the wolf. Make a list of verbs (such as the ones listed in the Exploration) that summarize the wolf's movements.

Kinesthetic Tune-Up

Stretch
Twist
Shake
Flop
Swing

Exploration

Explore the following verbs, which are movements of the wolf.

"I'll huff, and I'll puff, and I'll blow your house down!"

Sneak
Huff, puff, blow
Climb (up a stove pipe)
Slide (down a stove pipe)
Land (in boiling water)
Yowl (from the burn)
Run

[*Ask individual students to demonstrate different ways to express these verbs. If desired, the whole class may copy these demonstrations.*]

Culminating Form

Create a sequence of these movements and show them to others. This can be done in small groups or as a whole class with one half showing the other half. See culminating forms in The Moving Body (Chapter 14) for detailed descriptions of Staying and Going or Moving within a Time Pattern formats for sequencing basic movements.

Closure

Choose one of the following movements to close each lesson.

Bit-by-bit relaxation followed by rounding the spine
Lying leg stretches

Lesson Notes

If you would like to add a southwestern flavor to the lesson, use the story version *The Three Little Javelinas* by Susan Lowell. In Part 1, substitute the materials and tactile qualities as follows: instead of straw, sticks, and bricks use tumbleweed (light, prickly, entwined, tumbling), saguaro rib, and adobe brick. Call the pigs "javelinas" and the wolf a "coyote," but keep the same words in the chants. The third lesson will be about movements of the coyote instead of the wolf.

CURRICULAR LESSON: THE LION AND THE RAT

This well-known fable is used as the basis for contrasting qualities as it describes the main animal characters, the lion and the rat. Emotions and descriptive details are abstracted from interactions between the lion, the rat, and other animals of the story. The safe and skillful expression of these qualities is practiced through attention to the force element and how it feels to express different emotions in movement. The story is danced with guiding narration.

CONCEPT SPOTLIGHT 19.6

Lesson Concepts

Strong/gentle (re: animal qualities)
Size, weight, speed (re: animal qualities)
Expressing emotions
Narrative story

Lesson Plan

Introducing the Concept
Using the story of *The Lion and the Rat* (Appendix F), you will express the feeling of moving like animals from the story. Instead of acting out or trying to look like the animals, we will identify their qualities together so you can express them in movement. While you listen to the story, think about the way these animals move and the feelings they might experience during the story. Listen for action words, emotions, and describing words because these will give you ideas for movement. [*Read aloud the story of* The Lion and the Rat.]

Of the two main characters, one is strong, the other gentle. Which is which? These are the qualities you will express in your dance. You will also use your expression of force qualities to relate to the emotions of the characters.

Kinesthetic Tune-Up
Sit in a clump or circle.
Press your palms together firmly. Feel the arm muscles working.
Rest.
Repeat, and this time direct energy from your center of gravity (abdomen) into the
     palms so that your whole body feels the tension.
Rest.
Repeat again, but this time release the amount of tension slightly so that your palms
     barely touch.
Move your arms with your palms lightly touching. This has a looser feeling in the
     muscles. The ability to control how much tension and relaxation you use in your
     movements will help you in this lesson.
Stand and scatter.

Basic Body Movements   Do these movements briefly in preparation for exploring animal qualities:

Stretch
Shake
Close, open
Chop
Float
Cringe
Tip-toe
Pounce

Individual Exploration
Force Qualities

Make strong, forceful movements, engaging the abdominal muscles and keeping the center of gravity underneath the torso.
Make the same movements with very little force, moving gently. The center of levity in the chest will rise.

Movement Qualities of the Rat   Everyone assumes the part of the rat. Stay in one spot and find movements (not just shapes) to express these things about the rat:

Strength: Does a rat move strongly or gently? Loosen your muscles as you did in the tune-up to help you move gently.
Size: Without trying to look like a rat, use your movements to express the smallness of the rat.
Weight: Is the weight of a rat light or heavy? Show that with your movements. Express the feeling of lightness.
Speed: Does the rat move quickly or slowly? Show that quickness in movement, without trying to look like a rat.

Feelings Expressed by the Rat   Express the following emotions that the rat might feel in the story. [*Discussing or brainstorming feelings drawn from words in the story is helpful.*]

Fear: How do you suppose it feels when the rat finds himself between the lion's paws? How do your muscles feel when you are afraid? Use that awareness to help you express this emotion. What movements might express fear (shaking, freezing still, hiding)?
Relief and gratitude: How might the rat feel when the lion lets him go unharmed? Do your muscles feel different when you express this emotion? Find movements to express relief or thanks (releasing into a drop or relaxing with hand on heart; grateful slow bowing).
Worry: How does the rat feel when he discovers the lion in trouble? Is there a movement you can find to express worry (hand-wringing expressed with the whole body, clenching tight, hands on head and curling forward)? Keep that feeling as you express the action of "gnawing." Gnaw with your whole body.

[*While watching students move, look for abstract expression rather than dramatic representation. You may notice particularly expressive ideas that can be pointed out or adopted as "character movements" to be used in the culminating dance.*]

Movement Qualities of the Lion   Everyone assumes the part of the lion. Find movements that express these things about the lion:

Strength: gentle or strong?
Size: small or large?

Weight: light or heavy? Although a lion weighs a lot, it moves very
    lightly on its feet. Think of stalking.
Speed: quick or slow or both?

Feelings Expressed by the Lion   Describe and express the feelings
expressed by the lion. Use the whole body, not just the face and arm
gestures.

Pride at being the lord of the jungle
Compassion when he lets the rat go free
Humor at the rat's promise to repay the lion's kindness (express
    laughing in silence, using the whole body)
Rage at getting caught in the net (express this without sound)
Helplessness when he cannot escape

Movement Qualities of the Other Animals   Everyone takes the part
of different animals of the forest. Find movements to express these things about the
animal you have chosen:

Strength
Size
Weight
Speed

Geena expresses the rage of the lion with movement but no sound.

Feelings Expressed by the Other Animals

Worry that the lion is trapped
Weakness/helplessness since they cannot help
Joy/freedom when the lion is released

Culminating Forms
Dance the Story

Divide into three groups. One group will be rats, one will be lions, one will be other
    animals. [*The dance can be repeated three times so that all students have an
    opportunity to dance each part.*]
Lions take their place in the center of the room (or stage), allowing space for the rats
    to move among them. As the teacher narrates the story, character groups enter
    and exit on cue.
At the end of the story, all the animals (lion, rat, other animals) join together in a
    dance of freedom, jubilation, and friendship. Find an ending that expresses this
    joy. (Suggestions: uplifted arms, skipping among each other, connected group
    shape, everyone hold hands.)

Closure
Choose one of the following movements to close the lesson.

Bit-by-bit relaxation followed by rounding the spine
Hook-up lying on the floor

Lesson Notes

- Encourage students to use the whole body movements they discovered during
  their explorations for the final dance. Minimize gesture and miming, and use
  sound judiciously because it can easily overpower the movement expression.

Appendix A

Biographical Sketches of Influences

FIGURE A.1   *Rudolf Laban (1879–1958)*

RUDOLF LABAN was born in 1879 in Bratislava, Hungary. The son of a military governor in the Austro-Hungarian Empire, he traveled with his father to the Balkans, learning folk and Sufi dance there. He briefly studied as a military cadet but gave that up to study architecture and visual art at Ecoles des Beaux Arts in Paris from 1900–1909. Laban's study of dance took place outside of academia. Laban began at this time his own independent observation of movement and experimentation with improvisation. By 1912 Laban had decided to devote his life to dance and movement. His early pursuits included investigating simple notation systems; separating dance from music, drama, and mime; and improvising in groups.

Laban's observation of human movement, anatomy, psychology, and crystalology were the basis for the three branches of his movement analysis framework Labanotation, a system for notating movement that is widely accepted for notating dance scores; his theory of Effort, or Eukinetics, which analyzes the dynamics of movement; and Space Harmony, a theory of the spatial relationships of movement (Maletic, 2005).

Laban presented his first formal dance work in 1912 and opened his first dance school in 1913. He became widely known as a trailblazer of modern dance in the early twentieth century in Central Europe across which, by 1927, there were twenty-one Laban dance schools. Early on he was associated with Dadaist artists, and his work flourished within the German expressionist zeitgeist of the Weimar Republic between the World Wars. Between 1912 and 1936 he created more than a hundred dance works, ranging from his own solo dances and works for his dance company to festivals, pageants, and dance dramas involving amateur dancers. German expressionist choreographer Mary Wigman was one of his most acclaimed protégées.

Laban championed dance for the community, originating the dance form of "movement choirs" for large groups and establishing movement choir groups at many of his schools. In 1929 he directed a workers' dance festival for 20,000 participants from many different guilds in Vienna. His professional dance company, *Tanzbühne Laban,* toured extensively throughout Europe. From 1930 to 1934 Laban was director of movement for the Berlin State Theater.

The Nazi regime viewed Laban's work as something that could be used to their advantage and tried to exploit it, assigning Laban the task of creating a massive dance extravaganza for the 1936 Berlin Olympic Games. However, Nazi official Josef Goebbels attended a rehearsal and, upon seeing the true spirit behind Laban's work, forbade the performance. Laban's work was banned, and he was placed under house arrest that year. In 1937 Laban escaped from Germany to Paris, finally arriving in England in 1938, a sick and disillusioned man.

After a slow recovery, Laban collaborated with F. C. Lawrence, applying his understanding of Effort to maximize efficiency of workers in England's wartime factories. He organized his movement principles into a course of study termed Modern Educational Dance, which was widely adopted in English schools as part of a progressive curriculum for general education of children. This work has greatly influenced the fields of physical education, dance therapy, and creative dance. In 1946 the Laban Art of Movement Guild was founded to promote Laban's work. Laban continued to teach in collaboration with Lisa Ullmann and to write and lecture on his work until his death in England in 1958.

Laban was a man of prolific inspiration whose work was continued and developed by many collaborators during and after his life. Study of his comprehensive theories of movement and Labanotation are required in many university dance programs. Several organizations continue Laban's work: Laban, the Laban Guild and the Labanotation Institute based in England; and the Dance Notation Bureau, Laban/Bartenieff Institute of Movement Studies and Motus Humanus, which are based in the United States. The Web site www.motushumanus.org provides more information about current applications of Laban's theories and has links to other sites and organizations.

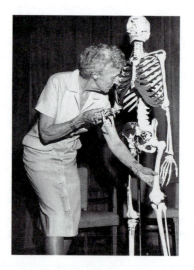

FIGURE A.2 *Margaret H'Doubler (1889–1982)*

MARGARET H'DOUBLER was born in Beloit, Kansas, to a prominent Swiss-American family. Her father was a highly innovative inventor and photographer. She majored in biology at the University of Wisconsin in Madison, and one of her main interests was the physical education courses offered there. Upon graduation in 1910 she was hired as an instructor in the new Department of Women's Physical Education. H'Doubler was a wildly popular teacher, and her classes were always brimming in whatever sport she taught.

In 1916 H'Doubler took a sabbatical from teaching to study at Columbia College in New York City and was deeply involved in the philosophy of education debate there. While in New York, H'Doubler was assigned the task by her department head Blanche Trilling of finding a dance form suitable and valuable for women to study in a university setting.

H'Doubler was bitterly disappointed in her investigations. She was uninterested in the dance-as-performance that she encountered in New York. Her most exciting discovery was the work of Alys Bentley, who began music classes with students moving while lying on the floor. This triggered a flash of insight and inspiration for H'Doubler. She applied Bentley's idea to dance and had students begin movement class while lying on the floor wearing blindfolds to heighten their kinesthetic sense. This allowed them to discover body coordinations by paying attention to movement sensation without concerns of balancing in gravity.

H'Doubler returned to Madison and began teaching her own exploratory approach to dance in the summer of 1917. Shortly thereafter, in 1925, H'Doubler published *The Dance and Its Place in Education*. This tentative beginning blossomed into the University of Wisconsin–Madison's dance program and the first university dance major in the world in 1926. Graduates of that program went on to establish dance programs in colleges and universities across the United States. H'Doubler also organized the Orchesis Dance Club, where students created their own choreography. Orchesis Dance Clubs became a common fixture in many colleges with or without dance programs.

H'Doubler's approach to teaching emphasized using dance as a medium for personal growth more than as a way to train professional dancers. She addressed the domains of thinking, feeling, and moving through dance. Influenced by her scientific background, H'Doubler felt that dance study should be grounded in science and that dancers needed to understand the anatomical basis for movement. She often used a skeleton in class to introduce movement explorations. H'Doubler approached creativity from a biological standpoint, asserting that because all living things adapt to survive, creativity is an inherent biological principle. From this basis she developed the belief that creative activity should be available to everyone.

Although H'Doubler distanced herself from most theatrical dance of the time, she did admire and establish personal connections with Mary Wigman and the German choreographer and associate of Laban, Harald Kreutzberg. In their dance she saw an emphasis on individual expression similar to her own convictions. The connection to German modern dance was also strengthened when Louise Kloepper, the first American to graduate from the Wigman School, joined the Wisconsin faculty and collaborated with H'Doubler in developing the dance program there. H'Doubler retired from full-time teaching in 1954 but continued to give workshops for Wisconsin students for many years. In her later life, H'Doubler lived in Tucson, Arizona, and was occasionally a guest teacher in Mettler's summer courses at the Tucson Creative Dance Center in the 1970s.

For more information on Margaret H'Doubler's life and work, see *Moving Lessons: Margaret H'Doubler and the Beginnings of Dance in American Education*, by Janice Ross (2000), and *Margaret H'Doubler: The Legacy of America's Dance Education Pioneer*, edited by Wilson, Hagood, and Brennan (2006).

BARBARA METTLER grew up north of Chicago near Lake Michigan in a family that practiced arts of all kinds within the home. Close to nature as a child, Mettler created her own dances freely but was uncomfortable with most formal dance classes she encountered. An exception to this was a course she took with a dance teacher from the University of Wisconsin. As a young woman, she was inspired by a performance of a group led by Isadora Duncan's daughter, Irma Duncan, but was discouraged from pursing that avenue, being told she was already too old.

While touring Germany, Mettler found a toehold for her artistic searching when she visited the Mary Wigman School in Dresden. Mettler returned to study dance there and graduated from the Wigman School in 1933. Beyond her studies at the Wigman School, she was highly affected by the artistic freedom and democratic spirit of the German Weimar Republic. This was at the height of Laban's work in Germany, which influenced Mettler through her dance study with Wigman.

Mettler was an independent dance pioneer who directed Mettler Studios for more than sixty years. Through her studio, Mettler offered ongoing dance classes and an intensive summer program each year. She also published nine books, produced films and

APPENDIX C
Formats for Group Work

The following guide shows different structures for addressing movement material in group dances. Use them for planning group explorations or culminating forms. Most of the formats can be done in duets, small groups, or large groups, although circles obviously require more than two dancers. Page references lead to an example where the formats are used in a lesson.

ALL DANCERS DOING SAME MOVEMENT

	Page
In Unison	
Facing each other (duets, mirror relationship)	207
Line, one behind the other	250
Line, side by side	250
Circle	208
With a leader	207
Without a leader	207
In Echo Format	
With sound	263
Without sound	207

DANCERS DOING DIFFERENT MOVEMENTS

	Page
Responding	
Moving and being moved (activity and receptivity)	188
Alternating movement or shapes (alternate response)	193
Relating	
Complementary	193
Contrasting	182
Using a specific theme	214

ORGANIZATIONAL FORMS

	Page
A and B alternating movement	173
Alternate in-place and traveling	181
Entering and exiting patterns (Jogging Dance format)	201
Repeatable series	223
Taking turns around a circle	208

APPENDIX D
Creative Dance Performance Objectives

The following charts are examples of ways to organize movement material into performance objectives. The elements of dance are each addressed separately. Categories that cross over all the elements include Group Work, Overall Dance Skills, Artistic Commitment and Motivation, and Verbal Demonstration of Conceptual Understanding. Within each category, Mettler's progression of working from freedom, to awareness, to control is used to further organize performance objectives. The goals in this group of performance objectives are broad and widely applicable. They can be used to get an overall grasp of what to look for and develop in dancers and may be adapted for use in many settings including pretesting, ongoing informal evaluations, formal summary evaluations, and even to identify students with special talent in dance. They are, however, by no means exhaustive. These objectives resemble (or can be translated into) models set out by individual states, national standards, and the illustrated assessment models in this book. Specific lessons may call for inclusion of other performance objectives.

THE BODY
Freedom

- Uses the whole body in movement, including bending and twisting the torso
- Stretches fully
- Performs swinging movements easily, drops weight, releases knees
- Is able to express relaxation while resting and in movement

Awareness

- Expresses awareness of movement feeling

Control

- Moves and stops easily and safely
- Controls release of tension when alternating loose and tight positions; can release tension gradually into complete relaxation
- Balances on one foot
- Performs age-appropriate locomotor movements
- Distinguishes between movement of the whole body and isolated parts of the body
- Changes level with ease and control

FORCE ELEMENT
Freedom

- Moves with a wide range of force qualities, especially forceful and forceless
- Allows one movement impulse to naturally flow from the previous movement

Awareness

- Is aware of the level of force being exerted and its appropriateness for a given situation

Control

- Can express and combine all force attributes—forceful/forceless, sudden/gradual, pinpointed/scattered—to express a wide range of emotions and movement qualities
- Expresses both activity and receptivity

TIME ELEMENT

Freedom

- Moves with a wide range of tempos: slow and fast

Awareness

- Matches the beat pattern with music
- Differentiates steady and mixed beat patterns

Control

- Maintains a steady beat in movement without assistance of accompaniment
- Groups and subdivides beats
- Creates and repeats variations on beat patterns

SPACE ELEMENT

Freedom

- Enjoys moving in a wide range of spatial qualities, especially large/small and straight/curved

Awareness

- Is aware of spatial relationships
- Is aware of the group shape when working in a group

Control

- Maintains self-space; does not bump into others
- Changes level with ease and control
- Holds clear positions at all levels
- Describes clear pathways in movement
- Is able to express full range of spatial attributes
- Can make spontaneous spatial adjustments

GROUP WORK

Freedom

- Initiates movement ideas within group dances

Awareness

- Is aware of other dancers when working in a group
- Is aware of group spatial configurations
- Is aware of themes as they develop

Control

- Does not bump into others
- Can be both active and receptive according to the needs of the dance
- Contributes to clarifying group forms
- Works cooperatively with others

Overall Dance Skills

Freedom

- Moves without inhibition
- Unites breath and vocal sound with dancing
- Solves movement problems in unique and nonstereotypic ways
- Inspires new ideas through movement exploration

Awareness

- Is aware of force, time, and space elements within a given movement or in a whole dance

Control

- Moves without talking to other students
- Can make both subtle and large distinctions in movement
- Differentiates qualities of movement (all movements don't look the same)
- Performs before peers and maintains focus
- Recalls movement sequences

Artistic Commitment and Motivation

- Maintains concentration and focus both while moving and while observing movement
- Moves with expressive commitment
- Perseveres when learning new material and when solving movement problems
- Applies knowledge from previous lessons

Verbal Demonstration of Conceptual Understanding (orally or in writing)

- Uses dance vocabulary accurately and comprehensively
- Is able to detail the difference between different kinds of movement and different movement qualities
- Accurately analyzes own and others' dance work
- Describes the feelings and images that occur while moving
- Creates similes and metaphors from movement experiences
- Is inspired to invent original movement problems

APPENDIX E
Quick and Easy Activities

Simple movement structures can be used regularly in the classroom to connect students to their kinesthetic sense and keep their kinesthetic intelligence active. Quick and easy activities (often derived from the lessons) can be done in the space available, without rearranging classrooms. They can be done at the beginning of the day, immediately preceding instructional or creative activities, before periods of stress (such as testing), or as a break after hard concentration. Many of these activities can be used as creative dance lesson openers or closures and are also ways to ease a group into longer movement lessons. If these activities are done frequently, your class will readily be able to use their bodies both to learn material and to express themselves fluently in movement.

GETTING THE BODY AND BRAIN MOVING

Yawn and Stretch   Simply yawning and stretching the arms, shoulders, neck, and torso can offer a welcome break from long periods of sitting. Do this sitting or standing.

Body Parts   With eyes lowered or closed, move each part in turn: shoulders, head, upper spine, arms, whole spine, legs, and feet.

Basic Body Movements   Choose three or four movements for the class to explore briefly or to repeat in sequence. For example: stretch, flop, shake, swing. These can be done standing by desks or sometimes even sitting. You can have a grab bag of cards with names of actions written on them to provide variety in this activity. These basic movements are good choices: stretch, bend, twist, shake, toss, undulate, bounce, swing, open/close. See The Moving Body (Chapter 14) for the lesson that introduces these movements.

Shake and Stop   At transition times or after students have been sitting and concentrating for a long time, do a series of shaking movements alternated with stopping on signal. This can be done with the whole body or parts of the body.

Sensing a Space Bubble   Indicate the edges of personal space with the hands, then do "painting" movements on the surface of that sphere with different body parts. See Management and Safety Strategies in Chapter 12 and The Moving Body lesson in Chapter 14.

Echo Clapping   Simple beat patterns clapped by the teacher and echoed by students quickly sharpen the attentiveness of a class. See Focus Tools in Chapter 12.

Tactile Awakening   Have students lower their eyes while tapping on their own body and noticing the sensation of each tap. The tactile sense can also be stimulated with somewhat more vigorous patting movements and gentle squeezing or brushing the surface of the body. See Focus Tools in Chapter 12.

Developmental Patterns   Here are suggestions for developmental movements that can be used sequentially or singly. They are arranged from least to most complex. Experiment with having students do these at a low level or lying, sitting, or standing. They are further discussed and exemplified in Chapter 4 and in The Moving Body lesson adaptation Developmental Movements/Evolution in Chapter 14.

Expand and Contract Lying on the back, open and close from the center of the body out to the extremities and back to the center again. The image of a starfish moving may be helpful here.

Arch and Curl Move the spine, bringing the head and tailbone toward and away from each other, curving, arching, bending sideways, and undulating. In the sitting position this can be rounding the spine forward, then arching backward (called the Energizer in BrainGym). When standing, bend the knees slightly. Children may enjoy the image of an inch worm or a slithering snake.

Both Sides the Same (homologous) Try any bilateral symmetrical movement in which the limbs of the body do not cross the vertical midline. For the lower body this includes knee bends (*pliés*) or squatting, bouncing, or jumping on two feet. BrainGym has a homologous movement called Double Doodles in which both hands "draw" lines in space on either side of a midline, creating a symmetrical design. This can be done with two pieces of chalk on a board, crayons on paper, or simply in the air. Jumping jacks combine upper and lower body homologous movement. Frogs and rabbits typically jump with both sides doing the same action.

Single-Sided Movement (homolateral) Sitting or standing, lift and lower the arm and leg of the same side; repeat on the other side. Lying on the belly, crawl with same arm and leg moving forward. On hands and feet, move forward first with the hand and foot of one side, then the other. Walk with the leg and arm of the same side moving forward together like Frankenstein.

Book Folding Lying, sitting, or standing, fold one side of the body over the vertical midline to meet the other side. This resembles the covers of a book opening and closing. Rocking and rolling from side to side with this action begins cross-midline movement, without counterbalancing, and provides a transitional coordination between homolateral and cross-lateral patterns.

Cross-Lateral Movement(contralateral) Many common movements involve contralateral coordination. Do the first four of these slowly at first to establish the neuro-muscular pathways that promote integrated use of both sides of the brain.

- *Lazy Eights* (from BrainGym): Draw a figure eight lying on its side with each hand separately, both hands together, and with other body parts such as the eyes, the nose, elbows, knees, or feet. See Focus Tools in Chapter 12 for details.
- *Twist and Kick*: Twist the torso side to side. Then kick one leg at a time diagonally across the midline. Combine these two so that the upper body twists one way and the lower body twists the other way. The opposite arm and leg will cross the midline in opposite directions.
- *Alternate Toe Touching*: Standing or sitting, lean forward. With one hand, touch the opposite toes (or knee). This is sometimes called the windmill.
- *Cross crawl* (from BrainGym): While standing, touch the opposite elbow and knee (or foot and hand) in front of or behind the body. This requires a shift of balance from one leg to the other. See Focus Tools in Chapter 12.
- *Crawl*: crawl on hands and knees.
- *March*: March and swing the arms in opposition. (This is the natural coordination.)
- *Walk*: Walk with a bouncy step, and swing arms in opposition.
- *Skip*

SPECIFIC STRETCHING MOVEMENTS AS CLOSURES

For detailed descriptions of these activities, see the Lesson Template, Closures in Chapter 11.

Standing calf stretches
Sitting stretches
Lying leg stretches

ACTIVITIES FOR WINDING DOWN, COLLECTING FOCUS, OR CLOSURE

Refer to the Lesson Template, Closures in Chapter 11 for further descriptions of these activities. For details on tight and loose movement, see the Interactive Forces lesson in Chapter 14.

Open and close whole body
Tight and loose, standing, lying, or sitting in chairs
Bit-by-bit relaxation
Rounding the spine
Bit-by-bit relaxation followed by rounding the spine
Hook-up
Floppy test
Lying down resting and attending to breathing
Memory integration

BRIEF GROUP WORK

Equal Pushing   Two people push palm to palm with the intent of exactly matching the amount of force exerted by the other person. Rather than trying to push each other over, the idea is to be sensitive to each other and balance the two opposing forces. See Focus Tools in Chapter 12 and the Strong and Gentle lesson in Chapter 16 for detailed descriptions of the exercise.

Unison at Tables   Sitting students each take a turn leading their table in unison movement. Then the whole class can follow a leader that not everyone can see. This is a good icebreaker for introducing movement. See the lesson adaptation to Finding Unison in Chapter 14 called "Ice-Breaker" Unison at Tables.

SHORT CURRICULAR APPLICATIONS

Once students are familiar with movement exploration, they can use movement to answer questions and demonstrate concepts without going through a full lesson. These movements can be done sitting or standing, by the whole class, by a few students, or by single individuals. Here are some examples:

- Make or draw letter shapes with the body using single letters or spelling words, printed or cursive.
- Show the meaning of vocabulary words in movement.
- Use claps or simple sudden movements to express the syllables in words.
- Show addition or subtraction with numbers of movements.
- Measure distances covered with walking or other traveling movements.
- Rotate fractional distances by making one-half, one-quarter, and three-quarter turns in specified directions.
- Intersperse reading of stories with movement expressing feelings or actions mentioned in the narrative.
- Make movements or shapes showing the design or meaning for specific punctuation marks.
- Demonstrate chemical reactions with partners or in small groups.
- Show spatial relationships connected with a topic using different parts of the body or two or more people.
- Demonstrate the day's weather in movement.

APPENDIX F
Teaching Resources

LITERARY RESOURCES

Baker, K. (1991). *Hide and Snake*. Orlando, FL: Harcourt Brace Jovanovich.

Baylor, B. (1973). *Sometimes I Dance Mountains*. New York: Charles Scribner's Sons.

Bober, Natalie (Ed.). (1990). *Let's Pretend, Poems of Flight and Fancy*. New York: Penguin Books.

Bornstein, R. (1978). *The Dancing Man*. New York: Seabury.

Carle, Eric. (1984). *The Very Busy Spider*. New York: Philomel Books.

Carle, Eric. (1987). *The Very Hungry Caterpillar*. New York: Penguin Putnam.

Finch, Mary. (1999). *The Little Red Hen and the Ear of Wheat*. New York: Barefoot.

Frost, Robert. (1997). Fire and Ice. In *Frost*, selected and edited by John Hollander.
   New York: Knopf. (Orig. Pub. *Harper's Magazine*, December 1920)

Golding, William. (1954). *Lord of the Flies*. New York: Perigee.

Gorbachev, Valeri. (retold and illustrated). (2001). *Goldilocks and the Three Bears*.
   New York: North-South Books.

Hoban, Tana. (1990). *Exactly the Opposite*. New York: Greenwillow Books.

Isadora, Rachel. (1976). *Max*. New York: Macmillan.

Lowell, Susan. (1992). *The Three Little Javelinas*. Flagstaff, AZ: Northland.

Mayo, Diana. (Illustrator). (2001). *The House That Jack Built*. New York: Barefoot.

Pasternak, Boris. (1958). *Doctor Zhivago* (Trans. Max Hayward & Manya Harari).
   New York: Pantheon.

Piper, Watty. (1981). *The Little Engine That Could*. New York: Platt & Munk. (Orig. pub. 1930).

Silverstein, Shel. (1974). *Where the Sidewalk Ends*. New York: HarperCollins.

Stevenson, Robert Louis. (1978). *A Child's Garden of Verses*. Racine, WI: Western.
   (Orig. pub. 1885)

Van Allsburg, Chris. (1988). *Two Bad Ants*. Boston: Houghton Mifflin.

Wildsmith, B. (1963). *The Lion and the Rat*. London: Oxford University Press. [Aesop's fable]

Wood, Audrey. (1982). *Quick as a Cricket*. Singapore: Child's Play.

Zemach, Margot. (1988). *The Three Little Pigs: An Old Story*. New York: Farrar, Straus, and Giroux.

For Science:

Lawrence Hall of Science, University of California at Berkeley. (2002). *Full Option Science System*.
   Berkeley, CA: Delta Education.

CULTURAL RESOURCES
Folk Tales and Legends from Different Cultures

These are traditional stories retold by the listed authors.

Aardema, Vera. (1975). *Why Mosquitoes Buzz in People's Ears*. New York: Dial Press. [West Africa]

Aardema, Vera. (1981). *Bringing the Rain to Kapiti Plain*. New York: Dial Press. [Kenya]

De Paola, Tomie. (1981). *Fin M'Coul: The Giant of Knockmany Hill*. New York: Holiday House.
   [Ireland]

Diakité, Baba Wagué. (1997). *The Hunterman and the Crocodile*. New York: Scholastic Press.
   [West Africa]

Doucet, Sharon Arms. (1997). *Why Lapin's Ears Are Long and Other Stories of the Louisiana
   Bayou*. New York: Orchard Books. [Creole and Cajun, United States]

Gerbrands, A. A., and Forge, A. (1973). *Asmat-New Guinea*. In E. Evans-Pritchard (Series Ed.) &
   A. Forge (Vol. Ed.), *Peoples of the World: Vol 1. Australia and Melanesia including New Guinea*
   (1st ed.). London: Danbury Press. [Fumeripits legend, Asmat-New Guinea]

Grimm, Jacob, and Grimm, Wilhelm. (1998). *The Bremen Town Musicians: A Tale* (Trans. Anthea
   Bell). New York: North-South Books. [Germany]

Lorenz, Albert. (2002). *Jack and the Beanstalk: How a Small Fellow Solved a Big Problem.* New York: Abrams. [England]
Maguire, Jack. (1992). *Creative Storytelling: Choosing, Inventing, and Sharing Tales for Children.* Cambridge, MA: Yellow Moon Press. (Orig.pub. 1985) [many cultures]
Mahy, Margaret. (1990). *The Seven Chinese Brothers.* New York: Scholastic Inc. [China]
McDermott, Gerald. (1975). *The Stonecutter.* New York: Viking Press. [Japan]
McDermott, Gerald. (1993). *Raven.* San Diego: Harcourt Brace Jovanovich. [Pacific Northwest Native America]
McDermott, Gerald. (1994). *Coyote.* San Diego: Harcourt Brace. [Southwest Native America]
Oughton, Jerrie. (1992). *How the Stars Fell into the Sky.* Boston: Houghton Mifflin. [Navajo-Native America]
Philip, Neil. (2003). *Horse Hooves and Chicken Feet.* New York: Clarion Books. [collection, Mexico]

Other Cultural Resources

Baylor, Byrd. (1972). *When Clay Sings.* New York: Scribner.
Baylor, Byrd. (1974). *They Put on Masks* New York: Scribner.
Evans-Pritchard, Edward. (Series Ed.). (1973). *Peoples of the World.* London: Danbury Press.
Harris, Jane, Pittman, Anne, Waller, Marlys, and Dark, Cathy. (1999). *Dance a While: Handbook for Folk, Square, Contra, and Social Dance* (8th ed.). San Francisco: Benjamin Cummings.

Videotape/DVD
Dances of the Seven Continents for Kids and Teachers. (2006). Volumes 1 and 2 [DVD]. Hightstown, NJ: Princeton Book Company.
Grauer, Rhoda (executive producer). (1992). Dancing in One World [motion picture] from the PBS series *Dancing.*
Wyoma. *African Healing Dance.* (1998). [motion picture]. Boulder, CO: Sounds True.

Dances from Many Cultures

This list was compiled by dance anthropologist Joann Keali'inohomoku.

Burchenal, Elizabeth. (1918). *American Country-Dances.* New York: G. Schirmer.
Burchenal, Elizabeth. (Ed.). (1924). *Rinnce na Eirann: National Dances of Ireland.* New York: A. S. Barnes and Co. Piano arrangements by Emma Howells Burchenal.
Burchenal, Elizabeth. (Ed.). (1933). *Folk-Dances and Singing Games.* New York and Boston: G. Schirmer and Boston Music Co. Twenty-six folk dances of Norway, Sweden, Denmark, Bohemia, Hungary, Italy, England, Scotland, and Ireland, with the music, full directions for performance, and numerous illlustrations.
Burchenal, Elizabeth. (Ed.). (1942). *Folk Dances of the People.* New York: G. Schirmer. A second volume of folk dances and singing games, containing twenty-seven folk dances of England, Scotland, Ireland, Denmark, Sweden, and Germany.
Cohen, Selma Jeanne. (Founding Ed.).(1998). *International Encyclopedia of Dance* (6 volumes). New York and Oxford: Oxford University Press.
Giurchescu, Anca, and Bloland, Sunni. (1995). *Romanian Traditional Dance: A Contextual and Structural Approach.* Mill Valley, CA: Wild Flower Press.
Herman, Mary Ann. (1957). Folk Dance, Trademarks, *Dance Magazine* [four parts, in March, April, May, and June].
Herman, Mary Ann. (1998). Folk Dance Sounds. In Selma Jeanne Cohen et al. (eds.), *International Encyclopedia of Dance* (Vol. 3, pp. 38–39).
Hinman, Mary Wood. (Ed.). (1923–1928). *Gymnastics and Folk Dancing* [5 volumes]. New York: A. S. Barnes & Company.
Jensen, Mary Bee, and Jensen, Clayne R. (1966). *Folk Dancing.* Utah: Brigham Young University Press.
Kennedy, Douglas. (1949). *England's Dances: Folk-Dancing To-Day and Yesterday.* London: G. Bell & Sons, Ltd.
Lawson, Joan. (1953). *European Folk Dance: Its National and Musical Characteristics.* New York, Toronto, London: Pitman.
Leach, Maria. (Ed.). (1972). *Standard Dictionary of Folklore Mythology and Legend* [2 volumes]. New York: Funk & Wagnalls. (Orig. pub. 1949)

Martin, Gyorgy. (1974). *Hungarian Folk Dances.* Hungary: Corvina Press.

Odom, Selma Landen. (1987). Sharing the Dances of Many People: The Teaching Work of Mary Wood Hinman. In Christena Schlundt (compiler), *Dance History Scholars Conference Proceedings* (pp. 64–74). Irvine, CA: University of California.

Pekara, Jean. (1985). The Legacy of Elizabeth Burchenal. *Viltis: A Magazine of Folklore and Folk Dance 44* (2), 8–10.

Playford, John. (1999). *The English Dancing Master: Or Plaine and Easie Rules for the Dancing of Country Dances, with the Tune to Each Dance.* Hugh Mellor and Leslie Bridgewater, editors. Hightstown, NJ: Princeton Books. (Orig. pub. 1651)

Seeger, Mike. (1992). *Talking Feet: Buck, Flatfoot and Tap: Solo Southern Dance of the Appalachian Piedmont and Blue Ridge Mountain Regions.* Berkeley, CA: North Atlantic Books.

Sharp, Cecil J. (1927). *The Country Dance Book* (3rd ed.). London: Novello and Company. (Orig. pub. 1909)

Sharp, Cecil J., and Oppe, A. P. (1972). *The Dance: An Historical Survey of Dancing in Europe* [1st ed. reprinted with a new introduction by Richard Rastall]. Wakefield: EP. (Orig. pub. 1924)

Thurston, H. A. (1954). *Scotland's Dances.* London: G. Bell and Sons, Ltd.

Tolman, Beth, and Page, Ralph. (1937). *The Country Dance Book. The Old-Fashioned Square Dance, Its History, Lore, Variations and Its Callers, Complete and Joyful Instructions.* New York: A. S. Barnes.

Viltis: A Magazine of Folklore and Folk Dance. Published by Vytautas F. Beliajus 1940–1994, and Madison: International Institute of Wisconsin, Madison 1994–1998. Available from University Microfilms, Ann Arbor, MI.

Vissicaro, P. (2004). *Studying Dance Cultures Around the World: An Introduction to Multicultural Dance Education* (foreword by Joann Kealiʻinohomoku). Dubuque, IA: Kendall/Hunt.

Cultural Dance Web Sites

Shannon, Laura. Links a Great Circle: An Internet Magazine for Circle Dancers, www.dance.demon.co.uk

Shannon, Laura. Simple Dances: Where Do They Come From, Where Do They Lead? www.dance.demon.co.uk

Cross Cultural Dance Resources, www.ccdr.org

MUSIC RESOURCES

Listed here are some of our favorite pieces of music or artists for use with creative dance. This is but a sampling, and teachers should search for and use music that appeals to them.

Specific Music Referenced in Lessons

Eric Chapelle, "Skippy," *Music for Creative Dance*, Vol. 1. [U.S.], Ravenna Ventures, Inc., 1993.

Eric Chappelle, "Whales," *Music for Creative Dance*, Vol. 2. [U.S.], Ravenna Ventures, Inc., 1994.

Philip Glass, *Einstein on the Beach* [Contemporary classical], Electra Nonesuch, 1993.

William Ackerman, "Ventana" [Contemporary classical], Windham Hill Music, 1984.

Follow the Drinking Gourd [Traditional, African American spiritual]

Artists

Altan [Ireland, traditional]

Baka [Australia]

Eric Chappelle [Music for creative dance, U.S.]

Early Beatles [England, rock and roll]

Enya [Ireland, Contemporary pop]

Benny Goodman [U.S., Big band era]

Peter Jones [U.S., Jazz]
Ray Lynch [U.S., New Age]
Miriam Makeba [South Africa]
Ladysmith Black Mambazo [South Africa]
R. Carlos Nakai [Contemporary with Southwest Native American flute, U.S.]
Gabrielle Roth [U.S., New Age]
Babatunde Olatunji [West African percussion]
George Winston [U.S., Jazz]

Environmental Sounds

Ocean waves
Whales

BIBLIOGRAPHY

WORKS BY OR RELATING TO RUDOLF LABAN

Bartenieff, I. (with D. Lewis). (1981). *Body movement: Coping with the environment.* New York: Gordon and Breach.

Dell, C. (1970). *A primer for movement using effort shape and supplementary concepts.* New York: Dance Notation Bureau.

Hodgson, J. (2001). *Mastering movement: The life and work of Rudolf Laban.* London: Methuen.

Hodgson, J., and Preston-Dunlop, V. (1990). *Rudolf Laban: An introduction to his work and influence.* Plymouth, Great Britain: Northcote House.

Hutchinson-Guest, A. (1977). *Labanotation* (3rd ed.). New York: Theatre Arts Books.

Hutchinson-Guest, A. (1983). *Your move: A new approach to the study of movement and dance.* New York: Gordon and Breach.

Laban, R. (1956). *Principles of dance and movement notation.* London: Macdonald & Evans.

Laban, R. (1971). *The mastery of movement* (3rd ed.). Edited by Lisa Ullmann. Boston: Plays, Inc.

Laban, R. (1974). *The language of movement: A guidebook to choreutics.* Boston: Plays, Inc.

Laban, R. (1975). *A life for dance, the autobiography of Rudolf Laban.* Hightstown, NJ: Princeton Book Co.

Laban, R. (1988). *Modern educational dance* (3rd ed.). Plymouth, UK: Northcote House. (Orig. pub. 1948)

Laban, R., and Lawrence, F. C. (1974). *Effort: Economy in body movement* (2nd ed.). Boston: Plays, Inc.

Lamb, W. (1965). *Posture and gesture: An introduction to the study of physical behavior.* London: Gerald Duckworth.

Maletic, V. (1987). *Body-space-expression: The development of Rudolf Laban's movement and dance concepts.* Berlin: Mouton de Gruyter.

Maletic, V. (2005). *Dance dynamics: Effort and phrasing.* Columbus, OH: Grade A Notes.

Moore, C., and Yamamoto, K. (1988). *Beyond words: Movement observation and analysis.* New York: Gordon and Breach.

Preston-Dunlop, V. (1980). *A handbook for modern educational dance* (2nd ed.). Boston: Plays, Inc.

Web Sites

Dance Notation Bureau, www.dancenotation.org

Integrated Movement Studies, www.imsmovement.com

Laban (UK), www.laban.org

Laban/Bartenieff Institute for Movement Studies, www.limsonline.org

Laban Guild (UK), www.labanguild.f9.co.uk

Laban-Ausbildung (Germany), www.laban-ausbildung.de

Labanotation Institute, University of Surrey (UK), www.surrey.ac.uk/Dance/General/Laban.html

Motus Humanus, www.motushumanus.org

WORKS BY OR RELATING TO MARGARET H'DOUBLER

Brehm, M. A. (1988). *Margaret H'Doubler's approach to dance education and her influence on two dance educators.* Doctoral dissertation, University of Wisconsin–Madison (University Microfilm International, 8810005).

Brehm, M. A. (1990, March). Margaret H'Doubler's ideas on the role of dance in education: Using art and science to promote individual growth. *Wisconsin Academy Review, University of Wisconsin–Madison* (pp. 48–51).

Gray, J. A. (1978). *To want to dance: A biography of Margaret H'Doubler.* Doctoral dissertation, University of Arizona, Tucson (University Microfilm International, 783903).

Gray, J. A., and Howe, D. (1985). Margaret H'Doubler: a profile of her formative years, 1898–1921. *Research Quarterly for Exercise and Sport,* 93–101.

Hagood, T. K. (2000). *A history of dance in American higher education: Dance and the American university.* Lewiston, NY: E. Mellen Press.

H'Doubler, M. (1925). *The dance and its place in education.* New York: Harcourt, Brace.

H'Doubler, M. (1932). *Rhythmic form and analysis.* Madison, WI: J. M. Rider.

H'Doubler, M. (1950). *A guide for the analysis of movement.* Madison, WI: Kramer Business Services.

H'Doubler, M. (1998). *Dance: A creative art experience.* Madison, WI: University of Wisconsin Press. (Orig. pub. 1940)

Moore, E. A. (1975). Recollection of Margaret H'Doubler's class procedure: An environment for the learning of dance. *Dance Research Journal, 8*(1), 12–17.

Ross, J. (2000). *Moving lessons: Margaret H'Doubler and the beginning of dance in American education.* Madison: University of Wisconsin Press.

Wilson, J., Hagood, T., and Brennan, M. A. (Eds.) (2006). *Margaret H'Doubler: The legacy of America's dance education pioneer.* Youngstown, NY: Cambria Press.

WORKS BY OR RELATING TO BARBARA METTLER

Brehm, M. A. (1997). Creative dance experiences which build community. *Proceedings of the 30th annual conference, Congress on Research in Dance: Dance, culture, and art-making behavior.* 17–36.

Brehm M. A., and Kampfe, C. (1997). Creative dance improvisation: Fostering creative expression, group cooperation, and multiple intelligence. *China–U.S. Conference on Education: Beijing, People's Republic of China* (pp. 15–22). Greensboro NC: ERIC/CASS.

Canner, N., and Klebanoff, H. (1975). ….and a time to dance. Boston, MA: Plays, Inc.

Cashman, J. (1998, Summer/Fall). The making of a kinesthetic community: The legacy of Barbara Mettler. *Contact Quarterly, 23*(2).

Mettler, B. (1970). *Children's creative dance book.* Tucson, AZ: Mettler Studios.

Mettler, B. (1975). *Group dance improvisations.* Tucson, AZ: Mettler Studios.

Mettler, B. (1980a). A dancer's history: Autobiographical sketch. Retrieved January 12, 2006, from www. barbaramettler.org

Mettler, B. (1980b). *The nature of dance as a creative art activity.* Tucson, AZ: Mettler Studios.

Mettler, B. (1981). Artist or educator: Autobiographical sketch 2. Retrieved January 12, 2006, from www.barbaramettler.org

Mettler, B. (1983). *Dance as an element of life.* Tucson, AZ: Mettler Studios.

Mettler, B. (1988). *The language of movement.* Paper presented at the Congress on Research in Dance Conference, Mexico City.

Mettler, B. (2006). *Materials of dance as a creative art activity* [commemorative ed.]. Tucson, AZ: Mettler Studios. (Orig. pub. 1960)

Newsletter for People in the Field of Creative Dance. (1996–present). Providence, RI: International Association for Creative Dance.

Victor, D. (2000, May/June). Dancing life … living dance … creative dance is for everyone. *The Bridge Magazine,* 42–43.

Victor, D. (2006, Winter). Dancing in the kinesthetic spirit. *Sacred Dance Guild Journal, 48*(2), 4.

Web Sites

Barbara Mettler, www.barbaramettler.org

International Association for Creative Dance, www.dancecreative.org

ADDITIONAL REFERENCES

Alexander, F. M. (1984). *The use of the self.* Downey, CA: Centerline Press.

Battista, M., Clements, D., Russell, S. J., Sarama, J., and Tierney, C. (1998). *Investigations in number, data, and space: Flips, turns and area.* Menlo Park, CA: Dale Seymour.

Baum, S. M., Owen, S. V., and Oreck, B. A. (1996). Talent beyond words: Identification of potential talent in dance and music in elementary students. *Gifted Child Quarterly, 40,* 93–101.

Boorman, J. (1969). *Creative dance in the first three grades.* New York: David McKay.

Boorman, J. (1973). *Dance and language experiences with children.* Orlando, FL: Harcourt Brace.

Brandt, R. (Ed.). (1998). *Assessing student learning: New rules, new realities.* Arlington, VA: Educational Research Services and Alliance for Curriculum Reform.

Brooks, C. (1986). *Sensory awareness: Rediscovery of experiencing through the workshops of Charlotte Selver* (3rd ed.). Great Neck, NY: Felix Morrow.

Calais-Germain, B. (1993). *Anatomy of movement.* Seattle, WA: Eastland Press.

Cohen, B. B. (1993). *Sensing, feeling, and action: The experiential anatomy of body–mind centering.* Northampton, MA: Contact Editions.

Cone, T. P., and Cone, S. (2005). *Teaching children dance* (2nd ed.). Champaign, IL: Human Kinetics.

Damasio, A. (1999). *The feeling of what happens: Body and emotions in the making of consciousness.* New York: Harcourt Brace.

Dennison, P., and Dennison, G. (1994). *Brain gym teacher's edition (revised).* Ventura, CA: The Educational Kinesiology Foundation.

Dimonstein, G. (1971). *Children dance in the classroom.* New York: MacMillan.

DuBose, L. (2001). Dance movement treatment perspectives. In J. Robert-McComb (Ed.), *Eating disorders in women and children: Prevention, stress management, and treatment.* New York: CRC Press.

Duncan, I., and Rosemont F. (Ed.). (1994). *Isadora speaks: Writings & speeches of Isadora Duncan.* Chicago: Charles H. Kerr.

Faber, R. (1994). *The primary movers: Kinesthetic learning for primary school children.* Unpublished master's thesis, American University.

Fee, F. M. (1971–1972). Discovering rhythm through the senses. *Dance Research Monograph One,* 65–72.

Feldenkrais, M. (1977). *Awareness through movement.* New York: HarperCollins.

Findlay, E. (1971). *Rhythm and movement: Applications of Dalcroze eurhythmics.* Princeton, NJ: Summy-Birchard Music.

Gardner, H. (1999). *Intelligence reframed: Multiple intelligences for the 21st century.* New York: Basic Books.

Gardner, H. (2004). *Frames of mind: The theory of multiple intelligences* (3rd ed.). New York: Basic Books. (Orig. Pub. 1983)

Gerbrands, A. A., and Forge, A. (1973). Asmat-New Guinea. In E. Evans-Pritchard (Series Ed.) and A. Forge (Vol. Ed.), *Peoples of the World: Vol 1. Australia and Melanesia including New Guinea* (1st ed.). London: Danbury Press.

Gilbert, A. G. (1977). *Teaching the three r's through movement expression.* Englewood Cliffs, NJ: Prentice Hall.

Gilbert, A. G. (1992). *Creative dance for all ages.* Reston, VA: National Dance Association, American Alliance for Health, Physical Education, Recreation and Dance.

Gilbert, A. G. (2003). *BrainDance: Variations for infants through seniors* [motion picture]. Reston, VA: National Dance Association, American Alliance for Health, Physical Education, Recreation and Dance.

Gilbert, A. G. (2006). *Brain compatible dance education.* Reston, VA : National Dance Association, American Alliance for Health, Physical Education, Recreation and Dance.

Griss, Susan. (1998). *Minds in motion: A kinesthetic approach to teaching elementary curriculum.* Portsmouth, NH: Heinemann.

Hackney, P. (2002). *Making connections: Total body integration through Bartenieff fundamentals.* New York: Routledge.

Hagood, T. K. (2001, May/June). Dance to read or dance to dance? *Art Education Policy Review, 102*(5), 27–29.

Hall, E. T. (1966). *The hidden dimension.* Garden City, NY: Doubleday.

Hall, E. T. (1977). *Beyond culture.* Garden City, NY: Anchor Press/Doubleday.

Hanna, J. L. (1999). *Partnering dance and education: Intelligent moves for changing times.* Champaign, IL: Human Kinetics.

Hanna, T. (1988). *Somatics: Reawakening the mind's control of movement, flexibility, and health.* Reading, MA: Addison-Wesley.

Hannaford, C. (1995). *Smart moves: Why learning is not all in your head.* Arlington, VA: Great Ocean Publishers.

Hartley, L. (1995). *The wisdom of the body moving: An introduction to mind–body centering.* Berkeley, CA: North Atlantic Books.

Hay, J., and Reid, J. (1978). *The anatomical and mechanical basis of human motion.* Englewood Cliffs, NJ: Prentice-Hall.

Jaques-Dalcroze, E. (1930). *Eurhythmics: Art and education.* New York: A. S. Barnes.

Jensen, E. (2000). Moving with the brain in mind. *Educational Leadership, 53,* 3.

Jensen, E. (2001). *Arts with the brain in mind.* Alexandria, VA: Association for Supervision and Curriculum Integration.

Joyce, M. (1994). *First steps in teaching creative dance* (3rd ed.). San Francisco, CA: McGraw-Hill.

Klatt, F. (1923). *Die schopferische pause.* Jena, Germany: Eugen Diederichs Verlag.

Kornblum, R. (2002). *Disarming the playground: Violence prevention through movement.* Oklahoma City, OK: Wood and Barnes.

Littlewood, W. C. (with Roche, M. A.), (Eds.). (2004). *Waking up: The work of Charotte Selver.* Bloomington, IN: Authorhouse.

Lloyd, M. (1998). *Adventures in creative movement activities, a guide for teaching.* Dubuque, IA: Eddie Bowers.

Martin, J. (1986). *Introduction to the dance.* Hightstown, NJ: Princeton Book Co.

Mirus, J., White, E., Bucek, L., and Paulson, P. (1993). *Dance education initiative curriculum guide.* Golden Valley, MN: Minnesota Center for Arts Education.

Montgomery, K. (2001). *Authentic assessment: A guide for elementary teachers.* New York: Addison-Wesley Longman.

Mueller, J. (2003). *Authentic assessment toolbox.* Retrieved November 11, 2005, from http://jonathan.mueller.faculty.noctrl.edu/toolbox/whatisit.htm#names

National Center for Education Statistics. (1999). *Eighth-grade findings from the national assessment of educational progress* (NCES 1999-485). Washington DC: U.S. Department of Education Office of Educational Research and Improvement.

National Dance Association. (1994). *National standards for dance education: What every young American should know and be able to do in dance.* Reston, VA: National Dance Association, American Alliance for Health, Physical Education, and Dance.

National Dance Association. (1995). *Consortium of National Arts Education Associations Opportunity-to-Learn Standards for Dance Instruction.* Reston, VA: National Dance Association, American Alliance for Health, Physical Education, and Dance.

National Dance Education Organization. (2005a). *Standards for dance in early childhood.* Retrieved January 12, 2006, from www.ndeo.org/standards.asp

National Dance Education Organization. (2005b). *Standards for learning and teaching dance in the arts.* Retrieved January 12, 2006, from www.ndeo.org/standards.asp

Newman, C. (2004, August). Why are we so fat? *National Geographic, 206*(2), 46–61.

Pomer, J. (2002). *Perpetual motion, creative movement exercises for dance and dramatic arts.* Champaign, IL: Human Kinetics.

Ratey, J. (2001). *A user's guide to the brain: Perception, attention, and the four theatres of the brain.* New York: Pantheon Books.

Sagan, E., Sagan, J. B., Leath, A. A., Jr., and Graham, J. (1967). *Creative behavior and artistic development in psychotherapy.* Oakland, CA: Institute for Creative and Artistic Development.

Schmid, D. W. (2003). Authentic assessment in the arts empowering students and teachers. *Journal of Dance Education. 3*(2), 65–73.

Smith, R. (2001, May/June). The Harvard REAP study: Inherent "versus" instrumental values. *Art Education Policy Review, 102*(5), 11–14.

Stevenson, L., and Deasy, R. (2005). *Third space: When learning matters.* Washington, DC: Arts Education Partnership, CCSSO Publications.

Stinson, S. (1988). *Dance for young children: Finding the magic in movement.* Reston, VA: National Dance Association, American Alliance for Health, Physical Education and Dance.

Taylor, G. (2003). *Informal classroom assessment strategies for teachers.* Lanham, MD: Scarecrow Press.

Tombari, M. L., and Borich, G. D. (1999). *Authentic assessment in the classroom: Applications and practice.* Upper Saddle River, NJ: Prentice-Hall.

Vissicaro, P. (2004). *Studying dance cultures around the world: An introduction to multicultural dance education* (foreword by Joann Keali'inohomoku). Dubuque, IA: Kendall/Hunt.

Zakkai, J. (1997). *Dance as a way of knowing.* Portland, ME: Stenhouse.

Web Sites

ArtsEdge (Kennedy Center for the Performing Arts), www.artsedge.kennedy-center.org

Brain Gym, www.braingym.com

Cross Cultural Dance Resources, www.ccdr.org

National Dance Association, www.aahperd.org/nda

National Dance Education Organization, www.ndeo.org

Opening Minds through the Arts Project, www.omaproject.org

INDEX